REDPOINT

REDPOINT

The Self-Coached Climber's
Guide to Redpoint
and On-Sight Climbing

DAN HAGUE &
DOUGLAS HUNTER

STACKPOLE
BOOKS

Published by
STACKPOLE BOOKS
5067 Ritter Road
Mechanicsburg, PA 17055
www.stackpolebooks.com

Printed in the United States of America

First edition

Front cover photo of Tom Adams on Golden 5.14b, The Cathedral, St. George, UT by Nathan Smith—Pull Photography

Cover design by Wendy A. Reynolds

10 9 8 7 6 5 4 3 2 1

Library of Congress Cataloging-in-Publication Data

Hague, Dan.
  Redpoint : the self-coached climber's guide to Redpoint and on-sight climbing / Dan Hague and Douglas Hunter.
     p.   cm.
  Includes bibliographical references and index.
  ISBN-13: 978-0-8117-0764-0 (pbk.)
  ISBN-10: 0-8117-0764-4 (pbk.)
  1. Rock climbing—Training. I. Hunter, Douglas. II. Title.
GV200.2.H33   2011
 796.522'3—dc22
                                                                    2011008652

Contents

Warning

This book contains much useful information about the sport of climbing. Before engaging in this potentially hazardous sport, however, you must do more than read a book.

This sport requires skill, concentration, physical strength and endurance, proper equipment, knowledge of fundamental principles and techniques, and unwavering commitment to your safety and that of your companions.

The publisher and author obviously cannot be responsible for your safety. Because climbing entails the risk of serious and even fatal injury, we emphasize that you should not begin climbing except under expert supervision. No book can substitute for proper training and experience under the guidance of a qualified teacher.

Introduction

Over the past several decades, the concepts of redpoint, on-sight, and flash have been widely and vigorously debated and refined until today they set the standards by which we measure climbing achievement. Central to the debate is the meaning and purpose of an ascent and the validity of different notions of style. In recent years these concepts have stabilized, but for most of climbing history there was no such thing as a redpoint or a flash, and early on their acceptance was not assured. The following definitions will help you understand the concepts and activities in this book. We'll also sketch out some of the history that helped shape American climbing as it stands today.

Clean Climbing

In the early '70s during the rapid transition away from the use of pitons, a clean ascent was simply one in which only removable, nondestructive protection was used. Today a clean ascent retains the older meaning on traditionally protected climbs, but since so few climbers use pitons now, it's assumed that trad climbers use clean methods—with the exception of big wall, aid climbing where pitons are still sometimes employed. In general, clean has also come to mean relying only on your own power, climbing without physical aid of any kind, including pulling on a quickdraw or using rope tension to help support body weight. Redpoints, on-sights, and flashes are all examples of clean climbing in the latter sense, but no ascent of a sport route is clean in the original sense because of the use of bolts that permanently alter the rock.

Redpoint

A redpoint is a clean ascent made after one or more previous attempts on a route, either working burns— attempts made for the sake of learning the route and its details—or a failed attempt to send the route first try.

A redpoint of a sport route can be achieved with all the quickdraws already in place so that the climber simply clips the rope as he goes. Alternatively, the climber can both hang the draws and clip the rope, although at an earlier time the former was mocked as a "pinkpoint." In situations where the climb's first bolt is high off the ground or there is a risk of injury if the climber should fall before reaching the first bolt, stick clipping the rope through the first quickdraw is a standard practice, even though previous generations considered doing so aid. Stick clipping the rope into bolts above the first is usually frowned on unless there are extraordinary circumstances such as poor bolt placement or additional danger.

Although the term *redpoint* is often considered synonymous with sport climbing, Pat Ament in his 2002 book *Wizards of Rock: A History of Free Climbing in America* states, "For gear-protected climbs, such as cracks, a redpoint ascent is one where all gear is placed during the final lead." Climbers sometimes refer to completing a boulder problem as a redpoint, and while it may sound odd, the term can be applied to bouldering. Throughout the book, we frequently use redpoint in the context of traditional climbing and bouldering.

Flash and On-Sight

A flash is a clean ascent of a route done on the first try. Flashes fall into two categories, those in which the climber receives no outside information about the route, known as an on-sight flash or simply on-sight, and those where he does, commonly called a flash.

For a *flash* or *beta flash* you may review all available information before making the attempt. You can inspect the route from the ground, while lowering off a nearby climb, or even by rappelling down the route to inspect the holds and place the draws. You can watch others climb the route and consult with those who've climbed it before. You can study photographs or videos and read detailed descriptions of the route. You are free to gather as much information as you like, as long as you don't touch the holds.

A *beta flash* can even include coaching from the ground—someone who knows the route well gives you hold-by-hold, move-by-move instructions as you progress up the route. Although significantly easier than an on-sight, a beta flash is still a challenge.

An *on-sight flash* or just *on-sight* is a clean ascent of a route done on the first try without the aid of outside information about the route other than its location, name, grade, and on sport routes, the number of draws. You may not be given detailed descriptions of the route, its moves, or characteristics. You can't watch others on the route, examine photos or video of climbers on the route, or discuss it with anyone who has been on it. It is also off-limits to boulder out the first few moves before the attempt. To attempt an on-sight means having no information from other sources at all. This definition is strict and requires you to be careful in your use of a guidebook because some provide detailed information that you would have to avoid.

You can study the route from nearby hillsides or large boulders near the climb. Some climbers will even use binoculars or climb nearby trees to get a better view. What you can't do is rappel down the route or lower off a nearby climb for a closer inspection, nor can you touch the holds prior to making your attempt. Keep in mind, though, there is no time limit on how long you can study a route. While many attempt on-sights after inspecting the route for just a few minutes from the ground, longer periods of study are not unheard of. You may study a route for hours or on different days or at different times of day so the light is different, and, if leaves obstruct your view, you can even wait for the season to change and the leaves to fall. Don't attempt the on-sight until you are satisfied with your inspection and plan for the route.

There are those who feel you should have no information of any sort about the route prior to attempting an on-sight, that you should tie in and start to climb without examining the route or its moves. Some also claim that true on-sights are not possible in most climbing situations because chalk and tick marks identify crucial holds. Such objections are not without merit, as they remind us of elements that make the climber's job easier, and those who follow the stricter rules aspire to a very demanding standard, but at this point the climbing community has largely settled on the idea that inspecting and interpreting the route on your own with no outside assistance is OK. In fact, the visual inspection of a route is central to the challenge and enjoyment of on-sight climbing.

Another aspect of on-sighting that is still debated is climbing back down to the ground for a rest. Some argue that a climber struggling low on the route can climb back to the ground for a rest if he climbs down under his own power—rather than jumping down—and does not have additional information about the rest of the route. Others argue that if the climber comes down to the ground for a complete recovery and does further study of the route, he is really making a new attempt thereby invalidating the on-sight. Both have their positive points, but the strictest rule, developed in the early days of on-sight competitions, is that coming back down to the ground for any reason whatsoever is not allowed.

The rules for what constitutes an on-sight are strict because it's the ultimate test of what you can achieve based on your own experience, ideas, creativity, fitness, adaptability, and ability to read a route. You must collect, interpret, apply, and adjust to information entirely on your own. Information from other sources demeans this test, and thus changes the nature of the achievement from an on-sight to a flash. An on-sight is a solitary achievement.

History

The emergence of rock climbing and its development as a sport is an intriguing story defined by the passions of climbers seeking out new challenges in each era. It's defined by different visions of what climbing is and why it matters, by the sometimes violent clash of philosophies and methods that have been part of rock climbing from the beginning, and by the experiences of individuals. The stories of a few climbers over the last several decades illustrate how conceptual and philosophical changes led us to the generally accepted rules that shape climbing today, and in understanding where we began and the changes that took place, we gain a greater understanding of how the tactics described in this book fit into the sport of climbing as it's defined today.

Prior to the late 1950s rock climbing was considered a part of mountaineering. It was believed that skills on rock were necessary because one never knew when technical rock climbing might be encountered in the mountains. Rather than being considered a distinct sport, with its own values, goals, and methods, rock climbing was widely thought of as a subset of mountaineering. Climbers applied the same conceptual framework used in the mountains to the rocks; success meant reaching the summit of a mountain or cliff by whatever means necessary, so aid and free climbing techniques were frequently combined in the process.

By the late 1950s the strong link between mountaineering and rock climbing began to dissolve. This decoupling can be seen in the experience of Gunk's legend Jim McCarthy who started climbing with Hans Krauss in 1951. Krauss, an avid mountaineer and one of America's rock climbing pioneers, passed on a number of ideas to McCarthy: He taught that aid and free climbing were both necessary skills and that climbing in the Gunks was practice for the mountains and would help them achieve bigger climbs in the Rockies or the Tetons. McCarthy enjoyed doing new rock routes, even in the beginning, and his enthusiasm drove the pair to complete many first ascents in the Gunks. Despite the fact that rock climbing consumed a considerable amount of their time, they didn't consider it most important to their experiences as climbers because they were always thinking of the mountains.

McCarthy's thinking began to change in 1957 with his first ascent of Yellow Belly, a well-known Gunks 5.8. At the time, McCarthy and others felt that 5.7 was the limit on technical rock. To try to climb harder routes would have been to undertake a risk too great for the reward. Although that might sound odd to us today, at the time, climbing equipment was crude: Pitons were the only form of protection, modern harnesses didn't exist yet, footwear typically consisted of hiking boots or sneakers, chalk and belay devices had not been introduced, and because of the great risks involved, taking a lead fall was considered something to be avoided at all costs.

Yellow Belly was a breakthrough for McCarthy; the route's crux represented the hardest moves he had ever done, and it got him thinking about difficulty. He began looking around the Gunks and realized that "we could be doing things a lot harder than we were," and in the years to come he pursued harder rock climbs for their own reward. His style of climbing also began to change; whereas most of his early first ascents had been done first try, the more difficult and demanding climbs he now sought out sometimes required multiple attempts. McCarthy was not alone in this, and with time more and more climbers became willing to invest multiple attempts on a single route.

With this emphasis on difficulty and change in style McCarthy became a catalyst for change in the Gunks where his success in raising standards had a significant impact on the actions and attitudes of the next generation of climbers who were also captivated by the pursuit of rock climbing difficulty.

Meanwhile another climber active in the 1950s had a different idea of what rock climbing should be. John Gill, who is often thought of as the father of hard bouldering, was a gymnast before he became a climber, and he drew parallels between the two. In his words, he began "to perceive climbing as a kind of gymnastic sport with boulders treated as apparatus. These ideas percolated in the relative isolation of the Deep South where climbing as a sport was almost completely unknown. Had I been around climbers of that era I might not have become quite as independent a personality—I felt free to imagine what climbers might be capable of, rather than simply following contemporary perceptions."

Gill remembers, "There was little if any discussion about what climbing was all about in the 1950s . . . My first serious discussions about just what the sport was all about occurred in the Tetons, with [Yvon] Chouinard telling me that 'bouldering' was what I was doing and that he and his friends played on boulders as a way of sharpening their abilities to climb the big walls, or free lines that had previously been aided . . . When I explained what I thought climbing could become—demonstrated by my accomplishments on the pebbles—most were polite, but dismissive of such ideas . . . And when I talked about how gymnasts polished their routines so that they became choreographed artistic demonstrations, eyes glazed over."

McCarthy's and Gill's stories represent those of a handful of climbers in the late 1950s and 1960s. On shorter routes and boulder problems, some climbers were exploring the athletic potential of free climbing. Gill and McCarthy were compelled by the search for difficulty and realized that to complete a hard free climb, it might be necessary to attempt and refine moves over the course of several tries before a clean ascent could be achieved. This facilitated the split from mountaineering as rock climbing difficulty was pursued for its own rewards.

When reflecting on changes that started to take place in this era, it's common to emphasize big wall, aid-climbing ascents in the Yosemite Valley and the idea that risk and adventure were essential elements of the climbing experience, but McCarthy and Gill give a different perspective. At the time the small and poorly connected American climbing community was not universally focused on or even aware of what was happening in Yosemite. Individual climbers across the United States were formulating their own ideas about rock climbing apart from the grand scale of big walls and mountaineering, and that broadened their horizons beyond risk, adventure, and getting to the top. Experiences such as McCarthy's and Gill's exemplify the kind of thinking that helped rock climbing emerge in its own right; they were two of the first to explore the athletic challenges of rock climbing.

Throughout the 1960s more people were attracted to rock climbing, its transition into an independent sport continued, and the standards of difficulty continued to rise into the 5.10 range. During this era the accepted style was "ground up" in that each attempt on a route began when the climber left the ground and either reached the top of the pitch or fell. There was no such thing as asking the belayer to "take," and hanging on the gear for the sake of resting or inspecting the route or practicing sections was considered bad style. As soon as a climber fell, he was lowered to the ground.

But by the late 1960s a problem emerged. The repeated hammering and removing of pitons in the cracks of Yosemite and the Adirondacks, among others, was taking its toll—chipping away the rock, making the cracks wider, and creating openings big enough to use as handholds.

While traveling in Europe, a few American climbers had been exposed to removable protection that didn't damage the rock, a good solution to the growing problem in America. By 1972 the Chouinard Equipment catalog featured nuts and hexes as well as several articles about why it was important to climb in a clean style using only protection that could be placed and removed without damaging the rock.

In 1971, Royal Robbins published his book *Basic Rockcraft*, one of the first how-to, technical rock climbing manuals, in which he addressed the issue of style: "In rock climbing it refers to the methods and equipment used and the degree of 'adventure' involved in an ascent. Adventure here means the degree of uncertainty as to the outcome." Robbins also voiced his objection to the use of bolts because by using them any wall, no matter how devoid of features, could be climbed. There was no uncertainty as to the outcome, and as he put it, "There would be no adventure in such an endeavor, and it would be in the worst possible style."

Robbins' objection to bolts was based on their use in big wall, aid climbing. By the time Robbins wrote those words, a few routes had been put up in Yosemite that relied on many bolts to aid through long blank sections of rock. Robbins felt that such climbs were in poor style because they removed adventure—that is, uncertainty—from the equation. He also objected to the way bolts eliminated the need to work with the features of the rock; a bolt could be placed anywhere regardless of the rock's features or weaknesses. Robbins, however, did not distinguish between aid and free climbing with regard to bolts. That distinction would only become meaningful later.

These examples showcase an awakening in the climbing community. In the late '60s and early '70s climbers began thinking about and discussing how climbing should be done in new ways. Central to the discussion was what made an ascent meaningful, the nature of a route, and what constituted good climbing practice. This new dialogue transformed the sport and later influenced the development of sport climbing.

Through the 1970s new equipment was introduced, climbers continued to push the standards of difficulty, and rock climbing was widely pursued for its own challenges and rewards. Clean climbing became the norm and ascents that combined aid and free techniques became less common as free climbing took center stage. By the 1970s many first ascentionists had the specific goal of freeing old aid lines or creating new free climbs, an emphasis that informs most rock climbing today.

During the 1970s the predominant style of climbing continued to be ground-up, but a new practice called yo-yoing emerged as part of ground-up style. One or more climbers worked over a number of tries to place the gear at higher intervals on the route. A climber would climb as high as he could, place higher protection, and if he fell, he'd be lowered to the ground so the next climber could try the route. The next climber would then either pull the rope, starting anew from the ground, or tie in with the rope still through the highest piece of protection, top-rope up to the current high point, and begin leading from there. The practice of leaving the rope through the highest protection gave the practice the name "yo-yo." Working in this manner, the climbers would eventually get all the protection in place and reach the top of the pitch. In areas like Joshua Tree in California and the Gunks in New York where there were many single pitch climbs, yo-yoing was often a group activity, with climbers hanging out at the base of the route waiting their turns. Longtime Gunkie Russ Clune remembers it fondly: "Yo-yoing created a bond, because it was a team effort; everyone worked together. Whoever got to the top first did it on the backs of everyone else who was putting effort into that work."

Yo-yoing fostered team efforts and promoted community, but the problem was that it combined top roping and leading. It meant that later attempts on the route could be far less strenuous than earlier attempts since most of the gear was already in place. A climber could claim a first ascent in which he actually top-roped most of the route and had to place little or no protection during the ascent.

Due to the prevalence and problems of yo-yoing, claiming you had done a route in the 1970s and early '80s often led to a lot of questions from other climbers concerning the number of attempts made, what gear was used, how much of the gear you placed yourself, how much gear was placed during the ascent, and whether or not the rope was pulled between attempts. Climbers were using a variety of methods and didn't have a uniform vocabulary like we do now for categorizing an ascent. It became more widely recognized that an ascent where the climber placed all the gear could make the climb much more difficult than top-roping a portion of it, so the legitimacy of many ascents was questioned.

At about the same time the methods and style of climbing began shifting in another direction that would come in conflict with the ground-up styles prevalent in the 1970s. In 1981, Russ Clune was one of the first American climbers to visit the Rhineland Pfaltz in Germany, where he saw climbers hanging on fixed ropes using Jumar ascenders to practice the moves on routes prior to attempting a free ascent from the ground. Clune decided to try this method himself, and in a few hours he completed the second 5.12 of his climbing career. His first 5.12 had taken days of effort in the ground-up style, but the second was completed in an afternoon by first working out the moves. Clune reflects, "It's when I saw firsthand what could be achieved with a change in tactics." Yet he didn't rush to apply this method when he returned to the United States: "It was logical to us that if you hung on the rope you could shorten the amount of time it would take to do a route. But that wasn't the point of climbing; the point of climbing was to do a route a certain way."

Hanging on the rope was a form of aid climbing, and Clune, like many other Americans at the time, considered aid climbing unacceptable in free climbing even if it would eventually lead to a free ascent. Clune reflects, "What we didn't know at the time was that the sport was about to embrace difficulty at the expense of what we thought of as good style."

An important factor that initiated the move away from previous notions of good style was that harder climbs in many areas occur on less-featured rock and can be hard to protect, if they can be protected at all. Climbers who wanted to challenge themselves on harder routes had to take substantial safety risks. While some believed facing the risk of serious injury was part of the adventure inherent in the sport, others valued athletic difficulty and viewed physical risk as an impediment to the pursuit of excellence.

Perhaps the first place in the United States where climbers started to venture onto rock that could not be protected by clean trad gear was Smith Rock in Oregon.

Alan Watts and a group of other climbers were developing their talents at a rapid rate and running out of new routes in the process. Watts recalls that he "spent two years climbing increasingly disgusting cracks . . . so I turned to the blank faces of the Dihedrals out of desperation for something new. It wasn't until I started rappelling unclimbed faces at Smith did I realize how featured they were. But many of these routes couldn't be done on lead without just drilling a bolt ladder. So I started rappelling routes and hand-drilled bolts." Watts developed a hybrid style: He'd place bolts on rappel, preview routes, and hang on his protection for the sake of resting, but the end he was working toward was a free, ground-up ascent. Essentially Watts was moving in the direction anticipated twenty years earlier by John Gill when he correlated climbing with rehearsing and refining a gymnastic routine.

At the time, Watts' tactics—placing bolts on rappel, previewing, cleaning, and what we now call working a route—were considered a violation of good style. Nonetheless, Watts felt he was adapting to the new challenge of the long blank faces of Smith Rock. Further, he had no knowledge of the style of climbing that Russ Clune had seen in Germany two years earlier or the tactics that were being used on the hardest climbs in France.

Watts and others were independently developing their skills and climbing methods in ways that were very similar to what was being done in Europe at the same time. But there were differences: Watts was placing clean protection when he could, and he also felt compelled to adhere to the established ground-up methods accepted at Smith Rock to the extent possible. Thus he always placed clean protection as he climbed, and he didn't just leave in it place as if it were a bolt. He placed quickdraws, nuts, or cams on lead during each attempt, and he cleaned the draws as he lowered down from unsuccessful attempts. Whereas in other regions yo-yoing would have been considered acceptable, at Smith Watts and others were blending the new methods with the old in their own way.

It wasn't until he was going for the first ascent of the East Face of Monkey Face (5.13c/d) in 1985 that Watts changed his style to incorporate the yo-yoing so common elsewhere. East Face of Monkey Face was very close to Watts' athletic limit and was protected

largely by nut placements. He was having a difficult time placing the gear as he went without pumping out. He kept reducing the number of placements he used and did what he could to make placing gear and clipping easier, but he was still coming up short. Watts describes what happened next: "Around the same time, Heinz Zak, the renowned Austrian photographer, visited Smith. We spent a day taking pictures on the route. He informed me that other routes around the world (including Wolfgang Gullich's Punks in the Gym, the first 5.14a in the world, done in 1985) were done with a yo-yo. So in the end, I just lowered off after clipping the second bolt [which was high on the route] and settled for a relatively uneventful yo-yo ascent." Thus his first ascent included a significant amount of top roping, and he avoided having to place the gear that had given him so much trouble on other attempts.

During the years that Watts was putting up the first sport climbs at Smith, other climbing areas were also seeing significant development, and yo-yoing was being widely used and questioned. In 1983 Drew Bedford was working on the first ascent of Pump or Jump (5.11d) in Ferguson Canyon near Salt Lake City. He fell repeatedly at the same spot and, in keeping with the style he embraced at the time, pulled his rope from its high point before making another attempt. Despite Bedford's best efforts, Steve Hong snagged the first ascent of the route by yo-yoing. Hong left the rope through its high point and top-roped a significant portion of the route for the send. While Bedford accepted the ascent, he did have questions about its style. "To me that was not kosher," Bedford recalls. He'd been trying to do the route in what he considered the best style, and it didn't occur to him that a yo-yo could qualify as a first ascent. Bedford's uncertainity about yo-yoing was typical of many climbers during this era, but it wasn't until a few years later that he saw the solution.

In 1986, when Bedford met Kurt Albert and Wolfgang Gullich in the Yosemite Valley, he heard from them the explanation of what they were calling a "rotpunkt" or redpoint. Albert had been freeing many existing aid routes in Germany's Frankenjura. His method was to hang on the rope over a number of attempts to discover, practice, and refine workable sequences in order to eventually make a ground-up, free ascent. After achieving the send, Albert would paint a red dot at the base of the climb, or fill in an existing red circle, signifying to others that a free ascent had been made. The entire process of working and then sending a route eventually came to be called redpointing.

Bedford immediately took to the redpoint concept. He recalls, "I had always been aiming for the redpoint but didn't have a word for it. It also reaffirmed for me that yo-yoing wasn't legitimate." Bedford recognized, as did many others, that the concept of the redpoint cleared up the problems associated with yo-yoing and validated using one set of tactics to learn a route and a different set for the free ascent. Bedford was one of many American climbers to learn about redpointing between 1985 and 1987, and his eventual adoption of it reflects the wider evolution of the sport. The redpoint in particular freed climbers to pursue the hardest climbs without being limited by what felt like arbitrary rules. To many the challenge and self-fulfillment in climbing was not found in taking physical risks, but rather in the pursuit of athletic excellence, in learning and executing movement to the best of one's abilities.

In the United States, redpointing developed along with bolted sport climbs, but on-sights and flashes had a different origin. The idea that a climber could walk up to a route and send it first try without knowing much about it was considered excellent style, even in the '60s and '70s. The distinction between flashes and on-sights was brought about in part by the development of climbing competitions. First in Europe and then in the United States, climbing competitions developed a specific set of rules about what climbers could and could not do. The French *a vue* climbing, in which the climber can have no previous knowledge of the route prior to his first attempt to free climb it, was popularized through competitions and translated into English as "on-sight." In an on-sight competition the climbers could not look at the route or watch other climbers on it prior to their attempt. Further, after a climber left the ground he could not step back down.

In 1988 and '89, the transition to sport climbing was happening at a rapid pace, and some areas such as the New River Gorge in West Virginia, Red Rocks in Nevada, and American Fork in Utah saw nearly all new route activity take the form of bolted sport routes. By 1990 American Fork was quickly gaining a reputation as a sport climbing mecca with the hardest and steepest routes in the country. An important development that occurred as part of the rapid expansion of sport climbing was the refinement of tactics; climbers were getting better at learning routes and then redpointing them. Climbers were also working out the rules for redpoints. For example, at the time a distinction was drawn between a redpoint and a "pinkpoint" in which the quickdraws are preplaced on the route, eliminating the need to place them while climbing. When a climber would complete a sport route with the draws already in place, the ascent was considered a lesser achievement. But pressure arose quickly to dispense with this distinction, and it was not long before a consensus developed that cleaning some routes was far more trouble than it was worth, and by 1993 it was broadly understood that an ascent made with the draws in place could be called a redpoint.

By the early 1990s sport climbing was widely embraced, and its methods and tactics were being worked out. Climbing gyms were being built around the country, and climbing pedagogy started to emphasize sport climbing, athletic training, and the development of movement skills in ways that were not previously imaginable.

Since the early 1990s the concepts used to describe different styles of ascent have gone through some refinement. These different styles form the conceptual model for climbing today. We have witnessed firsthand how the tactics used in these different ascents have changed and become more robust over the last twenty-five years. At first redpoint tactics consisted simply of being allowed to hang on the rope rather than returning to the ground; being able to tell the belayer to "take" was itself a radical innovation. Over time climbers have developed rigorous methods for making the process of learning and memorizing a route as easy as possible. This book elaborates the best tactics that have been developed over the past twenty-five years to enhance learning, create higher level performances, realize greater enjoyment, and ultimately send harder routes in fewer attempts.

CHAPTER 1
Assessing Your Abilities

Many climbers don't set goals because they don't have the knowledge and experience to set them. Others have specific redpoint, on-sight, or bouldering goals but have trouble answering basic questions about their performance history and current skills, so they have no way of knowing if their goals are realistic or achievable. Many meander from climb to climb with little idea of where they have been or where they are going, and these climbers can become frustrated about not meeting their expected performance. Effectively improving performance comes from diligently applying effort toward specific goals.

The best way to improve in any arena is by first thoughtfully assessing your past performance and current abilities. To set good goals and reach your potential as an athlete, you'll need to accurately evaluate your strengths and weaknesses, performance history, and emotional response to climbing. For example, if your season goal is to redpoint a beautiful 5.12a that has inspired you ever since you first saw it, it's critical to know how many 5.11s you've sent in the last year, when you sent them, their characteristics, and how long it took you to complete them. If the last 5.11 you did was a 5.11c eight months ago that took seventeen tries over nine days, you have some work to do before attempting that 5.12a. The point is that the best indicator of what you will be able to achieve in the next six to twelve months is the climbing you have done in the past year, and therefore, assessing your performance history and current abilities is essential to setting challenging yet achievable goals.

This chapter has a number of assessment categories, questions, and activities. Adapt them as needed to your situation and create a profile of who you are now as a climber. Completing the assessment will show how you became the climber you are today and is the first step in the process of creating the climber you want to be. Take the time to be candid with yourself so you can gain an understanding of your climbing and correct deficiencies before they interfere with your goals. If you have never performed a formal assessment, chances are you don't yet know enough about your climbing to set and achieve realistic, high-quality goals.

Likes and Dislikes

Start your self-appraisal by writing down your likes and dislikes. Answer the following questions for three of your favorite climbs or boulder problems of any grade: What are their characteristics? For example, were they long endurance routes or short and bouldery? Cruxy or continuous? Was the crux near the top, middle, or bottom of the route? Was it steep, vertical, or slabby? Did it have off-widths? Cracks? Be specific and give details: describe holds, features, rests, the style of the route, the setting, the nature of the protection, and anything that stood out to you as enjoyable. Use the following template, which you'll also find as a PDF file on the DVD.

An honest assessment of your likes and dislikes can reveal your strengths and weaknesses. In general, people prefer things they are good at and shy away from those in which they are weak. Make a note of any strong likes or dislikes on the form below and then run the list by your climbing partners and ask their opinions—they've seen the types of climbs that attract you and the climbing skills at which you excel. Look for patterns. What are the common threads that run through the climbs? Do all your favorites involve crimpy cruxes or have hands-down rests? Are they all crack climbs or low-angle slabs? Fill out the following worksheet using the patterns you discovered. Not all the distinctions will apply to you, so disregard those that aren't relevant to your situation. Also, no doubt some of these characteristics were likely obvious to you before completing the assessment. Most climbers have a strong general sense of their preferences. Nonetheless, there are things that are easy to overlook.

The real utility here lies in uncovering likes and dislikes that you didn't openly acknowledge previously so that you can make plans to correct them. "I hate slopers!" is a common lament. The question is, how does hating slopers affect your climbing performance, and are you going to do something about it other than avoiding them? The good news is that with practice things you dislike, or even fear, can become things you look forward to. You'll get a real sense of accomplishment when you master something that you once disliked or even dreaded.

If you don't correct deficiencies, they may end up hindering your progress when you encounter them on future climbs. They can end up making routes harder than they should be by creating additional physical or emotional cruxes.

On the positive side, understanding what you love can help you choose which harder routes to attempt. Really loving a route or boulder problem and appreciating its moves, features, setting, and holds can be

What angle do you enjoy? Dislike?

Self-Assessment Worksheet: Most and Least Favorite Climbs

Answer the following questions for three of your favorite climbs or boulder problems of any grade.

Climb _____ Grade _____

Trad _____ Sport _____ Boulder problem _____ Other _____

1. Describe the characteristics of the route. Was it short, long, continuous, steep, a slab, a crack, a face?

2. What was the general nature of the holds?

3. Where was the crux?

4. Was the physical crux the same as the redpoint crux?

5. What was resting like on this route?

6. In general, how would you describe the nature of the movement? Was it static or dynamic? What did you like about it?

7. What was the nature of the protection on this route?

8. For boulderers, what was the landing like and how tall was the problem?

9. How accurate would you say the grade was?

10. What else was important or enjoyable about this climb?

Now list three of your least favorite climbs or boulder problems of any grade. What are the characteristics of these climbs? Use the following questions to specify the things that you found unpleasant.

Climb _____ Grade _____

Trad _____ Sport _____ Boulder problem _____ Other _____

1. Describe the characteristics of the route. Was it short, long, continuous, steep, a slab, a crack, a face?

2. What was the general nature of the holds?

3. Where was the crux?

4. Was the physical crux the same as the redpoint crux?

5. What was resting like on this route?

6. In general, how would you describe the nature of the movement? Was it static or dynamic? What made it unpleasant for you?

7. What was the nature of the protection on this route?

8. For boulderers, what was the landing like and how tall was the problem?

9. How accurate would you say the grade was?

10. What else was important or least enjoyable about this climb?

Self-Assessment Worksheet: Likes and Dislikes

1. What type of climbing do you prefer?

   Trad _____   Sport _____   Bouldering _____   Other _____

2. What route characteristics do you prefer?

3. What are your preferences concerning crux placement?

4. What are your preferences for resting? What lengths will your go to in order to get a good rest? Do you tend toward specific types of rests, such as stems or heel hooks?

5. What are your preferences for protection and landings? Figure out the point at which protection or landings become a distraction, inhibiting your performance because you are thinking more about the fall than the climbing.

6. Do you prefer grades that are soft, hard, or accurate?

7. What type of holds do you like: slopers, crimpers, pockets, pinches, cracks, underclings?

8. Is there is a specific reason why you like these holds?

9. What type of holds do you dislike?

   Is there a specific reason why you don't like them?

10. What type of stone do you prefer: limestone, sandstone, granite, conglomerate?

11. Is there a specific reason why you like this kind of rock?

12. Is there a type of stone you dislike? Is there a specific reason why you don't like it?

13. What are your favorite places to climb? Places you hate to climb? Can you identify specific reasons for these preferences?

14. Are there particular movement skills you like or dislike, such as heel hooks, knee bars, hand or foot jams, turning? Give specific reasons if you can.

15. Are there other likes and dislikes that affect you as a climber?

significant motivations. Knowing your likes and dislikes gives you a list of items to work on as well as a list of characteristics to look for in harder projects that will keep you motivated even when things are not going your way.

Are there hold types—for example, slopers or crimpers—that you like more than others?

Emotional Strengths and Weaknesses

You have to not only evaluate your climbing skills but also take a hard look at your emotional abilities. We use the term abilities here because we believe emotional skills are not fixed but rather can be strengthened through training. The ability to control fear, focus intently, keep a positive attitude when things are not going well, be analytical but not judgmental, and keep climbing despite fatigue or external distractions is just as important as strength and endurance. Again, be honest with yourself and note any weaknesses, and don't be embarrassed to ask your climbing partners to be frank as well.

Can you gather yourself before an attempt so you're focused and relaxed?

Self-Assessment Worksheet
Emotional Strengths and Weaknesses

1. On a scale of 1 to 10, how do you feel about leading?

   1 = you don't like it and try to avoid it
   10 = you love leading and try to avoid top roping

   1   2   3   4   5   6   7   8   9   10

2. Is leading second nature to you or do your palms sweat at the mere idea of tying into the sharp end? Why do you feel the way you do about leading? Have there been specific experiences that led you to feel as you do?

3. How far above your last piece of protection are you comfortable climbing?

4. How far above your last protection point do you start wanting another clip? How does the difficulty of the climbing affect your comfort level?

5. Do you fear possible falls? If so, is there something specific you are afraid of or is this a generalized fear?

6. Do you fear the possible injuries you could sustain from falling? (This is a different question from #5; some climbers simply fear the drop but not the consequences.)

Does leading cause you so much additional stress that it affects your climbing?

Success and Failure

The questions on the next worksheet address an important but often ignored aspect of climbing psychology (see *The Self-Coached Climber* for a longer discussion). Often, strong feelings about success and failure serve as self-fulfilling prophecies and have a significant impact on climbing performance. In other cases these fears can be powerful factors that influence decisions in one direction or another regardless of your fitness, experience, and apparent motivation levels. Once again, be candid with yourself and look for patterns.

Examining Your History

Top climbers keep a history of their on-sights, flashes, and redpoints, and many keep journals to track the weather, their feelings, their physical state, and many other factors each day they climb. All this information helps them understand the different and important aspects that affect performance.

Your redpoint history is a potential wealth of information regarding your abilities even if you don't keep a journal. Begin by recalling your three best and three worst redpoint experiences. Be specific; you need to remember definite routes and experiences well in order to answer the following questions about each one. Additionally you might consider examining your on-sight and flash histories in the same way; the patterns that emerge may be different from those discovered from your redpoint history.

Self-Assessment Worksheet
Success and Failure

1. Describe the last time that you felt you failed at something as a climber. This could be anything within climbing, including a big redpoint, a competition, or a bad day at the crag.

2. What is your attitude toward success? What does it mean to you? How do you define success? When selecting a route or boulder problem for redpoint, do you seek out problems that you are certain you can send or routes where you're not sure, or do you have a different approach? If thinking about success or failure influences your route selection, describe how.

3. Do you fear succeeding? Succeeding can mean you have to move on to another, potentially more difficult climb. Some climbers don't want the pressure to push on, so they just keep making failed attempts on the same project over and over.

4. Are you relaxed while on redpoint, or do you tense up and worry?

5. How fast can you memorize sequences?

6. Can you concentrate on and visualize sequences just before a redpoint burn?

7. Can you focus on the climbing and ignore distractions while you're on the rock?

8. Can you keep climbing once you're pumped?

Self-Assessment Worksheet
Examining Your History

1. What type of climb was it?

   Steep _____   Vertical _____   Slabby _____   Combination _____

2. What was the type of rock?

3. What were the critical holds like?

4. Where was the crux on the climb?

5. What moves do you remember most and why?

6. On a scale of 1 to 10, how well protected was the climb?

   1 = run out and not well protected
   10 = a lace up

   1   2   3   4   5   6   7   8   9   10

7. Did the protection affect your mental state?

8. How were you feeling physically that day?

   1 = tired and not feeling well
   10 = very well rested and feeling great

   1   2   3   4   5   6   7   8   9   10

9. Did you get enough sleep the night before?

10. What was your training and climbing like the week before?

11. What did your warmup consist of that day? How many climbs and what grades?

12. How excited were you as you put on your shoes just prior to leaving the ground?

   1 = completely relaxed
   10 = on-edge, jittery, palms sweating, and hair standing on end

   1   2   3   4   5   6   7   8   9   10

13. What was the weather like?

14. Who were you climbing with? What was it like to be climbing with that person? Were they
    a positive, negative, or neutral factor in your performance? Give an example if you can.

Compare the answers for your three best and worst climbs and look for any patterns that emerge. What factors were consistent in each set of answers? Those factors can also be indications of strengths and weaknesses in your abilities and areas that you can target for improvement or lean on in times of stress. You may also see some keys to success that you can control, such as choosing appropriate climbing partners.

Another method accomplished climbers use to examine their histories is compiling an experience pyramid. A climbing pyramid is a list of all the routes you've sent in the past year in descending order of difficulty. For example:

Climb	Date sent	Grade	Attempts
Buzz Kill	6/1/2009	12c	8
Thunderstruck	5/20/2009	12b	4
Reckless Abandon	5/15/2009	12b	3
Control	4/15/2009	12a	2
Freaky Stylie	4/1/2009	12a	4
Mensa	4/5/2009	12a	2
Erotica	4/1/2009	12a	3
Under the Milky Way	4/20/2009	11d	2
World at War	4/20/2009	11d	1

A number of other 11ds . . .

You can construct separate pyramids for sport routes, trad routes, and boulder problems. You should create a separate pyramid for your on-sights and flashes, if you have enough history with these, to see if any patterns emerge that differ from your redpoints. Don't include any routes or problems you are working on but have not sent. Once you complete the list, look for patterns, especially among the harder grades where you are likely to discover your climbing strengths. Ask yourself the following questions about these routes or problems:

1. What was the wall angle? How steep was the climb, especially at the crux?

2. Was there a predominant type of hold, and what were the holds like at the crux?

3. How long was the route?

4. Where was the crux located (high on the route or low)?

5. Was the route sustained or was it broken by good, solid rests?

The routes listed in the example pyramid above tend to be vertical with small crimpers at the crux, showing that the climber has a predisposition for vertical routes and small, crimpy holds. This reveals a strength both in this hold type and wall angle and, conversely, a possible weakness in slopers and steeply overhanging walls.

The shape of the pyramid can also reveal some interesting things about your climbing. It's common to see a pyramid with one climb at the highest grade, two at the next highest, then four, and then eight (1-2-4-8). A pyramid with this shape shows solid progress and a good foundation for advancement to a higher grade. If, however, the pyramid were tall and skinny, such as 1-0-1-2, it would indicate that you need more experience in the intermediate grades. A flat pyramid (1-6-15-lots) highlights either a climber who has plateaued or one who has developed a very solid experience base and needs to push on to higher grades. The difference between a climber ready to move on and a climber at a plateau is in the number of attempts on the routes at the top of the pyramid. More than ten attempts indicates a plateau, fewer than ten says move up.

Physical Conditioning Assessment

What follows is a framework for evaluating physical conditioning in four areas: aerobic, anaerobic, maximum strength, and stamina. Each area has an activity, the results of which you compare to the chart on the next page that cross-references performance in that area with a targeted climbing grade. In this way you can assess your physical abilities against those required by your goals and targeted projects. You can also easily see if you lag behind in one area.

Aerobic Conditioning

Aerobic conditioning is your ability to produce muscle energy using your body's aerobic restoration system. Aerobically-produced energy is significantly more efficient than anaerobic. As the intensity of an activity increases, such as climbing on smaller holds or a

Performance Guidelines

Consistent Redpoint Goal	Sub-level	Local Aerobic level — Continuous Climbing Level	Local Anaerobic level — Highest Intensity: 4X4	Local Anaerobic level — Mid-level Intensity: Laps on Routes	Strength — Max Bouldering Level	Stamina — C.I.R. Bouldering	Stamina — C.I.R. Routes
5.10	5.10a	5.7/5.8	N/A	5.9-	VB-V1	VB	5.8+
	5.10d	5.8/5.9-	VB-V0	5.9/9+	V0/1	V0	5.9/9+
5.11	5.11a	5.9-/5.9	VB-V1	5.10a/b	V1/V2	V0	5.9+-5.10a
	5.11d	5.9+	V0-V2	5.10b/c	V2/V3	V0/V1	5.10c-5.11a
5.12	5.12a	5.10a-c	V0-V2	5.10d-5.11b	V3/V4	V2	5.10d-5.11b
	5.12d	5.10d-5.11b	V1-V4	5.11c-5.12a	V4/V5	V3	5.11c/5.12a
5.13	5.13a	5.11b/c	V2-V4	5.11d-5.12b	V5/V6	V3/V4	5.12a/b
	5.13d	5.11c-5.12b	V4-V7	5.12b-5.13a	V8-V9	V5/6	5.12c-5.13a
5.14	5.14a/b	5.12b-c	V5-V8	5.12d-5.13a/b	V9-V11	V7-V9	5.13a/b

These general guidelines are consistent with solid performances such as on-sights, or fast redpoints, as well as with continued improvement to the next level.

They do not represent the minimum requirements necessary to climb at a specific grade.

steeper face, your muscles' need for energy will at some point outpace the aerobic system's ability to provide it. At that point, known as the anaerobic threshold, the anaerobic system kicks in, but at a cost. Anaerobic energy production yields large quantities of byproducts that cannot be removed as fast as they are produced. The byproducts accumulate, which produces the familiar burning and eventual failure of a severe pump. Crossing the anaerobic threshold, moving from aerobic to anaerobic energy production, means the clock begins to tick. It's best to delay the onset of anaerobic energy production as long as possible, and you can accomplish this by conditioning your local aerobic system. We commonly think of aerobic conditioning as systemic, involving the cardio-pulmonary system, for activities such as distance running or bicycling. Climbing typically doesn't tax the cardio-pulmonary system, but aerobic conditioning on a local level, for instance the forearms, is very beneficial.

Activity 1: Aerobic Conditioning Assessment

To assess your local aerobic condition, find the highest grade you can climb continuously for twenty minutes without developing a pump. Climb up and down routes the entire time; the climbing should feel easy and your forearms should not feel pumped, stiff, or tight. You should be able to use any holds equally well at this level, even those you don't like. Keep moving and rest as little as possible; if you find you need to rest, the intensity (difficulty) is too high. It may take a few tries to discover what grade level defines your aerobic level, so be patient.

A note for on-sights and flashes: Endurance is especially important to on-sighting and flashing since the duration of an ascent will almost always be longer than a redpoint of the same route. The longer duration means you'll need to stave off a pump longer, recover from a pump mid-route better, and climb longer while pumped to on-sight well. This makes aerobic conditioning crucial to success for on-sight climbers.

A note for boulderers: The role of endurance in bouldering is limited. While there are a few endurance boulder problems, your anaerobic threshold is probably not going to impact your performance on the vast majority of problems. However, endurance might affect

how you recover between problems. The climber with better local aerobic fitness may have an advantage when it comes to recovery and productivity during the course of a day. This is especially true for bouldering competitions in which your rest period is timed or when the number of problems you complete is part of the scoring system. In these situations, it's not the climber who can do the most difficult boulder problem who has the advantage; rather, the climber who can do the most problems at a relatively high level may be in a better position to win. The ability to recover is affected by both your local anaerobic and aerobic fitness. As a result, those who compete in bouldering competitions may want to consider some aerobic and anaerobic conditioning if the comp formats favor the climber who can recover more quickly.

Anaerobic Conditioning

As a roped climber, you'll regularly exceed your anaerobic threshold even if you have a superbly conditioned local aerobic production system. The good news is that you can improve your anaerobic capacity through conditioning. To assess your ability to process and tolerate anaerobic activity, perform the following activity and cross-reference it on the conditioning chart.

Activity 2: Anaerobic Conditioning Assessment

Pick four boulder problems of equal grade. Climb all four with a minimum of rest between each. Run, don't walk, between the problems and get off the ground as quickly as possible. Rest for two minutes and repeat the four problems. Repeat the climb and rest sequence until you have climbed the four problems four times. You want to find the highest grade problems you can do without pumping out and falling off. Ideally you want to just barely finish the last problem of the final set.

Alternatively you can pick a route to climb instead of four boulder problems. Climb the route and begin your rest period as soon as you weight the rope at the top. Two minutes later, begin another lap, and repeat until you've completed four. For optimal effect, the route should be hard enough that you can just barely complete the fourth lap. Pick a continuous route with poor or no rest stances; remember, this is a training exercise in which you want to stress your anaerobic system and then allow it to partially recover between laps.

Maximum Effort

You're looking for your consistent maximum bouldering level. What is the highest grade you can consistently send in six to ten attempts? It may take some thought and experimentation to figure out what this level is for you. Although not an actual measure of your maximum strength, maximum bouldering grade is actually more important to assess since it's a reflection of your current fitness and ability to deploy tactics and movement. Once you've figured out your consistent max compare it to the cross-reference conditioning chart.

Stamina

Stamina is a measure of how many high-intensity efforts you can put in on a given day. To be as productive as possible, you may need to make multiple high-intensity efforts in a day. Further, you want to know that even after several strong efforts you can still succeed on later burns; you need to be able to make a number of good attempts on your project in a single day. The stamina test is of particular interest to boulderers because experience suggests that there is a strong relationship between current stamina level and your bouldering, on-sight, and redpoint level. Compare the results from the following activity to the conditioning chart.

Activity 3: Stamina Assessment

First determine the highest grade for which you can climb a single pitch without developing a pump, and then do nine to twelve pitches at this grade. You may need to do routes more than one time if you are in a gym or at a small crag. Rest as much as you like between each pitch; there is no timed interval in this exercise. It may take a bit of experimentation to determine the grade and the number of reps you can do, but once you do, compare the results to the conditioning chart.

For boulderers the activity is a little different. Due to the higher intensity and shorter duration of boulder problems, getting a pump from a single problem is less likely. Usually if a boulderer gets a pump it's either from an unusually long problem or it's the result of doing problems in close succession. So to perform this activity correctly, find the highest grade at which you can complete twelve to fifteen boulder problems with a maximum of three tries each with as much rest as you like between each effort. Ideally all the problems should be just above your flash level. If you try a problem and fail, rest before trying it again, and if you don't complete a problem in three tries, move on to the next problem. Rest as long as you want; you don't want to get a pump by giving yourself too little rest. The activity can take two hours or more.

After the halfway point in the activity you will find it increasingly difficult to move the way you want due to fatigue, and you'll need more rest between problems. This is to be expected: while the difficulty of the routes is not high, doing them in large volume is challenging. Also, it's common to over- or underestimate the proper grade level for the activity. If you get to the tenth problem and you've done every problem in one or two tries and you don't feel that tired, keep going to see how the rest of the activity feels, but you may have underestimated your stamina level. If you feel yourself running out of energy before the halfway point and your movement is getting hard to control, then the grade is probably too high. In the best case you'll get through all the problems but the last few will be very hard, and you will be exhausted even though you never got a pump.

In both versions of this activity you need to scout out the crag or gym. After you have decided on the grade level, make a list of all the climbs or problems at that grade, decide which you'll be doing more than once, and establish an order for the climbs.

Assessment Implications

This assessment gives you a detailed view of your climbing strengths and weaknesses, providing a comprehensive picture of your climbing abilities, which becomes your starting point for improvement. We've found that it's most beneficial to improve your weak areas first, although you'll need to undertake training with an eye on your goals.

Goals help you determine which of your abilities may hamper your progress and would therefore be considered a weak area. For example, if you've been

Your ability to perform difficult moves on a roped route can be measured by your consistent maximum bouldering level.

bouldering heavily for several months to the exclusion of roped climbing, your local aerobic endurance and route stamina may need to improve if you'd like to send sport routes. But if your goal is to stick with bouldering, then your conditioning in these two areas may be perfectly adequate.

Performing an assessment is both a science and an art. What follows are the responses of real climbers to the self-assessments to which we respond with commentary and suggestions. It's not enough to do the assessment; you then need to process the information and use it to create an improvement plan. There are a number of ways to do this, and the following example shows how you might process your own assessment.

Assessment Conclusions

It can be hard to successfully identify your areas of proficiency and weakness. What you identify as strengths and weaknesses are often based on what you believe to be the most important attributes to climbing successfully. For example, climbers who believe that power is of singular import tend to believe that failure on a move or climb is caused by a lack of the right kind of strength. We tend to assess ourselves in ways that conform to what we believe about climbing and about ourselves. This is why it's important to ask other people about your climbing—they may have different attitudes and beliefs and, therefore, will interpret your climbing in different ways. The answers on the next page were pulled from responses to the questionnaires described earlier.

What can we say about this climber's strengths and weaknesses, and what recommendations do we have for improving? Since the climber doesn't list goals, we'll assume he wants to improve in general.

Assessment of past experience: A relatively tall, thin pyramid suggests this climber is ready to break out, but in the narrow niche of vertical climbs with crimpy climbing and possibly low-height cruxes. He'll need to broaden his climbing experience to access the entire crag of slab to severely overhung routes.

Assessment of strengths and weaknesses: The obvious strength here is with crimpers on vertical terrain in southern sandstone and the lack of lead-induced fear. Weaknesses are in the use of slopers, overhanging terrain, and any other type of rock. Simply broadening his experiences would benefit this climber greatly—he should take a few trips and climb on other types of stone. We recommend overhanging routes and climbing slopers.

Assessment of likes and dislikes: What we find when we compare the climber's likes and dislikes to his best and worst performances is not surprising, but it is instructive. Best and most enjoyable performances were on vertical routes and the familiar southern sandstone; worst are overhanging routes and slopers. He indicates that climbers in the area can be a distraction, especially when he dislikes them, leading us to conclude that he may have problems concentrating and focusing.

Assessment of physical conditioning: This climber is well-suited physically to the demands of vertical walls with good rests. The level of conditioning is consistent with low-end vertical 5.11s with an emphasis on technical movement and balance rather than bouldering strength, and the climber's preference for big rests reinforces this conclusion. Current maximum bouldering level at V1 won't allow much if any steep climbing since the movement intensity on these routes very often meets or exceeds that grade. We do, however, see a good base of local aerobic fitness and stamina upon which this climber can build.

Recommendations: Without a clear idea of where this climber wants to go, it's impossible to build a targeted improvement plan, but we can make some general recommendations.

Boulder: Since climbing involves the precise, movement-appropriate application of force, maximum strength is best developed by bouldering. The movement intensity of boulder problems often requires the climber to stretch his limits both in terms of strength and movement, making it the ideal activity for improving his ability to apply force in effective ways. He should add one or two bouldering sessions per week.

Climb slopers: Slopers are everywhere, and not being able to effectively use them will hamper the climber's progress. He must force himself to become comfortable with this type of hold. The best way to practice is during a weekly bouldering session.

Overhanging routes: Once he gains a bit of strength and comfort with overhanging walls by bouldering, he should begin getting on more and more overhung routes.

Sample climber preference assessment

1. **What type of climbing do you prefer?**

   Trad _____   Sport __X__   Bouldering _____   On-sighting _____   Other _____

2. **What route characteristics do you prefer?** *Vertical routes broken by solid rests.*

3. **What are your preferences concerning crux placement?** *Low on the route.*

4. **What are your preferences for resting? What lengths will you go to in order to get a good rest? Do you tend toward specific types of rests such as stems or heel hooks?** *I like a large ledge to stand on and other hands-down rests in the middle of the climb.*

5. **What are your preferences for protection and landings? Figure out the point at which protection or the landing becomes a distraction, inhibiting your performance because you are thinking more about the fall than the climbing.** *I don't like run outs greater than 10 feet, but I'm comfortable leading.*

6. **Do you prefer grades that are soft, hard, or accurate?** *Accurate.*

7. **What type of holds do you like: slopers, crimpers, pockets, pinches, cracks, underclings?** *The cruxes on my favorite routes tend to be crimpy.*

8. **Is there is a specific reason that you like these holds?** *They feel more solid to me. I always feel so tentative on slopers, as if I may slip off at any time.*

9. **What type of holds do you dislike?** *slopers*

   Is there a specific reason why you don't like them? *I feel unstable using them.*

10. **What type of stone do you prefer: limestone, sandstone, granite, conglomerate?** *I am most comfortable on my home stone, which is southern sandstone.*

11. **Is there a specific reason why you like this kind of rock?** *It tends to have lots of crimpers and I'm used to its gritty texture.*

12. **Is there a type of stone you dislike? Is there a specific reason why you don't like it?** *Limestone is somewhat polished and pockety or blocky. It's not at all like southern sandstone.*

13. **What are your favorite places to climb? Places you hate to climb? Can you identify specific reasons for these preferences?** *I like climbing in the Southeast on sandstone. I can't stand granite because it's slippery and has too many slopers.*

14. **Are there particular movement skills you like or dislike, such as heel hooks, knee bars, hand and foot jams, turning? Give specific reasons if you can.** *If there's a heel to be used, I'll use it! I rarely use knee bars or hand jams.*

15. **Are there other likes and dislikes that affect you as a climber?** *I don't really have any issue with leading on sport routes up to 10-foot run outs.*

    My best sends have been on southern sandstone on vertical routes when I'm climbing with my favorite partner. My worst experiences are with overhanging routes involving slopers and steep climbing or when climbing around people I dislike.

    What my partners say about my climbing: They say I complain about slopers and overhanging routes. I tend to shy away from routes with these attributes. They also say I don't have trouble leading and that I don't become gripped when I get above a bolt.

    My route pyramid for the past twelve months is:
    1 x 12a crimpy crux low on route with hands-down rest immediately above, sandstone
    0 x 11d
    3 x 11c all vertical routes on sandstone
    12 x 11b only two overhanging routes, the remainder tend toward vertical
    Continuous climbing twenty minutes at 5.9
    Maximum consistent bouldering grade: V1
    4x4 grade: V0-
    Stamina grade: 10b

Road trip: Traveling to new areas with different rock will broaden his abilities and make new areas enjoyable rather than frustrating.

Climb with others: He should practice climbing in crowded environments such as a gym so that he can learn to focus on the climb rather than the people around him.

The starting point in any serious improvement plan is to assess the current situation. Begin your journey to improving redpoint performance by taking the time to make a detailed and candid review of your climbing and you'll be rewarded with a more effective improvement program.

QUICK TICKS

✓ Begin by assessing your likes and dislikes both through a self examination and by asking others you climb with.

✓ Construct a route pyramid of climbs you've completed in the last six months.

✓ Evaluate your emotional responses to a variety of climbing stimuli.

✓ Determine your attitude toward success and failure.

✓ Evaluate your physical conditioning in the areas of strength, endurance, and stamina against standards for the grade.

✓ Use your assessment, along with goals, to guide the creation of your improvement plan.

CHAPTER 2
Setting Goals

U nderstanding your current abilities is simply the stepping-off point to improving your redpointing. Next you'll need to decide where you're headed, because your goal, in combination with your current abilities, determines what the road ahead will look like.

Matching Expectations to Reality

There's a fine line between a good goal and poor goal. Goals need to be challenging and achievable to be motivating. If the goal is too big, you never get there and eventually you lose motivation when you realize that you can't succeed. Too easy, though, and success is a given, so why try too hard?

How do you choose the right goal then? Your goals will be influenced by the following factors.

- Your current condition as described by your self-assessment from chapter 1.

- Your lifestyle. How much time and effort can you devote to climbing each week?

- Effort you've applied in the near past toward improving your climbing performance. If you've been working effectively and diligently at improving for some time, you can't expect big gains to come quickly.

- Number of years you've had performance increases. The greater your past improvement, the less you can expect to gain.

- Your age. While everyone is different, age does matter. It can mean longer recovery time, dealing with long-term pain or injuries acquired from other activities, and slower development of fitness levels. These physical issues can be offset somewhat by greater maturity, better focus, and knowing yourself well.

- Access to quality improvement resources such as a nearby crag or gym and climbing partners. Better access leads to better potential improvement.

In essence, the younger you are (within reason), the more time you can devote to climbing, the less effort you've already applied to climbing improvement, and the closer the quality resources, the more quickly and dramatically you can improve. Let's look at a couple examples.

John's 20 and has been climbing regularly for about a year. He'd like to improve, but school takes up much of his time and there are few good resources near his college. During breaks he has a good gym near home and time to travel to excellent outdoor crags.

    Current redpoint level: 5.9
    Current consistent bouldering level: V1
    Continuous climbing: 5.7
    Stamina: 5.8
    Resources: limited for much of the year
    Goal: consistent 5.11 redpoint ability this year

Jane is 42 and has been climbing for almost 15 years. She climbs four times a week, much of it indoors, and can travel to excellent crags three or more hours away.

    Current redpoint level: upper-5.10
    Current consistent bouldering level: V2
    Continuous climbing: 5.9
    Stamina: 5.10a
    Resources: good for training, adequate for outdoor redpoints
    Goal: send Freaky Stylie (12a) this year

Jack is in his mid-20s, single, and highly motivated to improve. He's been climbing for a few years and is now leading 5.12. He has a good gym near his home and quality outdoor resources within an hour's drive, and he can climb four or five days a week. He wants to climb 5.13.

    Current redpoint level: 5.12a
    Current consistent bouldering level: V4
    Continuous climbing: 5.9
    Stamina: 5.11a
    Resources: excellent
    Goal: send any 5.13 this year

Joanne is in her late 20s, married with no children, and highly motivated to improve. She's only been climbing for six months and is primarily interested in bouldering. She has a good gym near her home but outdoor resources are a few hours away, and she can climb four or five days a week. Her goal is to climb at the V5 level.

Current redpoint level: V2
Current consistent bouldering level: V2
Continuous climbing: unknown
Stamina: V0
Resources: good
Goal: send V5 consistently in six months

Are the goals realistic for each of these climbers? What can each expect in the way of improvement over the next year?

Because of resource and time constraints, John will have difficulty meeting his goal. He just can't climb consistently enough over the school year to make a big difference in his abilities. He does have a couple of things going for him: he's young with little climbing experience, which means that with a moderate application of effort his learning curve could be quite steep. Over the summer when he has access to resources and the time to use them, he just might be able to redpoint some 5.11s. Given John's situation it's probably unrealistic to expect anything more than this for the upcoming season.

Jane's been working on her climbing for quite a while, but her goal of a single, specific 12a is within her reach. Since she can devote the time and has excellent resources, she can tailor her training to match the demands of her targeted climb. Freakie Stylie is a vertical climb with a dynamic crux 60 feet off the ground. She can easily duplicate its requirements in a gym setting and train specifically for it. A pyramid of similar routes can be constructed leading to her targeted climb at its apex so she gains specific climbing experience. Her age and lengthy career suggest a flatter learning curve overall, but her experience will allow her to quickly apply practiced movement skills where required. Her physical conditioning is not what it needs to be to send Freaky Stylie, but she can build it with effort.

Jack has set himself a big goal—jumping an entire number grade in a single season is a tall order. In order to achieve it he'll need to apply significant effort in a very targeted way. First, he should choose a popular 5.13a that really motivates him. A popular route means it's probably good quality, and chances are Jack can find someone who's climbed it to help determine if it's a good route for him and to provide beta. Second, he'll need to create an improvement plan designed to prepare him for that specific 13a. His age, motivation, current abilities, and resources all suggest he just might be able to pull it off.

Joanne's goal of attaining a consistent V5 level in six months is well within the realm of possibility for her. Given the access to a good gym and enough free time to allow frequent trips to quality outdoor boulder fields, Joanne should be able to achieve her goal. Our recommendation would be twofold. First, she should take care not to get sucked into the all-too-common bouldering mentality of only working near her maximum level. At least twice a week she should perform a CIR/VIR bouldering block as described in *The Self-Coached Climber* to gain the depth and breadth of experience and stamina needed to advance to higher grades. Second, she should take frequent trips outdoors to push her limits, gain wider experience, and provide the mental stimulus to retain interest.

Long-Term Goal

After considering all the factors listed in the beginning of this chapter, your first task is to set a long-term climbing goal. Two years from now, where do you want to be? The goal can be a specific route ("I want to send The Beast!"), a grade ("I want to boulder V8."), a type of climb ("I want to send all the routes in the Hell Cave."), general improvement ("I want to become proficient at 5.12."), or just about anything else you can imagine as long as it's discrete, specific, and objective. A goal of simply "being better" is not specific enough; you can't tell when or if that objective has been achieved, so it's less motivating. Make your long-term goal discrete and exciting. Don't make your goal to "climb a 5.13"; rather, make it "I want to climb Apollo Reed."

Take some time and consider what you want to achieve. Be sure to give some thought to all the factors discussed above and the gap between where you are now and your possible goals. If you don't have the resources to reach the goal, you'll set yourself up for frustration. Don't get us wrong on this point; we love lofty goals. But recognize that any worthwhile goal takes commitment and that you'll need to pony up the time, sweat, and other resources to make it happen. It pays to think about this North Star, or long-term goal, carefully; once selected it drives your improvement efforts.

Short-Term Goals

The gap between your current performance level and the level you'll need for your long-term goal may be quite large and, at first glance, seemingly unachievable, but this alone should not deter you. Your next step after establishing a long-term goal is setting short-term, or interim, goals. Whereas the long-term goal might take several years to attain, short-term goals should be achievable in a period of three months to a year.

Apollo Reed (13a) follows the steepest section of the Coliseum at Summersville Lake in West Virginia.

Your interim goals should be challenging but achievable. Remember, if you set the goal too low, you guarantee success with little effort. Too high and only superhuman effort can get you over the top. Interim goals need to stretch you and require effort to reach. How much progress is reasonable for a single year or season?

Here are some rules of thumb: If you have plenty of time, are well motivated, can climb three or four days each week, have frequent access to outdoor routes and a training facility or crag, haven't trained hard in the previous six months to a year, and have good climbing partners, you could improve up to four letter grades or more (three V grades for boulderers) in a single year, especially if you're working in the lower grades. For example, improving from V0 to V3 or 5.7 to 5.10 in your first year is common and relatively easy, moving from 5.12a to 13a in a single year is more difficult but is being seen more frequently, as is getting to V5.

If you can only climb two or three times per week or you've already been working hard on your climbing over the last six months or year, you might need to step your interim goal down to a two-letter grade improvement.

Additionally if your current abilities fall in the 5.12 range (V5 for boulderers) or above, a four letter grade (three V grade) improvement may not be possible even if you satisfy all the prerequisites cited above. This is not to say that you shouldn't try; it's simply an acknowledgment that not everyone ends up climbing V8 or 5.13.

As with your long-term goal, your interim goals should be specific, even down to naming the routes that you'll send over the season. As we'll see in the next section, you can use progressive performance pyramids to provide continuous and specific improvement, culminating in achieving your short-term goal.

Once your initial interim goal is set, consider the second year or season and beyond. How much progress can you make toward your North Star, or long-term goal, each year? It is the stringing together of short term, achievable goals that makes your North Star reachable.

Progressive Performance Pyramids

Usually at this point, after having set a long-term goal and perhaps several interim goals, climbers diverge wildly in their approaches to improvement. Many engage almost exclusively in physical conditioning, believing that improved climbing performance is a simple matter of increased strength and endurance, while others climb whichever routes or boulder problems look interesting. You need a practical method to focus improvement on your interim goals and, ultimately, long-term goals by directing your efforts in the most beneficial way.

A performance pyramid is a listing of specific routes to send in four levels. By forcing you to send certain routes or boulder problems, performance pyramids produce the most relevant experience for achieving your goals, thereby speeding up your development in crucial areas of performance. All the routes on a given level carry the same grade, and each level is one letter grade harder than the tier below it: a base of eight climbs, a second tier of four climbs, a third tier of two climbs, and a top tier of a single route. For example:

12a

11d 11d

11c 11c 11c 11c

11b 11b 11b 11b 11b 11b 11b 11b

Begin by examining the gap between your current level of performance and your first interim goal; consider the nature of the climbs in the redpoint pyramid you listed in chapter 1, page 11. Are the routes in your history similar to your interim goal? If you have some experience with routes similar to your goal (the route at the apex of the pyramid) you'll have a leg up on the first pyramid; if not, you'll need to start at a lower grade and build experience with routes like it.

For example, assume your chapter 1 experience pyramid consisted of the following grades, and the routes were similar to your interim and long-term goals.

12a

11d 11d

11c 11c 11c 11c

11b 11b 11b 11b 11b 11b 11b 11b

Your first performance pyramid on the road to your ultimate goal might look this:

12b

12a   *12a*

11d 11d   *11d 11d*

11c 11c 11c 11c   *11c 11c 11c 11c*

11b 11b 11b 11b 11b 11b 11b 11b

The original historic pyramid consisted of:

one 12a
two 11ds
four 11cs
eight 11bs

The new performance pyramid consists of one 12b, two 12as, four 11ds, and eight 11cs.

However, since you've already sent a portion of this new pyramid, you won't need to start over, you simply include those routes already sent and add on any deficiencies. In this case you need to send the following grades, preferably in this order, before bumping your pyramid up a grade: four 11cs, two 11ds, one 12a, one 12b.

These routes should be similar to your goal, so choose carefully. You want to build a wealth of experience in a specific area in a relatively short period of time. For simplicity's sake we've simply listed grades, but you'll want to name the specific routes. In this way you remain focused on your long-term goal by choosing in advance routes that will give you the experience you need to advance to the next level.

Once you've clipped the anchors on the final route in this first pyramid, it's time to create the second. Here's what you'd have completed:

12b

12a 12a

11d 11d 11d 11d

11c 11c 11c 11c 11c 11c 11c 11c

The next pyramid is constructed like the first:

12c

12b   *12b*

12a 12a   *12a 12a*

11d 11d 11d 11d   *11d 11d 11d 11d*

11c 11c 11c 11c 11c 11c 11c 11c

Your new list of routes to send consists of four 11ds, two 12as, one 12b, and one 12c. This progression is perfectly reasonable for a single climbing season given the proper conditions as described above. Let's take a look at what you can accomplish in this scenario. To send the targeted 12c, you would have previously sent sixteen new routes to push your hardest climb up two letter grades. You would have sent four routes as hard or harder than anything completed previously. Lastly, you would have raised your base from 11b to 11d. This is significant progress for sixteen weeks, but well within reach for many climbers.

It's important to recognize the commitment and focus necessary to achieve this progress. There are significant challenges to holding true to your chosen course. Don't let your plans get changed by the whims of your partners or your own indecision or fear. Sometimes climbers stray off their pyramids simply because they are intimidated by the goals they have set. Maintaining discipline is important, but so is flexibility. If you go on a spontaneous road trip or a great new crag is discovered in your region, find a way to work these developments into your pyramid. Don't let your goals take the fun out of climbing! Rather, goals should be the source of fun and deep personal satisfaction.

You'll need to allow time to practice movement skills and work on supplementing the necessary physical capabilities. Likewise you'll need a good dose of motivation to stick with the program week after week.

Yes, this program takes effort, but you'll build a rapid portfolio of successful ascents. Those interim successes on the way to your ultimate goal are remarkably motivating and satisfying. Unlike other training regimens that require long periods of relatively poor performance to peak for a short time, the performance pyramid method consistently rewards your efforts with modest but important successes.

What if your chapter 1 pyramid doesn't look like the standard 1-2-4-8 or the routes aren't consistent with your goals? You'll need to step back a bit and fill in with climbs that will provide the essential experience. For example, suppose your pyramid from chapter 1 consisted of:

12a

11c 11c

11b 11b 11b

11a 11a 11a 11a 11a 11a

You'd want to gain quite a bit more experience before pushing on to 12b. We might recommend:

12a

			11d 11d	
	11c 11c		*11c 11c*	
	11b 11b 11b		*11b 11b 11b 11b 11b*	
11a 11a 11a 11a 11a 11a			*11a 11a*	

The next progressive pyramid would be the more standard:

		12b
12a		*12a*
11d 11d		*11d 11d*
11c 11c 11c 11c		*11c 11c 11c 11c*
11b 11b 11b 11b 11b 11b 11b 11b		
11a 11a 11a 11a 11a 11a 11a 11a		

In this way you can convert a nonstandard pyramid into one in which you gain the skills necessary to move toward your goals.

Pyramid Variations

You can use variations of the pyramid in a number of settings.

Short-term goals. You can use the pyramid structure to help reach short-term goals, such as when you're on a road trip and trying to familiarize yourself with the climbing at a new location or you just want to try something new to see how it works for you. Go well below your redpoint level, say two number grades, and put together a representative sampling of climbs in a 1-2-4 pyramid. If your redpoint level at your home crag is 12a, for instance, set your new crag familiarization pyramid at four 10as, two 10bs, and one 10c. The experience you gain from starting at a lower level will give you a broad base of support from which to tackle more difficult climbs.

Pyramids for bouldering. Bouldering is a special case when considering pyramids. We observe that the typical boulderer applies most of his time working on projects, often spending significant time on problems that take five or more tries to complete. Focusing on projects tends to limit the breadth and depth of experience and slows development of skills by reducing the quality and amount of climbing completed in each session.

Bad habits aside, boulderers can complete a large number of problems in one session. If you are working at the right level of difficulty, this fosters a high volume of high-quality practice in a short period of time, which aids in improving overall bouldering performance. Boulderers can rapidly gain a great deal of experience and push their levels higher by spending less time working projects and more time bringing up their base levels. This can be achieved by using flatter and broader pyramids as part of a short-term training structure rather than as a mid-range performance goal as you might do with a route pyramid. It may be more accurate to refer to this flattened pyramid as a block approach, reflecting a mix of Continuous and Variable Intensity Repetitions rather than a pyramid. See *The Self-Coached Climber* for descriptions of these workouts.

To create your first block, start at your current consistent flash level for bouldering. The first goal is to complete a large number of problems at this level in a single workout. For example, if your current flash level is V3, then your goal is to complete fourteen to sixteen V3s in a single session. You may repeat problems you have already done; in fact most of the problems may be repeats. The point is to do a large number of climbs at that grade in one session. After you are able to do a workout of fifteen V3s you are then ready to start building the next level by reducing the number of V3s in the workout and adding a number of V4s. Thus the next workout might consist of ten V3s and five V4s. In each subsequent workout you will remove a couple of V3s and replace them with V4s until you can do fourteen to sixteen V4s in a single session. After that, you start reducing the number of V4s in the workout and adding V5s.

Pyramids for trad climbers. Although many of the principles of progressive pyramids apply to traditional climbing, you may need to broaden the pyramid to take into account the challenge of placing protection. Gaining a deep understanding and extensive experience in placing gear is not simply an exercise in improving efficiency. Your safety is at stake if you come under stress during a difficult climb and then can't figure out the pro. Especially for areas or rock types new to you, learning to protect yourself adequately is an essential skill that cannot be bypassed.

Start with a wide variety of easier climbs, from finger cracks to off-widths, horizontals to pockets, and do lots of them. Many good texts and instructors are available for reference, but there is no good substitute for experience when it comes to placing pro. Keep in mind that, generally, as the grade increases, so does the difficulty of finding good gear placements. This is another reason to use a relatively broad pyramid, say 1-5-15. Give yourself the time to develop protection skills before you begin to tackle more difficult climbs.

Pyramids for on-sighting. By definition, the opportunity to practice on-sighting is limited. There are only so many routes to attempt at your on-sight level, and once you've given a particular route a go you can't go back and try to on-sight it later. You get just one shot. This means that most climbers are somewhat inexperienced at on-sighting, and as we explain in detail in chapter 8, the skills required differ from those necessary for successful redpoints. To acquire on-sight expertise, broaden your pyramid. Get lots of experience at a base level before attempting more difficult routes nearer your limit. This may mean you have to travel to find viable routes. As you travel, approach new routes, even at your warmup level, as on-sight attempts using the full methodology described later in the book. Warmups or routes below your current flash limit can provide opportunities for high-quality practice for on-sight tactics.

Pyramids for stamina training. Similar to bouldering pyramids or blocks, stamina pyramids are not used for the sake of creating and achieving short and mid-range performance goals. Stamina pyramids are used as a training structure for the sake of fostering a high volume of climbing at a specific level in a short period of time. This means that their shape is relatively flat, providing a great volume of work at about the same intensity.

Creating stamina pyramids for routes is very similar to the method for bouldering blocks described above. The goal is to complete a large number of routes in a single day or session that fall into a narrow range of difficulty. In order to be effective, this difficulty level needs to be at about your current flash level. Climbers who are fit may be able to work at a slightly higher level, while those who aren't will need to work a few letter grades below their flash level. The goal is to do ten to fourteen routes of a given grade in one session, not including the warmup and cool down. You can progress on routes the same way we suggested progressing in bouldering—that is, by reducing the number of problems at the lower level and increasing the number of climbs you do at the next level. So if you have been successful in doing twelve 5.11as in a single workout, then the next step is to attempt to do nine 5.11as and three 5.11bs until you are able to do ten to fourteen 5.11bs in a single workout.

You can also modify the workout so that the total number of routes is lower but the intensity is higher. Let's say that your current redpoint level is 5.12a and your current flash level is 5.11a. If you know several routes rated 5.11b or 5.11c well, you can try to do eight or nine repetitions of 5.11b and c in a single session. The key to this workout is familiarity with several routes of the right grade. Knowing the routes well enough to do them quickly does not lessen the impact of the workout. You still need to perform at a relatively high level for a large number of repetitions.

Planning is important for effective stamina workouts. You need to know the routes you will do and the order you will do them in before you start. Before heading out the door or as soon as you arrive at your destination, jot down the fourteen boulder problems or eight routes to be completed that day.

Completing a self-assessment and then setting challenging yet achievable goals sets your course, and interim goals chart each step along the way. This clarifies your path to improvement, allowing you to concentrate on weaknesses with the end goal in mind.

QUICK TICKS

✓ You can improve more quickly and dramatically if you are younger (within reason), can devote more time to climbing, have applied less effort to climbing so far, and have more quality resources close by.

✓ Set a specific long-term goal such as a particular route to send, and then create short-term goals that are incremental steps toward your long-term goal by using progressive performance pyramids.

✓ Begin by sending all the routes at the lowest grade and then move up a level to prepare yourself for the skills and conditioning more difficult climbs require.

✓ Post your pyramid where you're likely to see it: the refrigerator or a mirror. Mark off the climbs as you send them. You'll see your progress daily, and you'll be reminded of those climbs that remain to be sent.

✓ Reward yourself when you succeed, which should be regularly under this system. Take time to recognize your advancement by treating yourself.

✓ Track your progress indoors and out. Keep a log of when you send a route so you can look back at your progress and assess your improvement.

✓ Target high-quality routes. To make sure you enjoy pursuing your goals, spend time on the very best routes you can find; climb the classics in a variety of styles to maximize your learning and enjoyment. Avoid low-quality routes and routes that you know are soft for the grade.

CHAPTER 3

Choosing a Route and Planning Your Day

The New River Gorge and surrounding area has over five hundred sport routes covering many genres from slab to steep. There are even more around Salt Lake City. Wherever you climb the choices are likely to be daunting, and you want to be careful to choose routes that are inspiring, fun, and will help propel you toward your goals. How do you go about picking great routes when the choices can seem overwhelming?

You can narrow down the choices significantly by adhering to your goals. If those goals are specific to a route or a set of routes of a particular type, you can use the following steps to create a list with which to fill your pyramid.

1. What grade are you seeking? If you require four 11bs, two 11cs, and an 11d, that eliminates, at least for the time being, routes not of those grades.

2. What route characteristics do you seek? You're working toward a specific performance goal, so the cumu-lative skills, knowledge, tactics, and fitness you gain from routes lower on your pyramid should help you complete the more difficult routes. Variety can be good, although too much can dilute the experience you need. For instance, if your ultimate goal is a short route with lots of technical bouldering, you may not want to place multipitch slab routes on the lower levels of your pyramid. Here are some variables to consider when comparing routes and thinking about your pyramid as a whole.

• Wall angle. Steep, vertical, or slabby?

• Predominant hold type. Slopers, pockets, crimps?

• Endurance requirements. Are there good, solid rests or is the route continuous?

• Strength requirements. Is there a difficult crux with movement that is more difficult than the rest of the climb, or is the route more continuous in nature?

The Endless Wall at the New River Gorge is four miles long.

Discombobulated (11a), a New River classic, follows the prominent arête.

- Style of movement. Does the route consist of thuggy, technical, or other movement styles?

- Crux location. If there is a distinct crux, is it high on the route or low?

- Length. Is the route short or long?

- Safety or scare factor. How intimidating is the route from a safety perspective?

3. Assess the potential on-sight, flash, or redpoint project candidate for quality and your inspiration to climb it. Motivation is a key to success, and if a particular route has no interest to you—even if it fits nicely into your pyramid—then move on to another. Be careful here, though, that you don't eliminate routes just because they don't seem like something you'd like. We all tend to gravitate to those things we do well and shun those things we do not. Don't let your natural inclinations stand in the way of progress toward your goals; sometimes taking on a route outside of your areas of expertise can lead to the greatest learning. Try to choose higher-quality routes instead of the easy pickings. You'll end up with better experience and knowledge, and the climbing should be more enjoyable and the send more satisfying.

A word about intimidation and fear: If one of your weaknesses is a fear of falling on lead, you'll want to incorporate this into your selection criteria. Do you want to challenge yourself with more intimidating routes or hold off until you're better prepared? You can't put off dealing with this fear indefinitely, but you can be prudent about pushing your limits in a careful and controlled manner. See chapter 11 for more on overcoming fear.

Lastly, consider safety especially when choosing trad routes or boulder problems. There are many fine trad routes that are difficult to protect and plenty of great highball or bad landing boulder problems. Unless your goal is to broaden your experience in these emotionally challenging and potentially risky areas, it's usually best to err on the side of prudence and push the upper limits of your pyramid with high-quality, safe routes.

Give some consideration to the severity of falls when choosing routes.

Step one above is relatively easy to assess since most guidebooks are reliable sources of route grade, but steps two and three are much more difficult tasks. There are trustworthy sources for what you seek, but use discretion, as some of the information is subjective. Start by consulting local guidebooks, which may have useful nuggets in the route descriptions. Friends who have climbed the route or local experts who may have climbed just about everything in the area are other good sources. For potential flash or redpoint projects, a particularly useful tactic is to watch someone climb the route; you can usually tell where the crux is, the type of holds involved, and the movement required.

If your goal is a more general improvement, then choosing routes of different types would be the best approach. A general approach to improvement necessarily means working on your weaknesses, and this translates to choosing routes outside your preferences. Create a performance pyramid by selecting high-quality routes outside your expertise. You may need to take a step down in grade from your historic pyramid to gain necessary experience.

Take your time and choose pyramid routes carefully. Your progress and long-term goal are dependent on good learning experiences along the way.

Preparations

Enjoying a day of climbing and making progress toward meeting your redpoint or on-sight goals begins well before you rope up. To make significant progress on a redpoint project, complete one or more on-sights, finish a half dozen difficult boulder problems, or just do ten pitches in a day means using your time advantageously, and that requires preparation and focus.

Choosing a Partner

Choose a partner with an equal interest in performance. If you have goals and a plan, nothing is more annoying than a climbing partner who wastes your time. Choose your partners carefully—they can make the difference between a productive and enjoyable day and one that leaves you frustrated. They should also be pursuing a goal, be motivated, and understand that you both want to have fun and be successful. Climbing

Route Assessment Checklist

Grade: _____

Rate how each route meets your criteria. 1 = not consistent, 2 = somewhat consistent, 3 = consistent

	Route 1:	Route 2:	Route 3:	Route 4:	Route 5:	Route 6:	Route 7:
Crux location:							
Wall angle:							
Hold type:							
Endurance:							
Strength:							

Quality rating

1 = poor, 2 = fair,
3 = good, 4 = excellent

Inspiration rating

1 = low, 2 = medium, 3 = high

partners who are not equally motivated by daily goals often don't get along.

Consider your partner's personality. You need to like your partner as a person. Apply the following criteria and then try a few partners for a session at a gym or for an afternoon outing before committing to entire weekends.

Intensity level. Are you laid-back and carefree or focused and intense? Having a similar intensity level to your partner's can go a long way toward limiting potential tensions.

Supportiveness. Some of us like a little support from our partner, someone to cheer us on, be happy when we succeed, and console us when we fail. On the other hand, many climbers are driven internally and find external emotional support annoying. Choose a partner who matches your expectations of support and try to provide your partner with the degree of emotional buttressing he or she requires.

Communication and social skills. You'll be spending a good bit of time with your climbing partner, so communication and social skills are important criteria. Choose someone you can talk with comfortably and who respects you.

Attitude and recovery from failure. Attitude is infectious. The mindset of those around you can affect the way you feel about yourself and your surroundings. Negative people create a negative atmosphere that can poison an otherwise productive day. Choose partners who aren't prone to fits over disappointments and don't go sour after failing to meet expectations. Surround yourself with positive, uplifting people, and your performance and overall experience will improve.

Develop a list of several potential climbing partners. You'll likely narrow your steady partners to one or two, but climbing with others has advantages. You'll be exposed to different performance expectations, and you can still go climbing when your usual partners are unavailable.

Making the Most of Your Crag Time

If you're like most people, you've got a limited amount of time to spend climbing and you want to accomplish as much as possible in that time. Here are a number of things that experienced, goal-oriented climbers do to get the most out of each day.

Be ready when it's your turn to climb. When it's your turn to climb, climb. Don't waste time finding your rope, searching for draws, locating shoes, taping up, and so on. Keep yourself and your things organized so when it's your turn to climb you can get on the rock. If you're not organized, you waste not only your own time, but your partner's as well.

Be aware of your partner's needs and goals. Be prepared to move to a new climb and belay for your partner.

Keep an eye on the clock. It's easy to let time slip away when you're having fun. Have at least a general idea of what time it is and whether you are on schedule for the day. You can always change your plan if you need to, but keeping an eye on the time helps you stay on track or be more flexible if necessary.

Have contingency plans. You need to have a plan for the day, but other climbers or weather conditions may not cooperate, so be flexible. Have a backup plan ready for each step of the day. If your warmups are wet or busy, are there different routes you can do? If there is a long line for the project you want to get on, can you get on another route? Don't make the mistake of thinking that you must do a specific warmup route or rely on conditions being exactly as you want them to be. Hope for the best, but plan and prepare for the worst. Perfect conditions aren't necessary for success. Imagine that you are good enough to succeed in almost any condition.

Get to the crag early. The reality of climbing in America today is that at any popular crag the easier climbs are almost always crowded, especially on weekends. The less experienced climbers want to flash or redpoint them, and the experienced climbers want to warm up on them. By 10 a.m. on any nice Saturday, every popular 5.9 to 5.11 has a line at the base. Getting to these climbs late can double or triple the amount of time it takes to warm up. If you like a particular warmup route, or if you just want to be able to warm up at your own pace, get to the crag early. You can usually beat the rush to popular crags by simply getting up at a reasonable hour. If you are late to the crag, pay attention to what other parties are doing and which routes have the least traffic. It's not uncommon to find someone getting ready to hang draws on a route you want to do a quick lap on. Offering to hang the draws for them can be a benefit to you both.

Planning Your Day

Before you get in the car and start driving to the crag, you need a plan for the day. Making the plan a day or two before is typical among seasoned climbers and nearly unheard of among those less experienced. Getting to the parking lot and then asking, "What should we do today?" more often than not wastes time. Do you want a performance, working, training, active recovery, or movement learning day, or simply a light day of climbing and hanging out? Or will it be a mix? The answer doesn't matter as long as you know ahead of time and plan accordingly. Spend a few minutes considering which crags you will visit and when. What climbs will you do? Do you want to do them in a specific order? How long will you spend on each part of your day and on each route? Which climbing partner should you choose? Before you dump your gear in the trunk and drive off with visions of stellar sends in your head, consider the following.

Travel time. It takes time to get to your routes. Meeting up with partners, driving to the crag, and hiking can take a chunk out of your day. If you will be climbing with someone who is a slow starter in the morning, plan to meet at his place; otherwise you'll end up waiting somewhere checking your watch every two minutes while sending threatening text messages. If you'll be moving from crag to crag during the day, think about how much time packing, traveling, and unpacking are going to take.

Overall goal. The overall goal for your day—whether it's a performance, working, or training day, or a mix—influences everything else. Your goals for the day will determine crag and route choices, the type of warmup, the number of pitches, climbing intensity, and rest periods.

Decide on a primary goal before you go, and stick with it. If your goal for the day is to link several sections of your current project (a performance day), you'll need to plan on a lengthier warmup than if your

Before you begin driving to the crag spend time planning your day.

goal was to train for local aerobic endurance. You'd also avoid working another route before your linking attempts on the project.

If you're climbing several days in a row, you may want to reserve the first day for hard on-sights and red-point attempts and devote subsequent days to working, linking, or training. The first day, you are likely to be at your peak. Performance tends to decline without rest days, so the subsequent days of climbing in a row will usually be less productive.

A good warmup prepares both your body and your mind for difficult climbing.

Getting to and around the Crag

All your planning and packing is useless if you can't find your way to and around the crag. There are a number of sources that can provide directions and travel times, including guidebooks, the internet, and local experts. If you are unfamiliar with an area, consult several sources to plan your day.

A proper warmup. A proper warmup is essential for preparing your body and mind for intensive activity. Warming up reduces your risk of injury by increasing the flow of synovial fluid into the joints, producing a greater range of motion and increased flexibility. Warming up increases blood flow to muscles so that oxygen, fuel, and nutrients can be transported in greater quantity and waste products removed.

Further, warming up properly will put you in the right frame of mind for achieving your goals for the day. You can take a variety of approaches for this emotional part of the warmup, but the goals are similar: first, to get you in the state of mind that is most conducive to achieving your goal, and second, to foster a confident and flexible mental state. Establishing a series of small successes on warmup routes before attempting anything difficult helps you develop a positive, self-assured attitude that can last throughout your climbing day. You can also use your warmup for positive self-talk and visualization and adjusting your expectations.

Start slow, with a route three or perhaps four number grades, or a boulder problem four or even five grades below your project. Climb smoothly, concentrating on your movement to put yourself in the right frame of mind for the day. Do three or four routes or half a dozen boulder problems of increasing difficulty, with the last warmup three or fewer letter grades or a V grade below your project. For example, for a 13a project you might warm up on a 10a, a 10d, an 11c, and a 12b. A helpful warmup method is to use different routes to focus on different aspects of your climbing, especially those you need on your project. Focusing on general elements of movement, such as foot precision, gives you an overall sensation of smooth, controlled climbing on any warmup. Because it's often difficult to find a good range of grades at the same crag, you may need to move between crags to complete your warmup. Build this travel time into your plan for the day.

Rest twenty to forty minutes between roped climbs.

Activity 4: Warmup

For a day of outdoor climbing, try doing six warmup routes for which you have specific goals.

Routes 1 and 2 should be easy enough for you to move however you want. Choose any of a number of playful exercises, such as imitating a style of movement associated with an animal, like a monkey, or focus on moving in a smooth and continuous manner, or practice variations of dynamic movement. Have fun and play.

Routes 3 and 4 should be moderately difficult. Work on precision and focus on any movements that you need to improve. Use these routes to remind yourself of patterns of movement initiation, pacing, or precision that you need later in the day.

Routes 5 and 6 will be the most difficult climbs of the warmup and should be hard enough to require mental concentration and focus. Approach each route telling yourself that it will be difficult and require your best effort; don't take anything about them for granted. This will help put you in the mental state necessary as well as prepare you to move well for the more difficult routes of the day. These harder warmups require focus, but they should be easy enough that you can climb them without degrading your physical condition.

Attempts and rest periods. Once you're warmed up, how long should you rest before making your first real burn? There's a fine line between recovering and cooling off—rest too little and you're not fully recovered from your last climb, rest too long and you'll begin cooling off. A number of factors influence how long you should rest between climbs, including the weather (colder weather means you will begin cooling off sooner), your fitness, and the intensity of the last climb.

Make sure you always have the essentials for a day at the crag.

A good rule of thumb is that you want your forearms to completely de-pump without your joints beginning to stiffen. For roped climbs, that's usually somewhere between twenty and forty minutes, but with experience, you'll be able to feel the difference between not resting enough and resting too long. For boulderers, four to six minutes rest may be all that's necessary depending on the nature of the last effort; ten minutes rest is very long unless the problem you are working relies heavily on local anaerobic endurance.

Cool down. Leave time at the end of your day to do a couple laps on an easy climb of approximately the same grade as your first warmup route. Cooling down can reduce soreness and recovery time; the mild activity helps remove any remaining waste products from your muscles and replace nutrients.

Contingency plans. Popular climbs can be continuously busy with people lining up rope bags to get a run in, and the weather in many areas can turn dramatically in the course of a day. You need an alternative or flexible plan that provides options. Keep a mental list of acceptable warmup crags and routes, and adjust your plan as conditions develop. Here's a sample day plan with travel times, warmups, redpoint runs, cool downs, and contingencies.

8:00 a.m.: Leave house.

8:30 a.m.: Meet climbing partner and leave for crag.

10:00 a.m.: Arrive at parking area for crag.

10:15 a.m.: Arrive at base of first warmup. If busy, hike additional five minutes to alternative. Do two laps on first warmup.

10:45 a.m.: Leave for second and third warmups.

11:00 a.m.: Arrive at crag for second and third warmups. If busy, hike additional ten minutes to alternative. Do one lap on each.

11:30 a.m.: Leave for project.

11:45 a.m.: Arrive at base of project. Preplace draws on project as fourth warmup.

12:15 p.m.: Rest, eat, drink.

12:45 p.m.: Make first redpoint burn. If successful, clean route and move to next project on performance pyramid. If unsuccessful, repeat.

1:45 p.m.: Make second redpoint burn.

2:45 p.m.: Make third redpoint burn.

3:45 p.m.: Move to a fun route or another route that you want to work.

4:45 p.m.: Move to and complete cooldown route.

Efficient Packing

An efficient pack can shave minutes off your travel time and minimize frustrating gear searches. Where you pack specific items is not as important as packing consistently. If you're meticulous about storing your things, you'll be able to locate whatever you need in a matter of seconds.

Make sure you have quick access to liquids and food so that you don't have to unpack everything to reach them, and keep frequently used items in the outer pockets of your pack. See chapter 4 for packing lists and equipment information.

We've been accused of being over-the-top when it comes to planning a day of climbing. After all, climbing is supposed to be fun, right? Why plan so rigorously—that just seems like work! But if you're like us you have any number of demands on your time, including family, work, and friends, and a day of climbing can be a special thing you don't want to fritter away. You don't need a rigid schedule, but in order to get the most out of your time at the crag, at least put a little forethought into what you want to achieve and how you'll go about accomplishing it. Ultimately, the goal of planning is to increase the likelihood of success, the amount of climbing you can do in a day, and your enjoyment.

QUICK TICKS

✓ Begin choosing routes by narrowing the choices by grade, characteristics consistent with your long-term goal, and quality.

✓ Next create a performance pyramid made up of your route choices.

✓ Choose a partner who shares similar goals and motivations and who you can get along with over many hours.

✓ Make the most of your crag time by planning your day before you get in the car. Decide on an overall goal, where you'll warm up, how you'll prepare your redpoint project, and where and when you'll rest.

✓ Make a contingency plan in case crowds or weather affect where or when you can climb.

✓ Pack efficiently so you can easily find what you need when you need it.

Compared to many sports, bouldering and sport climbing have relatively small equipment requirements. In this chapter, we will show how your gear can be used to best advantage. Which belay device or shoes you choose to use is a personal decision based on functionality, your style of climbing, and personal preference, so we'll focus instead on the basic equipment you need and how best to use each piece.

The equipment you use will rarely make or break your chances of redpointing or on-sighting a route or boulder problem. Nonetheless, your gear should be suited to your needs and preferences. You've got to be comfortable with how to use it, and it can make the tasks you'll perform—such as belaying, cleaning, or working a route—easier or more comfortable.

Advertising hype and current trends in the climbing community often influence purchases. In the early 1990s ultralight equipment was all the rage in sport climbing. Manufacturers produced harnesses that weighed next to nothing and carabiners were shrunk to tiny size. The result was harnesses that were not comfortable for belaying or long sessions working a route and carabiners that were so small they were hard to clip. After a few years of "light is right," tastes swung back in the other direction and weight mattered less to climbers. Lately it's not without irony that we notice manufacturers headed back in the direction of superlight carabiners and other equipment. Don't be swayed by advertiser's hype. Tiny, lightweight carabiners may be exciting, but many climbers find them hard to use; you shouldn't waste your time with gear that you find hard to work with or that you don't trust.

In trad climbing, it's easy to become fascinated with each new innovation and to scrutinize all the different types of gear. But using trad gear is about skill, and laying out money for new gadgets is never a substitute for taking the time to become an expert at using the gear you already own; there are probably still a few climbers left who can protect cracks better with a rack of old hexes than most climbers can with the latest cams.

Serious climbers may acquire more equipment than those with simple recreational goals. A dedicated sport climber may require multiple ropes, eighteen or more draws, many pairs of shoes, and several harnesses and belay devices. The rack of a serious big-wall climber may completely fill the trunk of a car and take years to acquire. In either case the type and amount of gear you own should be a reflection of the volume and type of climbing you do as well as personal preferences, with the end goal being maximum preparedness and functionality.

Sport Climbing Equipment List

Climbing shoes

Harness (optional lighter redpoint harness plus a second more comfortable belay and route working harness)

Chalk bag, belt, and chalk, including an extra chalk reserve

Belay device with locking carabiner

12–18 quickdraws plus one or two long draws (24") (optional additional rack of 12 draws)

Rope (optional larger diameter route-working rope plus redpoint burn skinny rope)

Rope bag (one for each rope)

Pack

Leave it biners or quick links

Small nylon or natural-bristle brush

Skin repair and first-aid kit
    Athletic tape
    Nail clippers
    Small scissors
    Super Glue (cyanoacrylate)
    Band-Aids
    Neosporin
    Tweezers
    Lip balm
    Sunscreen
    Tape stickum or tincture
    Non-greasy, fast-absorbing skin cream such as Hoofmaker
    Ibuprofen

Insect repellent

Food and drink

Belay gloves

Rappel device if your usual belay device
is auto-locking

Stick clip

Knee pad

Clothing matched to conditions

Bouldering Equipment List

Climbing shoes (optional pairs for different
purposes such as steeply overhung routes
and technical faces)

Pad or pads

Chalk bag or bucket and chalk

Small nylon or natural-bristle brush

Skin repair and first-aid kit
Athletic tape
Nail clippers
Small scissors
Super Glue (cyanoacrylate)
Band-Aids
Neosporin
Tweezers
Lip balm
Sunscreen
Tape stickum or tincture
Non-greasy, fast-absorbing skin cream such
as Hoofmaker
Ibuprofen

Insect repellent

Food and drink

Telescoping paint pole with small brush attached
to brush holds at a distance

Clothing matched to conditions

You'll find a lot of variations on the basic equipment list, but this list will be more than sufficient for
most crags; however, just because you carry the proper
gear doesn't mean you'll use it correctly. Although
having the right equipment can certainly make life easier, using that gear correctly is what really counts.
Read on for current best practices.

The sport climbing essentials.

Quickdraws

To properly use a quickdraw, you first need to set it up
right. The upper, or bolt-hanger, carabiner should have
a straight or wire gate and be attached to the dog bone
(webbing sling portion of the draw) on the end that
allows it free rotation. The rope end of the draw should
have a bent gate or wire biner, if you prefer, and be
secured to the dog bone so that it cannot rotate. Most
dog bone slings have an end that allows free rotation of
one biner and another that more or less locks the bent-
gate or wire biner in position. The rope is clipped into
the bottom, or rope-end, biner.

The main dog bone variables are length, width, stiff-
ness, and how the biner on the clipping end of the draw

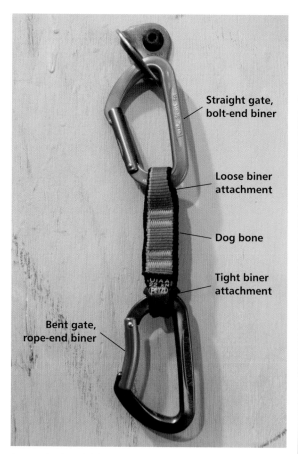

Straight gate, bolt-end biner

Loose biner attachment

Dog bone

Tight biner attachment

Bent gate, rope-end biner

A standard quickdraw.

is held in place. The length of the draw will increase or decrease rope drag in different situations. A wider draw is easier to grab and use as a handle when working a route. A stiffer sling can make a back clip more dangerous by holding the rope biner more firmly in place, rather than allowing it to twist, and increasing the likelihood of the rope coming unclipped. Whether the gates of the upper and lower biner should face in the same or opposing directions is simply a matter of personal preference.

As with most sport climbing equipment, the trend in recent years has been to ever thinner and lighter dog bones. While we applaud any reduction in unnecessary weight, a thin dog bone is difficult to grasp. It can be productive to grab draws when working a route, and since most redpoints are attempted with draws already in place a small weight savings may not be worth the tradeoff.

Quickdraw Carabiners

Choosing a carabiner is a matter of personal preference, but a few differences affect how they function in different situations. Modern quickdraw biners are roughly D-shaped, a very strong design as long as there are only two directions of pull along the long axis. Tri-loading (three directions of pull) and cross-loading (direction of pull across the gate and the spine) can significantly reduce carabiner strength.

Carabiners with a notched nose can occasionally catch on the edge of a bolt hanger and can be frustrating to remove. Key-gate biners won't catch. On some carabiners the nose extends beyond the gate, allowing you to more easily grasp and control the biner for faster clipping in pinch grip situations (see photo #2 on page 45). The biner is easier to grasp, and the rope requires less of a push to get into the basket.

Ounce for ounce, a wire-gate biner is typically stronger than a solid gate, and it can therefore be smaller and lighter for the same strength. Wire gates also provide more stable points of contact for the rope when it is pressed against the gate, making it easier to grasp and control the clipping biner. Also, the low mass of the gate means that a wire-gate biner is much less likely to open and the rope come free when it vibrates, which regularly occurs in falls as either the rope whips quickly across the biner or the spine impacts the rock.

Why carry more than twenty quickdraws? You may want to rappel down and equip your project first, in which case you'll have no draws for your warmups if you carry only twelve. You may also decide to leave your draws on a route that you'll return to over the next few weeks.

Rack your draws by attaching the upper, or bolthanger, biner to your gear loops. That way when you remove one to clip it into a bolt hanger, your hand and the biner are already in the perfect position. Racking draws using the rope-end biner means you have to flip the draw in your hand before you can clip it to the hanger. This may seem obvious, but racking wrong is a common mistake.

There is much debate over whether it is better to rack draws on gear loops with the bolt-hanger biner facing toward your body or away from it. Our experience suggests that neither way is better. What matters

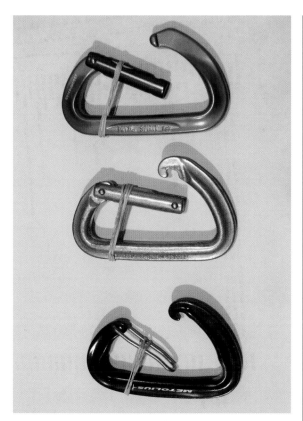

Notch and key-gate carabiners. The notch more easily hangs up on bolt hangers and the rope.

Comparison of a biner with a protruding nose (top) versus one with a relatively flat nose (bottom).

is what you prefer, especially in high-pressure situations; when you are pumped enough that you are likely to fumble with your gear and have a hard time clipping, which racking method are you more at ease and less likely to have problems with?

Clipping and Rope Management

Properly clipping the rope to a draw is an important element in overall climbing efficiency. Poor clipping means you have to hang on longer with one hand, sometimes to a poor hold, while you fumble to clip with the other. Clipping quickly can make the total effort required only slightly more difficult than top roping and can mean the difference between sending and failing. There are two techniques you can use, and which you choose depends on the orientation of the bent gate biner to your clipping hand.

Quickdraws properly racked with straight-gate biners attached to gear loops.

Clipping when the biner gate faces away from your clipping hand
for example, if you're using your right hand to clip a biner where the gate faces left

Reach down and grab a loop of rope between your thumb and index finger with your thumb and index finger pointed toward the ground.

Next, control the biner by placing your middle finger in the biner's basket and pulling down slightly to keep the draw from moving.

Then twist the rope over the nose of the biner, pushing it through the gate and into the basket.

The final result showing the rope in the biner.

Clipping when the biner gate faces toward your clipping hand

for example, if you're using your left hand to clip a biner where the gate faces left

Reach down for a loop of rope with your index finger and thumb pointed toward the ground. Pull up the loop and let it ride on the second knuckle of your middle finger.

Grasp the biner by placing your thumb on the spine and the tip of your middle finger on the nose.

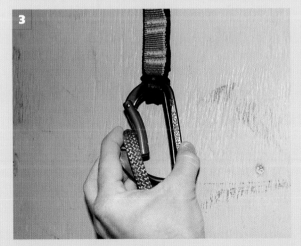

Push the rope off your middle finger and through the bent gate with your index finger.

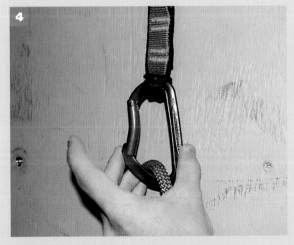

The final result showing the rope in the biner.

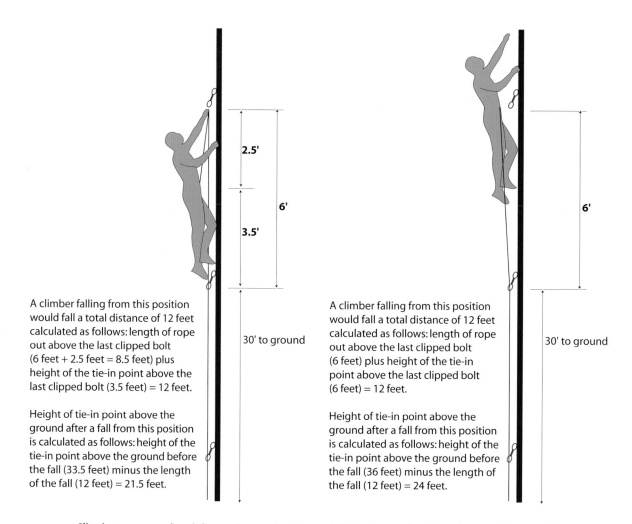

A climber falling from this position would fall a total distance of 12 feet calculated as follows: length of rope out above the last clipped bolt (6 feet + 2.5 feet = 8.5 feet) plus height of the tie-in point above the last clipped bolt (3.5 feet) = 12 feet.

Height of tie-in point above the ground after a fall from this position is calculated as follows: height of the tie-in point above the ground before the fall (33.5 feet) minus the length of the fall (12 feet) = 21.5 feet.

A climber falling from this position would fall a total distance of 12 feet calculated as follows: length of rope out above the last clipped bolt (6 feet) plus height of the tie-in point above the last clipped bolt (6 feet) = 12 feet.

Height of tie-in point above the ground after a fall from this position is calculated as follows: height of the tie-in point above the ground before the fall (36 feet) minus the length of the fall (12 feet) = 24 feet.

Clipping over your head does not result in a longer fall, but you will end up closer to the ground.

A word concerning clipping slack: It's a misconception that falling while clipping a draw over your head results in a longer fall than if you'd clipped from a higher stance. Actually, the distance you fall remains the same (see graphic above). The only difference is that you end up closer to the ground in the first scenario. This can be important if you're climbing above a ledge or you're close to the ground at the second or even third bolt. In addition, it's quicker and easier to clip a draw at your waist than over your head since you only need a single arm's length of slack instead of having to pull up a loop, grab it with your teeth, and

then pull a second loop. Also, you need to remember to spit the rope out as soon as you've grabbed that second loop. We once saw someone lose his two front teeth by falling with the rope in his mouth—don't let that be you!

You can sometimes improve your efficiency on a route by finding clipping stances closer to the bolts.

It's important to maintain proper quickdraw orientation so that once clipped, the rope runs from the ground behind the bent gate biner and out to you. Avoid a back clip in which the rope runs from the ground through the front and out the back of the bent gate biner. In a fall, a back-clipped rope can be pulled over a bent gate and come unclipped.

Normal 11- to 17-centimeter dog bones work well on most climbs, but a longer draw reduces rope drag in two situations: routes with roofs and those that meander. Routes with roofs often require the leader to clip a bolt near where the wall below the roof meets the roof. A normal-size draw on this clip forces the rope to turn two 90-degree angles as you move above the lip. The friction created by two 90-degree turns is substantial and can make pulling rope to clip above the roof much more difficult. Use a long draw instead so that the rope turns less sharply, reducing friction in the system and making the clipping and climbing easier above the roof.

As a general rule, you should keep the rope between you and the rock as you climb. If you're climbing to the right or left of your last clip, keep both feet to one side of the rope. Getting your leg between the rope and the rock exposes you to unnecessary risk; if you fall with the rope behind your leg, you might get a horrible rope burn behind the knee as your leg slides down the rope. Bad as that is, it pales to the second possible result, which is flipping upside down and falling headfirst. In a pendulum fall, you could swing into the rock headfirst. In addition to keeping the rope between you and the rock, pay attention to the direction a fall might take and adjust the position of your legs so that you won't catch the rope on your way down.

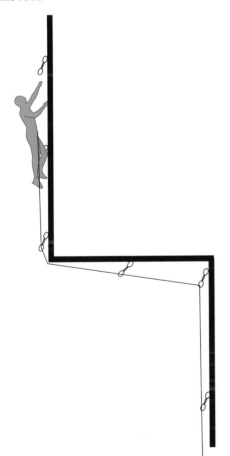

A roof protected with short draws. Note the increased friction (rope drag) in the system caused by the sharp angle in the rope.

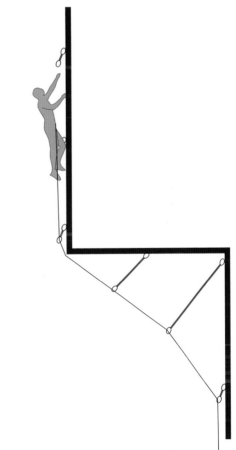

The same roof protected by longer draws. Friction is reduced by maintaining straighter rope travel.

Proper quickdraw orientation, with the rope running from behind the clipped biner out to the climber.

A back-clipped quickdraw. The rope can more easily come unclipped in a fall.

The general rule of keeping the rope between you and the rock almost always holds above the first bolt. If you stick clip the first bolt before you leave the ground, then keep the belay side of the rope to one side of your leg to prevent you from falling on the belay end of the rope. In such a fall the rope would go taut as the belayer locks off and you'd potentially fall straddling the rope.

Belay Devices

There are a dizzying array of belay devices on the market today, from inexpensive, simple tubular varieties to auto-locking types. Most do the job of stop-ping a falling climber well, but each type can aid your efforts in other ways. For example, you can't do a two-line rappel with an auto-locking device, so having a tube in your pack gives you the option of rapping off the top to preplace draws. On the other hand, an auto locker makes life much easier on your belayer when you're making learning runs. The constant taking, climbing, yarding, and other working activities are much easier to manage when the belay device assists in the work.

There are several other variables to consider when selecting a belay device. Keep in mind the essential tasks of the belayer: to provide the correct deceleration for a fall, quickly meet the needs of the climber, and

A climber between the first and second bolts. Keep the rope between you and the rock and the belayer off to one side.

A climber above the second bolt. Keep the rope between you and the rock.

reduce the amount of physical effort the climber needs to exert during routine tasks such as yarding and cleaning. A belay device's performance (and your skill in using it) should be measured by how well you can perform these tasks. Perhaps the most fundamental aspect is how quickly you can take in and feed out slack. Auto-locking devices can provide more resistance to feeding slack than non-auto-lockers, especially if the climbing rope is stiff or worn or iced over. Choose your belay device to match the conditions you will be working in. An auto-locker may be perfect for a single pitch of sport climbing with a new rope, but it might be the worst possible choice for a day of ice climbing with an older rope.

No matter what belay device you choose, practice with it and become an expert in all its uses before belaying for an on-sight attempt or a hard working burn. You should also be well versed in its limitations and most common errors. And possibly most important, make sure you read and follow the manufacturer's recommendations for use and heed warnings about misuse.

Rope

Dynamic climbing rope comes in a wide range of diameters from dental-floss thin to fat as a python. Your choice depends on what you'll use it for. In general, the

Below the first bolt, keep your leg between the rope and the rock or away from the belay end altogether.

thicker the rope, the longer it will last, but the more it weighs, although this is a loose correlation at best. Generally, a thicker rope is more difficult to clip and push through a belay device. Keep in mind that a rope's diameter is measured while weighted, so a loose-weave 10 mm, for example, will appear much thicker than a tight weave of the same stated diameter. Additionally, the coarseness of the sheath can also affect the feel and handling of a rope. Manufacturers of some belay devices, such as Petzl's Gri-gri, specify a minimum or maximum diameter that can be safely used.

All of these differences make it important to see and feel a rope before you buy it. A tightly woven rope is preferable in all diameters. A tight rope is thinner, allowing it to travel through belay devices and clip

more easily. Thin ropes (10 mm and under) are great for redpoint burns or on-sight attempts, while thicker rope will last longer under the greater stresses of learning runs. And be sure to get at least 60 meters (about 200 feet)—today's sport routes can easily extend to 100 feet in height.

Typically, rope wear is concentrated on the sheath in the first 15 feet from each end. This is where the rope crosses the highest biner during a fall or when the belayer takes tight to hold the climber in place. A rope wears out typically not because the core is shot or because it is worn evenly over the entire length, but rather because the sheath becomes heavily worn near the ends.

A few words on dry treatment: Ropes were first treated with a chemical to repel water so that in wet, cold environments, such as those found in ice or alpine climbing, the ropes wouldn't freeze into a hard, inflexible mass. Manufacturers now claim these treatments will extend the life of a rope by sealing out dirt particles and acting as a kind of lubricant between rope and carabiner. Dry treatment, however, doesn't come free; it can increase the cost of a typical rope by 10 percent or more. It's hard to say whether dry treatment will increase your rope's life enough to warrant the cost; in our experience it doesn't, but your mileage may vary.

A popular rope in the sport climbing world is the 10.5 mm by 60 meters. Known as a solid all-around rope, the 10.5 provides a reasonable compromise between longevity and weight. Anything bigger will last a long time but has limited usefulness in sport climbing due to its much heavier weight and difficult handling characteristics. An 11 mm rope won't travel through a belay device as smoothly as thinner rope and, for like materials, weighs over 20 percent more than a 10 mm cord.

Thin single ropes—down to close to 9 mm—have become commonplace in sport climbing. Thin rope weighs less and handles easily, including feeding through the belay device. But be cautious with extremely thin rope: Use only with approved belay devices and keep in mind that thinner rope creates less friction and will not lock down in any belay device as easily as a thicker rope.

Some climbers keep two ropes, a 10.5 mm or so for working routes and a thinner cord for making redpoint

Packing a rope bag

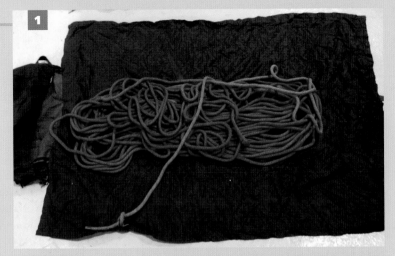

Flake the rope lengthwise down the middle of the tarp from the bag to the opposite end of the fabric. Secure the rope end on the bottom of the pile to one of the webbing loops to close the belay system and the end on top to the other loop so you can easily find it.

Fold the sides of the tarp to the middle so its width is the same as the bag.

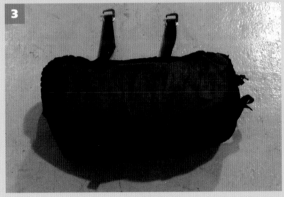

Roll the tarp up from the bagless end and stuff it into the bag.

Cinch up the drawstring, attach the compression straps, and pull them tight.

Knead the bag to settle the rope inside and draw the compression straps tight once again. Repeat step 5 several times.

or on-sight attempts. If your budget allows, purchase two ropes. Beat up your 10.5 to learn the route or do training runs and then break out the thin line (at 10 mm or less) just for redpoints or on-sights.

Rope Bag

A rope bag provides a number of advantages over coiling. First, a bagged rope can be compressed into a smaller, more compact unit, making it easier to pack and carry. Second, a properly bagged rope is instantly ready to use when you unroll the bag. Coiled ropes must be uncoiled and usually untangled before they can be used. Third, the tarp in the bag keeps the rope clean and dry while providing a handy platform for other gear.

To ready the rope for use, simply undo the straps, loosen the drawstring, and unroll the tarp. Untie the rope end on top of the flaked pile from the loop, tie in, and go. The rope will unfurl smoothly as you climb. When you're done with the climb, position the tarp directly under the anchors if possible—you can use the free end of the rope as a plumb line to determine where to place the tarp. A rope will naturally twist a bit over time if used in the same configuration, and pulling the rope from the free end allows the rope to untwist and return to its relaxed state.

Shoes

Today's climbing shoes tend to be designed with a particular type of climbing in mind rather than for general, all-around use, so serious climbers tend to own several pairs of shoes. Shoes constructed with a high arch and downturned toe are described as best for steep climbing, and stiffer shoes are said to work best for thin, technical faces. Shoes that are stiff and have larger rands as well as beefier uppers are made for cracks.

Shoes can be poorly suited to your purpose—just ask anyone who has had the misfortune of wearing slippers while crack climbing or downturned shoes on friction slabs. (We've done both!) In general, shoe companies attempt to make their products stand out in a crowded marketplace by filling a particular segment or use and may overstate the efficacy of a particular model.

Above all else make sure your shoes fit your feet; this is the single most important factor in determining the effectiveness of a given model. For most applications a climbing shoe should be tight but not painful. Your foot should move as little as possible inside the shoe; the more your foot can move around independent of the shoe, the less effective it will be at holding small or irregular holds. That said, you want to avoid pain. Discomfort is to be expected, but if you feel a pinching or cutting sensation, the shoe is either too tight or doesn't fit your foot properly.

For sport and bouldering shoes, your toes should press the inside front of the shoes and bend a bit at the knuckles causing small bumps in the top of the toe box. The upper material should be stretched taut across the top of your foot. The shoe should feel very tight, but you should not have pain that makes it difficult to stand on a hold.

You should be able to feel the shoe's arch under your foot. If the shoe's arch is too low, there will be a gap between your arch and the shoe; too high, and you'll feel an uncomfortable pressure under your arch.

The heel is a tricky fit. Most sport shoes have a slingshot rand, which forces your toes into the front of the shoe. This creates a tighter fit at the front but often leaves an air pocket directly behind and at the base of your heel. Due to the nature of slingshot rands, a small pocket is to be expected, but a large pocket can make holding heel hooks difficult. Anything more than $1/4$ to $1/2$ inch of space is excessive and should be avoided.

A very tight shoe helps you to use small holds. Remember that your shoes will stretch—more for leather and less for synthetic—so shoes that are extremely uncomfortable when new will many times stretch in places that result in a custom fit after a number of uses.

A shoe for dedicated slab climbing requires a somewhat different fit. Having one's toes right at the very front of the shoe is less important than how the shoe flexes and allows the maximum surface area of the ball of the foot to contact the rock. It may be helpful to have a little more room in the toe box.

Multipitch climbing where removing your shoes after every pitch isn't feasible requires a more comfortable fit. Yes, you'll sacrifice some performance for comfort, but at least your feet won't be scream-

A properly fit shoe with toes slightly buckled and upper material stretched taut.

ing in pain after you've worn your shoes for an hour or more.

Velcro or slip-on closures are convenient for the on-off nature of bouldering and indoor climbing, while lace-ups provide a more precise, solid fit. In addition, you might want a pair of very tight shoes for redpoint runs and a more comfortable pair for longer route working sessions.

Unless you have purchased and used a particular model previously, trying to choose a shoe and get a perfect fit is virtually impossible unless you can actually put the shoes on. Go to a bricks-and-mortar store where the staff knows how to fit climbing shoes, and try on different makes and models. Examine how each fits your foot, and if you can, try the shoe on an artificial wall in the store or gym before you buy.

Harnesses

Harnesses, too, are designed with specific purposes in mind. You might choose to have a comfortable harness with wide lumbar support, thick padding, and broad leg loops for learning burns and belaying, while reserving a light, thin harness for redpoints. Smaller harnesses don't just weigh less, they tend to be less restrictive as well.

Clothing

Some climbers can perform at high levels wearing whatever they like, but clothing can affect your performance. For example, jeans are less than ideal clothing for bouldering and face climbing because they are heavy, restrictive, and don't wick moisture well. On the other hand, off-width climbers who need to shove their legs deep into cracks value the durability and abrasion-resistance of denim. Climbers should choose their clothing based on the style of climbing with an eye toward clothes that don't bind or restrict movement and that are well suited to the environment.

Pay attention to clothing in cooler temperatures. Since it's common to take thirty minutes or more between efforts, you are at risk of cooling off and losing the benefit of your warmup. While ice climbing, it's easy to get overheated while climbing and then end up shivering, numb, and miserable while belaying. Sport and trad climbers can expect to cool off while belaying and may even get cold enough to lose the physical and emotional benefits of the warmup. This can even happen in moderate conditions. Bring along clothing to keep you warm between burns.

Take into consideration wind and the amount of time you'll spend in the shade, as well as weather conditions. If the temperature is going to be in the mid-60s but it'll be windy and shady at your crag, shorts and a tank top may be fine while you're climbing but you'll need a down jacket to stay warm between burns. Even during the summer, the wind can cool you off quickly, especially when you are working hard and sweating, so even if the temperatures are in the 70s or 80s, you may need additional clothing to stay warmed up.

Also consider more than just the kind of jacket you are wearing. Staying warmed up means insulating most of your body, so it's better to bring too much clothing than too little. You may want to bring warm socks, a fleece jacket and pants, a hat, gloves, a down jacket, and a wind barrier that you can layer as necessary over your climbing clothes. Further, the less you rely on cotton, the better. Cotton has very little insulating quality, dries slowly, and is a bad wind barrier. Use cotton only in the warmest conditions with no wind and when you won't be sweating. In warm envi-

Staying warm between burns may mean bringing a coat, hat, and gloves to the crag.

ronments light, loose-fitting, wicking clothing will let air circulate next to your skin, carrying away moisture and keeping you cool.

Accessories

There are a number of smaller, albeit important, accessories to include in your pack, such as a chalk bag, knee pad, and first-aid kit. Almost everyone carries a chalk bag, and you should look for a bag with a few key features. Make sure your bag has a loop for a small brush and that you use a separate belt for it. The chalk bag belt makes the bag more stable so that you can get your hand in and out more quickly. A chalk bag attached to the harness by a single biner can twist and flop around, making getting to the chalk a trickier proposition. A belt also lets you pull the bag to one side, providing easier access for one hand or the other.

For bouldering, many prefer a chalk bucket. This larger bag sits on the ground since boulder problems usually don't require you to chalk en route. The large size allows you to get both hands in the bag.

A small nylon or natural-bristle brush cleans chalk buildup from holds. Never use metal bristles because they can damage the rock by removing its texture.

Be sure to put together a small first-aid kit that includes items for repairing skin. You can sometimes treat a flapper, a flap of skin typically peeled from a fingertip, on the spot and keep climbing. A skin repair kit should include

Nail clippers (optional pair of small nail care scissors)

Athletic tape

Tape stickum

Tweezers

A properly set up chalk bag with belt and brush.

A large chalk bucket for bouldering allows you to chalk both hands simultaneously.

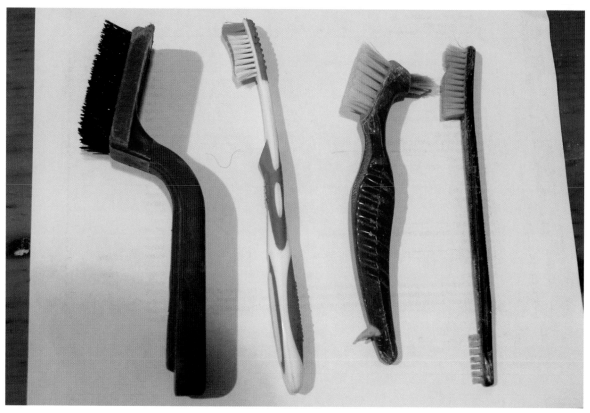

Any of these brushes will work well. Note that none have metal bristles.

Band-Aids

Neosporin

Ibuprofen

Super Glue (cyanoacrylate)

You can close small skin lacerations with Super Glue, which works surprisingly well—it causes less scarring, promotes faster healing, and is nontoxic. You can repair small tears and flappers by following these simple instructions:

1. Stop the bleeding by applying direct pressure to the area, using a paper towel or your shirt if necessary.

2. After the bleeding stops or slows markedly, wash out the wound with water, and then squeeze the wound together.

3. While holding the cut together, run a small amount of Super Glue down the length of the cut. Be careful not to get any glue on the fingers holding the cut closed or you will glue your fingers to the wound. Hold the wound closed for several minutes to allow the glue to dry. The glue will close the cut and stop any residual bleeding.

If you anticipate knee barring, a knee pad is indispensable. A pad lets you repeatedly apply great force to a knee bar without harming the skin above your knee. Climbers used to use the neoprene sleeves commonly used for knee support, and these continue to work well, but new products have a piece of sticky shoe rubber on the portion of the pad that contacts the rock as well as compression straps, which create a tight fit on the leg.

Food and Drink

Food doesn't get the attention it deserves among climbers. Some people have had successful climbing days while hung over, dehydrated, full of junk food, starving from lack of food, or ingesting little more than pot and beer. You might think that climbing performance is less dependent on diet than other sports such as distance running, where food and liquid intake are key. But inadequate hydration and poor diet are no help to climbers and may well hinder performance to some degree by not supplying the fuel, nutrients, and hydration necessary for difficult athletic activity. Although

Carry a knee pad. You never know when it'll come in handy.

we can't address broader dietary issues in depth here, a climber's diet should foster good nutrition and general health. Diet can influence how often you get sick and how quickly you recover from illness, both of which can impact your climbing and training schedule over the long term.

During a day of climbing, remember that hydration matters. Environmental factors such as wind, altitude, and dry air can contribute to water loss, and staying properly hydrated may take some effort. Even mild dehydration can lead to fatigue and degrade your performance potential. Thirst is a poor indication of the need for liquid intake, so drink regularly. Pack plenty of liquids: A single small water bottle is insufficient for a full day of climbing; most days you'll need at least two quarts and quite often more.

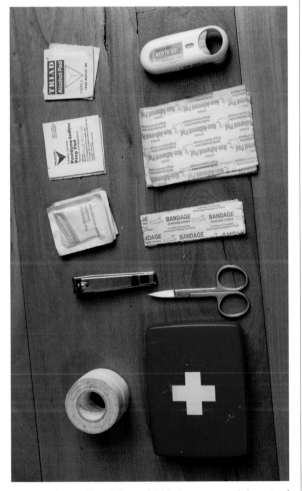

A properly outfitted first-aid kit is an essential part of your gear.

Avoid foods that give a quick burst of energy followed by a crash, such as candy bars and other snack foods that are low in nutrients and high in sugar and fat. Choose complex carbohydrates that you digest more gradually, providing your body with a metered energy source rather than a spike of sugar. Try whole wheat sandwiches or pasta. We are not opposed to energy bars, but many of them are just glorified candy bars with high calorie counts and a lot of fat and sugar. A typical day of bouldering, sport climbing, or trad climbing does not burn as many calories as quickly as you might think, so energy bars can give you far more calories than you need for climbing.

We are somewhat troubled by the marketing of products claiming to improve performance during a day of climbing by speeding recovery time between climbs, delaying the onset of a pump, and so on. Supplements are not regulated in the United States, and most of these products have not undergone rigorous testing to determine their efficacy. We find their claims to be dubious at best. Most supplements, rather than relying on any scientific proof, rely instead on testimonials by recognized names who are paid for their endorsement. It's important to remember that it is impossible for anyone to isolate and understand the effects of a product simply by incorporating it into his or her own daily routine.

QUICK TICKS

✓ Read the reviews, talk to your friends, and pick equipment that's right for you.

✓ We recommend wider dogbones to make grasping the draw easier.

✓ Choose key-gate or wire gate biners that are large enough to accommodate your fingers.

✓ Learning to clip properly means first controlling the rope-end biner and then clipping the rope into it.

✓ Use long draws to reduce rope drag when the route ascends a roof or zigzags.

✓ As you climb, keep the rope between you and the rock—avoid getting your leg behind the rope except when you're below the first bolt.

✓ Consider buying two ropes, a thicker rope for learning burns and a thin rope for redpoints, onsights, and flashes.

✓ Consider buying several pairs of shoes for different applications.

✓ Bring enough clothes to stay warm.

✓ Don't forget important accessories such as a knee pad and first-aid kit.

A skillful belayer has many jobs. The most important is to keep the climber safe—but a good belayer will also manage the rope in anticipation of the climber's needs and provide emotional support. An expert belayer rapidly feeds rope or takes in slack without needing to be commanded; there is never a shortage of line as the climber reaches for rope to clip nor a buildup of slack after the clip as the climber changes position in relation to his protection. A skilled belayer reacts quickly to commands, provides the proper slack in preparation for potentially dangerous falls, and applies a number of rope-handling techniques to assist the climber.

Clear Communication

The first step toward excellence in belaying is learning to communicate clearly and directly. The climber must be able to voice his desires so that the belayer always understands his needs. Not only is clear communication the foundation for safe climbing, but it improves the redpointing process by heading off miscues that must then be corrected. For example, if the climber gives the ambiguous "OK" upon reaching a bolt, the belayer may assume the climber is in straight and feed slack. If the climber meant instead for the belayer to take, the climber could end up hanging several feet below where he intended to stop, so he'll need to climb back up to the point he intended. "OK" is not an acceptable climbing command, and if someone you are climbing with uses it, be sure to ask him to clarify. Rather than "OK" or other ambiguous commands, use the following well-established language.

Climber: "On belay?" Belayer: "Belay on." This classic question / answer is often overlooked, but it's worth asking whether your belayer is ready to catch your fall.

Climber: "Take." Take all the slack out of the rope and provide tension. Hold the climber in his current position. The variation "take hard" means the same thing but emphasizes that the climber does not want to be lowered even an inch; he wants to be held exactly where he is. "Take hard" can also signal that the climber does not feel the belayer taking up slack fast enough or with enough force to accommodate for rope stretch.

Belaying is not a passive activity. This belayer is in good position to catch a fall or respond to the climber's commands. Note the proper stance with left foot forward, brake hand on the rope, and a watchful eye on the climber.

"Take" is a frequently misunderstood command. To most belayers "take" means locking off, but under this interpretation of the command the climber will end up a foot or more below the point he intended because the rope will stretch as the climber sits back in his harness. To regain his former position on the rock the climber has to yard up or climb. More precisely, the climber should hold himself in place on the rock and command "take" to his belayer, who immediately removes all the slack from the system and locks down his belay device. Next the belayer quickly backs away from the rock while sitting down in his harness to place tension on the rope. The belayer must do this quickly, and as soon as the climber feels the reassuring tug on the line, he lets go of the rock. Since all slack and rope stretch has been removed from the system, the climber is held firmly in place.

Sometimes climbers misuse the "take" command at the beginning of a lead fall—with an attentive belayer who takes the command seriously, this will result in a short, hard fall. There are times when a short fall is preferable, but sometimes climbers say "take" simply to signal that they are falling when a more dynamic belay style would be more appropriate.

Climber: "Clipping." Provide enough slack to clip the next draw.

Climber: "Watch me." The climber anticipates that a fall is likely, is trying something new, feels apprehensive about the upcoming moves, or needs to know that the belayer is attentive.

Climber: "Straight," "in direct," or "straight in." The climber has clipped in directly to a bolt and the belayer can relax tension on the rope.

Climber: "Back on you," or just, "on you." The climber is straight in to an anchor and wants to be held on the rope by the belayer. The climber uses this command after resting by having clipped in straight or after threading the anchor at the top of a sport climb. This is essentially the same as the "take" command but in a different context, and some climbers use "take" in this situation.

Climber: "Climbing." The climber is now back on the rock under his own power and should be belayed. Climbers often say this after resting on the rope following the take command.

Climber: "Slack." Feed some slack.

The Take Command

Proper execution of the "take" command. The belayer is in the proper position when the climber says, "Take."

The belayer takes up the slack.

The belayer pulls tight on the rope, backs up to increase the tension, and then sits down in her harness. The result is that the climber maintains his position on the wall.

Climber: "Up rope." Most often used in top rope situations when the climber can see excess and unnecessary slack in the system and wants it removed. Sometimes a climber uses this command when he pulls up a large amount of slack for a high clip and then steps up, developing a loop of slack between the protection and his harness.

Climber: "Lower." When the climber wants to be lowered, the belayer needs to know how far. Is he coming back to the ground, to the previous bolt, or down to a section of the route he wants to climb again on top rope? To be lowered back to the ground, climbers use expressions such as "dirt me" or "send me."

Climber: "Stop" or "hold." A climber says this while lowering to indicate where he wants to stop.

Climber: "Yarding." The climber wants to pull himself up using the rope. The belayer provides tension.

Climber: "Boinging." The climber can't reach the belayer's side of the rope or the rock (as in a fall on steep rock) and needs help. See page 80 for more on this technique.

Climber: "Rock!" A warning to the belayer and others at the base of a route concerning any falling object—rock, quickdraw, brush, shoe, etc.

Climber: "In straight," followed by, **"threading."** At the end of a route the climber is about to thread the rope through the anchors and is expecting the belayer to feed slack and keep him on belay during this process.

Climber: "Off belay." The climber is releasing the belayer from belay duty, and the belayer is expected to remove the rope from the belay device. When the climber and belayer are standing on the ground, the meaning of the command is obvious, but in the context of sport climbing, "off belay" is often misused. When at the anchors of a sport climb, only use the "off belay" command if you are planning on rappelling off the route and no longer want to be belayed at all. If you are planning to thread the anchors and then be lowered off by your belayer, do not use the "off belay" command. In this context, miscommunication will almost certainly lead to serious injury.

Belayer: "Belay off." The rope has been removed from the belay device and the climber is on his own.

Belayer: "Back clip" or "Z clip." Sometimes the belayer sees things the climber is unaware of, such as a potential Z or back clip. When the belayer sees an error like

this committed by the climber, the belayer should immediately warn the climber.

While commands are important, the quality of communication is what really counts. Climbers and belayers need to have a continual dialogue. While it is the belayer's job to anticipate the climber's needs, the climber should still tell the belayer what he wants or needs, especially in cases where the climber might do something out of the ordinary.

Feeding Out and Taking In Slack

Feeding out and taking in slack in appropriate quantities and at the right times are basic lead belay skills often poorly applied. A leader needs slack for a variety of reasons, including clipping, moving higher, threading anchors, and cleaning draws under tension. Timing and quantity are crucial: just ask the frustrated leader who struggles to pull enough rope to clip. If the belayer feeds enough slack but too late or feeds too little at just the right time, he shorts the leader.

In general the appropriate amount of slack between the climber and belayer is two to three feet, or a slight loop in the rope in front of the belayer. Less slack and the leader might encounter a downward tug if he moves quickly upward. Deficient slack during a fall can cause a short, hard fall, increasing the likelihood of ankle or knee injuries as the climber swings into the rock. Too much slack will make it more difficult for the belayer to respond quickly to some commands or may make an unexpected fall longer than necessary. Maintain two to three feet of slack as the leader climbs, feeding or taking in rope as required.

When the leader requires a fast feed of slack, as when clipping, the belayer should throw out two arms' lengths of rope as he anticipates the clip. If the clip is at the leader's waist, the belayer should feed a bit less, and if the clip is well over the climber's head, a bit more, but in general the belayer should feed two arms' lengths immediately before the leader reaches for the rope. The anticipation here is critical. If the belayer feeds just a moment too late, he shorts the leader. He can speed his delivery of clipping slack by simply stepping toward the rock while feeding rope.

Feeding quickly and on time requires practice and, in many cases, experience with a particular partner.

Feeding rope quickly

First reposition your hands according to the manufacturer's recommendations. (Here, with an auto-locking belay device.) Note that the belayer's thumb is holding the locking cam down while her brake hand remains on the rope.

Step toward the wall. This instantly provides the leader with two to three additional feet of slack.

Immediately throw out two arms' lengths of rope by pulling slack through the belay device with the left hand.

Reel in extra slack after the clip has been completed.

Generally, the proper amount of slack is two to three feet total and is indicated by one to two feet at the belayer's end of the rope.

As the climber moves up, the belayer feeds rope with both hands by simply pulling slack through the belay device with the left hand while the right hand follows along at the same rate.

Until the belayer learns the idiosyncrasies of the climber's clipping style, use the command "clipping" just prior to grabbing for rope so that the belayer's timing is right.

Practice with your chosen belay device because many require specific procedures for lead climbing. Not long ago the accepted method for feeding rope quickly with an auto-locking belay device, such as the Petzl Gri-gri or Trango Cinch, was removing your brake hand from the rope and clamping down on the auto-lock mechanism while pulling out slack with the other hand. This technique violates the most basic principle of belaying—the brake hand never leaves the rope—and is not acceptable. If you've been using this method, replace it with the new manufacturer prescribed methods.

Belay Techniques and Falls

Most times, the type of fall a climber experiences is determined by the amount of slack and how the belayer introduces it into the system. The belayer's actions, and sometimes the climber's, determine how the force of a fall will be distributed across the belay system and if and how the climber will impact the wall. There are two belay techniques for catching falls: One is a more static belay in which falls are shorter in length and impact forces are primarily absorbed by the rope and climber. The other is a dynamic belay, in which the belayer attempts to use his body to absorb some of the energy of the fall, resulting in a longer but softer and more comfortable fall for the climber. The drawback of a dynamic fall is that it is longer, which means the climber risks striking a ledge or other projection and has farther to climb to get back to his previous high point.

Determining which belay style to use for a potential fall begins with an inspection of the route and a conversation between climber and belayer before the climber leaves the ground. If the climber has been on the route previously, he can warn the belayer about certain difficult clips or dangerous falls and how to belay for each. Even if neither one has been on the climb before, certain potentially dangerous features are clearly evident, such as a ledge that breaks the climb into two sections. Climbing above the ledge would expose the leader to the potential of falling on it, and the belayer needs to be prepared to give a more static belay with less slack. Likewise pendulum falls can happen on a traversing route or section, so the climber and belayer need to agree on the belay tactic to use to minimize the possibility of swinging into a tree or inside corner. Climbing above a roof is another dangerous situation in which the climber might fall just far enough that his legs swing under the lip while his upper body remains above the roof; in this case the belayer must decide to use either a very static belay and keep the climber totally above the roof or a dynamic belay with added slack to allow the climber to fall completely below the roof.

Provide less slack if the climber is above a ledge or other projection.

For a climber above a roof, provide either more slack so that a fall results in his ending up completely below the roof or a very static belay so he stops completely above the roof.

Dynamic and Static Belays

A belayer can influence the nature of a lead fall by manipulating the rope. The goal of a dynamic belay, for instance, is to decrease the impact force the climber feels. There are two ways to accomplish this: In the most common, the belayer steps, hops, or even jumps up toward the first bolt at the moment when the falling climber begins weighting the rope. As the belayer jumps up and decelerates he adds length to the fall so that the climber has longer to decelerate. This lessens the force he feels. See appendix 2 for the physics behind belaying.

Timing is critical for a dynamic belay; the weight of the climber should pull the belayer higher and give the climber a longer deceleration. Jump too soon and the belayer falls back to the ground as the rope comes tight, effectively creating a static belay in which the climber decelerates quickly with greater force. Jump too late and the fall will be over by the time the belayer gets off the ground. One rule of thumb is to jump at the point when the falling climber passes the highest clipped protection. Be aware that this technique adds rope to the system, but don't think of it as simply leaving a larger loop of slack. A large "sport loop", or excessive loop of slack, does not provide a dynamic belay; it merely creates a longer fall.

Sometimes the belayer cannot step up or jump into a fall but will still need to provide a dynamic belay, like in a hanging belay or off a small ledge. In this less commonly used technique the belayer is anchored, and the only way to provide a dynamic belay is to let the weight of the falling climber pull some rope through the belay device before completely locking off and stopping the fall. The advantage of this method is that it does not require perfect timing; the belayer simply lets the rope slide through his hand and clamps down gradually instead of immediately locking down. The belayer needs belay gloves for this technique, and it can't be performed with an auto-lock belay device. In addition, practice and skill are required: If the belayer provides too little friction, the rope can very quickly scream through the belay device and the climber can fall uncontrollably. Seek professional belay instruction before attempting this type of dynamic belay.

Anchoring

Many climbers believe that anchoring the belayer to the ground or a tree provides a safety advantage, but this is not true. First, an anchored belayer cannot move around in response to the needs of the climber, and second, an anchored belayer will have a harder time providing a dynamic belay and can't get out of the way of rock fall or other hazards. Some belayers anchor in because they climb with a heavier partner and don't like being pulled off the ground during a lead fall, but being pulled off the ground provides a more dynamic belay, which is often beneficial. If the weight discrepancy between the climber and belayer is large, however, the belayer will always provide a dynamic belay even when it is disadvantageous. A difference of eighty or more pounds between climber and belayer makes for a far more challenging belay, and it takes a highly skilled belayer to handle such a large disparity. If this is your situation, it may be best to find a heavier belayer.

The belayer should only anchor if he is not on the ground or is at risk of falling off a ledge or slipping down a steep slab.

Belayer Position

A belayer has to perform a variety tasks and be attentive to different safety issues that can vary from route to route. He needs to position himself according to the

Climber below the first bolt with belayer positioned on the opposite side.

climber's location on the route and what might be needed at any given moment. Too many belayers place themselves in a disadvantageous position by sitting down or not moving around in response to the climber's actions, increasing the odds of belay mistakes or injury. At the beginning of a climb, the belayer may need to spot the leader until the first bolt is clipped. Before the climber leaves the ground, the belayer should feed out enough slack for the first clip so he doesn't have to stop spotting to feed rope. Immediately after the clip, he should move to the opposite side of the first bolt from the climber and pull in the remaining slack to make a rapid transition from spotting to belaying.

After the first clip, or in situations in which the first protection is preclipped, the belayer should keep the rope out of the climber's way and position himself on the opposite side of the bolt. The belayer stays in this position until the climber clips the second bolt because if the climber falls onto the first bolt, he can end up close to the ground and if the belayer has positioned himself directly below the first bolt, they could collide. The belayer can assist the climber by holding the rope off to one side and close to the rock so that as the climber passes the first clip the rope does not tangle in his legs or feet. On steeper routes the belayer can turn to the side or even put his back to the rock to maintain a line of sight to the leader. He should stand just to one side of the protection or bolt and close to the rock so that if the climber falls, he is pulled upward. On many routes the first two or three clips are the most dangerous part of the route. One reason for this is that the second bolt or protection point is far enough above the first that the climber risks falling to the ground if he pulls up slack to clip and then comes off. There is little a belayer can do about this because the climber is often too high for spotting and the belay will be ineffective due to the amount of rope out. To avoid potential ground falls, a climber might consider preclipping the first two bolts or pieces.

Even if the first two points of protection are placed close enough together, a lax belayer who leaves too much slack out or a leader who pulls too much rope to clip can cause a ground fall. On some routes, like those on the El Diablo wall in American Fork Canyon, a ground fall is inevitable if you come off while trying to clip the second or possibly third bolt; in these situations the belayer could only try to keep excess slack out of the system.

When the climber is low down on a route, he has very little rope out to absorb the energy of a fall. These short, hard falls have a higher impact; the climber often slams into the rock, the belayer lifts off the ground, and the climber can even crash into the belayer. The belayer needs a plan of action for each possible scenario before the climber leaves the ground; falls close to the ground require quick reaction time and typically have a smaller margin for error.

In most cases, the belayer should stand slightly to the side and near the wall and not some distance from the wall as is common practice. If a fall occurs with the belayer close to the rock, he is pulled up toward the first bolt, but if the belayer is out from the wall a fall can pull him off his feet, swinging him hard into the wall and possibly causing injury, or he could lose control of the rope. In the second scenario, the climber will also fall farther, and if he falls at the second or third bolt, he can, if the belayer is away from the wall, fall directly onto the taut rope stretched from the belayer to the first bolt.

After the climber is high enough that he doesn't risk a ground fall, the belayer can move away somewhat from the base of the rock to a position where he or she is best able to see and react to the needs of the climber. Typically he'll want to be close to the rock so that the direction of pull in the event of a fall is vertical. This gives him the opportunity to provide the dynamic belay described above; if he's standing away from the base, jumping up won't do any good and may pull him off his feet and drag him into the wall.

There is a wealth of advice admonishing belayers to be attentive, but what exactly does that mean? Let's examine some specific points you should be aware of.

Improper belay position too far from the wall.

Belayer positions

Right: The belayer stands to the side of the route. Note that in all positions the belayer remains slightly to the side and near the wall.

Below left: The belayer is turned 90 degrees to the wall so that she maintains her position near the wall but can still watch the climber.

Below right: On this steep climb the belayer has turned her back to the wall so she can watch the climber.

Wall Angle

Slab. If a climber falls on a less than vertical face, he can slide down the wall—even small projections can be dangerous in such a situation. The belayer should keep slack to a minimum since the farther the climber falls, the more chance he has of impacting or snagging a ledge, horn, or hold.

A climber who falls on very low-angle wall with a long runout can tumble down the face, a hazardous situation. If the belayer's movements are restricted, there's not much he can do. If, however, there is a clear path leading away from the base of the climb, the belayer can lock down his belay device and hightail it in the opposite direction as soon as the climber falls to

remove as much slack from the system as possible before the rope comes taut.

Vertical. Be aware of any projections because an unanticipated fall on a vertical wall means the climber will remain very close to the rock for the entire length of the fall. Vary the slack and dynamics to minimize the chances that a falling climber will strike ledges, horns, and other features.

Steep. An overhanging wall requires a dynamic belay since the climber is falling away from the wall. A static belay can cause a climber to swing back into the wall; the dynamics help dampen the impact of the fall so that the climber won't swing back into the wall.

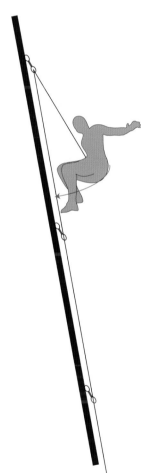

Low-angle climbs usually require less slack in the system to minimize the possibility of sliding into projections.

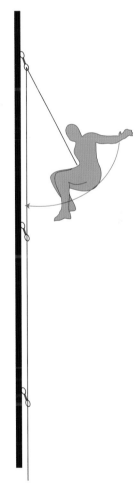

On vertical walls, vary the slack and dynamics to minimize the chances that a falling climber will hit projections.

A climber who falls farther on a steep wall will end up farther from the rock, making getting back on the climb more difficult. If the run is for redpoint, then a longer, softer fall is preferable. If it's a working burn, the climber may appreciate a shorter, harder fall so he has less work to regain the high point. The belayer should discuss such issues with the climber before the attempt.

Roof. Roofs present two fall risks. First, if the leader begins his way out the roof without having clipped ahead, he risks a severe pendulum fall into the wall, and the belayer can't do much to lessen its severity. Before the leader leaves the ground, discuss safe clipping through the roof as well as above it. Second, once the climber has clipped the first point of protection above the lip, he could fall with his head above and legs below the lip. Be sure to leave the appropriate

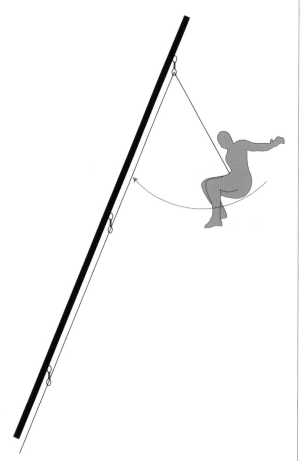

Dynamic belays are usually preferable on steep terrain.

length of slack so that a falling leader either ends up fully below the roof or fully above it.

Ledge or projection. If the climber is above any projection that he could impact in a fall, leave less slack out. A shorter, harder fall is better than landing on a ledge.

Climber Clues

You have scoped the route with your partner and discussed the various climbing and belay issues that might arise. He ties in and begins climbing, making clips as anticipated and climbing as you expected. Then something changes. You notice his movements become jerky, he's grunting and breathing heavily, and his footwork is no longer as precise. These cues tell you that he is reaching his limit and a fall is more likely. Here are some other things to watch for:

Leader stress. Be cognizant of your leader losing his composure. When this happens a fall is imminent, and you should be prepared to provide either a dynamic or static belay based on the situation. The signs of stress are a loss of precision, especially with the feet, "chicken wing" elbows, grunting or breathing heavily, "sewing machine" leg, and a slowing pace.

Leader errors. Be alert for your leader committing potentially dangerous errors such as getting the rope behind his leg, back clipping, Z clipping, or traversing off route. Give strong verbal warnings in all these situations, but be prepared for the worst case, in which the problem is not corrected and a fall ensues. A back clip could result in a longer fall should the draw come unclipped, Z clips usually produce relatively short, hard lead falls, and traversing off route can mean a wicked pendulum fall. If the climber's leg is behind the rope, he can flip upside down if he falls—to soften the fall and minimize the swing into the wall, provide a dynamic belay, but be aware of potential head impacts on projections and shorten or lengthen the fall to avoid them.

Belayer complacency. Be wary of becoming complacent when the leader appears to be having an easy time of it. Holds break, birds fly out of cracks, and feet can slip. Unexpected falls happen and the belayer's job is to provide as safe a fall as possible along the entire length of the route.

On-sight communication. Clear communication between belayer and climber is important in any situation

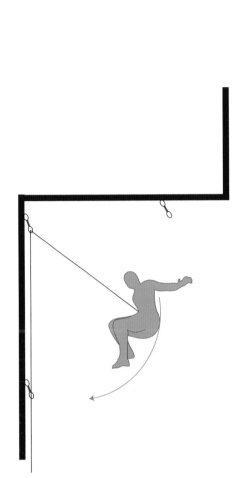

Before the leader leaves the ground, discuss clipping ahead in a roof to avoid a severe fall like this.

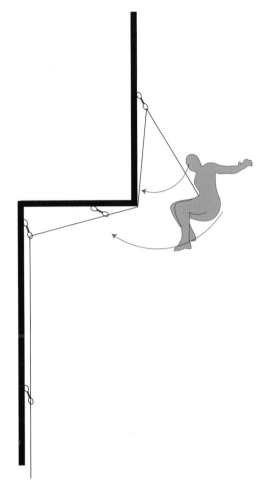

Provide the appropriate amount of slack so that the climber either stays fully above the roof or falls completely below it.

but especially so in an on-sight. Because the climber lacks information concerning the route, he is more likely to be unaware of dangerous situations that might arise than if he had worked the route for redpoint. It's therefore important to maintain a dialogue so the belayer is aware of possible hazards such as blocks marked with an X or rock projections that weren't visible from the ground.

Other Issues

Loose holds. Occasionally loose holds will be evident before they break off. The leader may tip you off to a loose hold, but typically they'll pop off without warning. Try not to stand directly below the climber so that

if he pulls a hold off it won't fall on you.

Weather. The belayer should watch for potentially dangerous changes in the weather, such as lightning storms.

The end of a route. As the leader approaches the end of the route, watch for several additional clues. The leader may be fatigued, the rope can begin to weigh heavily, and communication between climber and belayer can be difficult. For example, the second pitch of the Gunks classic Bonnie's Roof (5.8) ascends a large roof. If the leader climbs the entire second pitch to the belay at the top the crag, it will be nearly impossible for the climber and the belayer to hear one another, even when shouting. Agree on a plan for handling these situations before anyone starts to climb. You can solve this problem by climbing the route in three pitches rather than two; the leader can set up a belay just above the roof, where he can still be heard by his partner. Walkie talkies that are small and light enough to slip into a pants pocket are another solution. Perhaps the least effective solution is signaling each other using the rope. There are many possible problems with this last method, but it's better than nothing.

Sport routes present a different set of problems. The climber and belayer may have different ideas about what the climber is going to do at the anchors. Even if you've made plans, the climber may change his mind. If the climber says "off belay," immediately ask him if he is planning on rappelling down the route or he wants to be lowered. Never take a climber off belay if he's threading an anchor in anticipation of being lowered.

Rope Tricks

Working a route for redpoint presents technical challenges. The goal for learning burns is to acquire information as quickly and effortlessly as possible, and becoming skilled at this will help you advance. To that end, technical equipment handling skills can help you advance the rope to the next bolt, move up and down a section of a climb, decrease risks, and generally help get you to where you need to be with less effort.

Preplacing draws. Preplacing quickdraws can be an advantage on a learning burn, particularly in harder sections where the draws frequently serve as handles, giving the climber something to grab instead of taking a fall. Preplacing draws can also save you effort during a redpoint burn. No one differentiates between a redpoint and a pinkpoint—a term once used to describe a send where the climber didn't place the draws on the

Fixed draws are becoming more common on steeper routes.

full ascent—these days, so prehung draws gives you the added advantage of not having to take the time or effort to carry and place draws while attempting the send. You can sometimes preplace draws on rappel, or you may need to use a warmup burn. If you have a preference for clipping with the gate facing toward or away from your clipping hand, be sure to set the gate in the appropriate direction. Note that preplaced draws in and of themselves wouldn't negate an on-sight, but rappelling down a route for any reason would. So if you want to make an on-sight attempt with gear in place have someone else equip it for you.

Stick clipping. For some climbs with a high first bolt and bad landing, preclipping the first draw may be the only way to avoid possible injury. A stick clip is so named because its original, and still commonly used, configuration was simply a long stick with the draw (rope attached) taped to one end. The climber holds the gate of the upper biner open with a twig and then swings the stick up to clip the open biner into the first bolt.

There have been a number of innovations in mechanical stick clips over the years, and today a number of excellent products are available that make stick clipping quicker and more efficient. Stick clipping devices are relatively inexpensive and typically attach to the screw end of a telescoping paint or light-bulb pole. They vary somewhat, but most allow you to clip the first bolt, attach the rope to an already placed draw, and remove a draw. One of our favorites is the Superclip, whose simple design and all-metal construction make it more durable than its competitors.

The predominant reason to carry a stick clip is to attach a draw and the rope to the first bolt. Simply push the top biner down into the Superclip so the gate is held open (see picture), attach the rope, and clip the first bolt. Be sure you don't back-clip the first bolt or you'll have to pull the rope all the way through until you reach the other end.

To attach the rope to a prehung draw, push a bight of rope between the two tines, raise the pole so the biner is lassoed, and slowly draw the rope tight.

To remove a draw from a bolt, you first need to attach your rope to the bottom biner. If the first draw is sans rope, you'll need to clip a second draw with rope through the bottom biner to the prehung draw. Pull the rope tight to steady the draws and push the

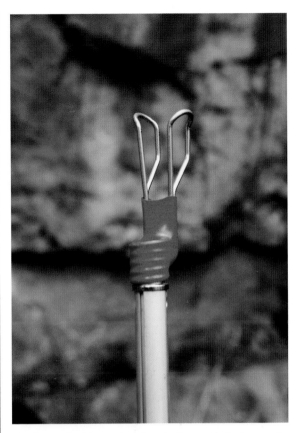

The Superclip (shown here) and other such devices make stick clipping easier.

Superclip onto the top biner to open the gate. Lift the draw off the bolt hanger.

There are other techniques for clipping the first bolt: If at the end of a burn you want the first draw clipped for the next run, unclip the second and possibly the third draw while lowering off. When you pull the rope, the lead end will fall to the ground, while leaving the first draw clipped.

If you lack the properly outfitted stick clip described above and a draw is already in the first bolt, how do you go about getting the first draw clipped before leaving the ground? The answer may be the difficult-to-master rodeo clip. Here's how you do it:

1. The draw must hang away from the rock. If the bottom biner touches the rock, find an alternative method.

Clipping the first bolt using a Superclip

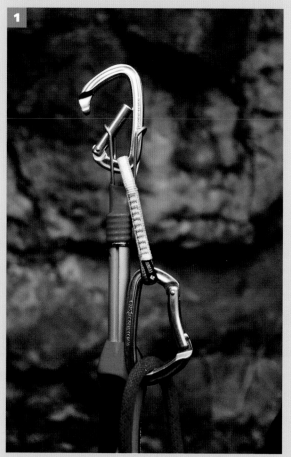

Insert a straight gate biner into the Superclip and clip in the rope. Be sure you're not back-clipping the rope.

Extend and lift the pole. Clip the straight gate biner into the bolt.

Pull straight down on your pole to remove the Superclip from the draw.

2. Stand under the draw and grab a bight of rope. Begin swinging the loop in vertical circles, starting small and gradually increasing the size until the end of the bight is near the bottom biner on the draw.

3. Try to catch the gate with the whirling rope. Ideally the loop will snap through the gate, but this is easier said than done—you've got to strike the biner gate just right to push it open and allow the rope inside.

Rodeo clipping is great for impressing the opposite sex, but inefficient since it can take many attempts to get the rope clipped. Our recommendation? Get a Superclip.

Going straight in. Take a load off your belayer while you rest en route by clipping in directly to a bolt after taking. Use a second draw rather than clipping your belay loop into the same biner as the rope. Attach a second draw to your belay loop and then grab the clipped draw. Find two footholds, thrust your hips upward, pull up on the draw, and clip the second draw to the first. Avoid pinching the rope. Once completed, tell your belayer, "I'm straight" or "Straight in."

A couple of cautions concerning going straight in: Be sure that when you begin climbing again you unclip your straight-in draw from the bolt. Do not climb while clipped straight in as this creates a very static system that can cause a biner to break during a fall. And don't go off belay; you're only attached to a single anchor.

Reducing rope drag over a roof. As the climber turns the roof, the rope will rub across the lip, and the higher on the headwall the climber gets, the more the rope drags. It can make it very difficult to pull rope to clip and can even impair climbing. You can reduce the drag on a small to medium roof (up to eight feet) by simply using longer draws on the last bolt or bolts before reaching the roof. Before placing a long runner at the beginning of a roof consider the costs and benefits of using draws of various lengths. The tradeoff is that placing a long runner can mean a longer fall if the transition from face to roof is difficult. On the other hand it might be the only way to reduce rope drag above the roof. Don't make the mistake of using a draw that's not quite long enough to reduce drag under a roof.

Clipping the rope to a prehung draw

Press a bight of rope between the Superclip's tines. Be sure that the rope strand closest to you is the end you plan to climb on; otherwise you'll be back-clipped and need to reverse the rope ends.

Lasso the bent gate biner with the bight and slowly draw the rope tight until it clips in.

Removing a prehung draw using a Superclip

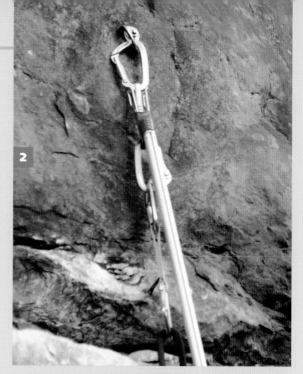

Pull the Superclip off the second draw. Grab both ropes and pull and hold the rope and draws tight. Push the tines of the Superclip onto the straight gate biner of the prehung draw.

Insert a straight gate biner into the Superclip and clip in the rope. Extend and lift the pole. Clip the straight gate biner into the bent gate biner of the prehung draw.

Release tension on the rope and lift the prehung draw off the bolt hanger.

You can leave the first draw clipped for subsequent attempts by simply unclipping the second and possibly third draw as you lower off.

On a large roof of ten feet or more you may need to use two separate ropes fed cleanly from two separate, flaked piles. For the first rope, tie a figure eight on a bight, clip a locking biner to the loop, and attach the biner to the belay loop on your harness. Tie in directly as you normally would with the second rope.

The belayer should have two belay devices, one attached to each rope. Both belay devices should be set up, threaded, attached to the belay loop of the belayer's harness, and ready to catch a fall.

Begin the route using the first rope and let the second hang loose to the ground. When you reach the lip, clip two draws to the bolt and then clip one rope into each draw.

After clipping in to at least two consecutive bolts with the second rope, the belayer carefully makes the transition from an active belay on the first rope to the second. While maintaining a brake on the first rope, he moves his free hand to the brake position on the second rope. After establishing a brake on the second rope, he takes his brake hand off the first. Pick up the first rope while you're lowering off.

Go straight in by clipping a draw to your belay loop and to the draw attached to the bolt.

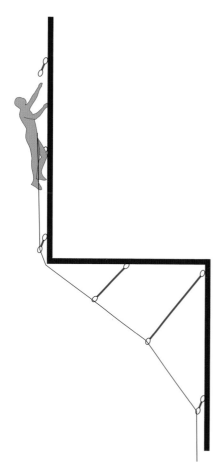

Use a long draw under a roof to reduce rope drag.

energy. It's a far easier task if the belayer uses his body to create tension than it is if the climber pulls his entire weight.

In some climbing situations a fall can put the climber in a position where he can't reach the belay side of the rope, such as a fall on a traverse or from above a roof that leaves the climber dangling in midair. If you can't immediately reach the belay end, try these techniques before resorting to the more tiring boinging method described below: Lean backwards in your harness until

After a fall you'll likely want to regain your position at the highest clipped bolt before pressing upward. To do that you can either reclimb that portion of the route or use one of the more efficient methods described below.

Yarding. Yarding is the best and most efficient way to regain the last bolt clipped. Yarding can help you recover lost ground with minimal effort. To yard, use the highest quickdraw as a pulley by pulling down on the belay end of the rope, thereby hoisting yourself up. If you can, push upward with your feet as you pull down on the rope. Your belayer should simultaneously pull hard on the rope to help you move higher. A good belayer makes yarding more effective by using his body weight as a counterbalance to pull the climber back up to his high point, thereby saving the climber's

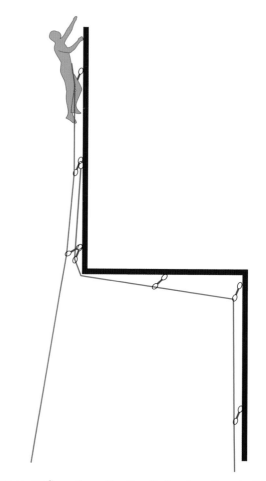

Rope configuration after the climber has clipped off the first rope. Note that he has clipped two bolts above the roof with the second rope before clipping off the first. There are two draws on the first bolt above the roof which prevents possible rope damage from having two ropes in the same biner.

Yarding up the rope

Grab the belay side of the rope and place your foot about waist high.

Pull down on the rope while pressing up with your foot. The belayer helps by pulling hard at the same time.

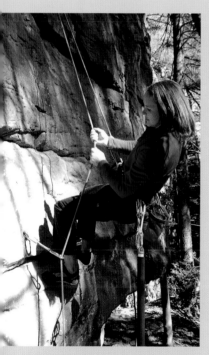

Stand up. The belayer pulls in hard to help you up and then hold you in place.

Reposition your hands.

Pull down again. Continue until you reach the position desired.

you're lying horizontally to extend your reach toward the rope or wall. Alternatively, if you can get a foot or hand to the rock, push off to create a swing. Increase the pendulum until you can grab the rope. Push off the rock in a direction opposite of that in which you want to swing. (If you want to move to the right, push yourself to the left.) You can also try to swing, then push. This is difficult, but if you're skilled at playground swings you may be able to create a small pendulum. As soon as you're close enough to the rock, push off to increase the swing distance.

Boinging. You may not be able to yard after you fall on steep rock if you end up several feet away from the rock and the belay side of the rope. To regain the last bolt try boinging. First, the belayer jumps in the air while maintaining tension on the line and pulling any slack generated through the belay device. This results in the belayer hanging in midair with feet off the ground and full weight on the rope and the climber no closer to the ground than before the belayer's jump. The belayer must do this perfectly or the climber will drop a bit each time the belayer jumps up.

With both the belayer and the climber hanging on the rope with their full weight, the belayer serves as a counterweight to the climber. The climber then grabs the rope at shoulder level or higher and pulls up on the

The belayer's first task in boinging is to get all her weight on the rope by simultaneously jumping up and pulling in slack. She jumps up while simultaneously drawing rope through the belay device until she's off the ground and hanging free with all her weight on the rope.

The belayer has all her weight on the rope and is ready for the boing.

The starting position for a boing: Both climber and belayer have all their weight on the rope.

Boinging

The climber reaches up, grabs the rope, and pulls himself up so that slack develops below his hands.

The climber quickly releases his grasp on the rope. Some of the slack is taken up by the belayer's weight and the climber ends up a bit higher.

Repeat until the climber can reach the belay end of the rope and begin yarding.

First, lower to the next-to-last bolt you clipped.

Next, go straight in.

Clip the stick to your harness.

Go back on belay, and then unclip the locker and untie the eight on a bight. Then ask your belayer to take and detach your straight-in draw.

3

Tie a figure eight on a bight on the belayer side of the rope and clip it to the belay loop on your harness. This provides you with two anchors. (Note that a tied-off, closed loop of rope is clipped into two different bolts.)

4

Go off belay and pull up slack on the belay end of the rope until a loop reaches the ground. Ask your belayer to attach the stick clip to the loop and then pull it back up.

7

Yard back up to your high bolt and go straight in.

8

Use the stick clip to advance the rope to the next bolt. Attach the stick to the bolt and continue climbing. (You can retrieve it on the way down.)

rope, creating slack between his hands and his harness, and then quickly letting go. The belayer will drop a few inches to a foot and the climber ends up that much higher. For this to happen, the climber must let go of the rope quickly as if it were scorching hot. Some climbers like to do a gymnastic "kip" when pulling up to give themselves an added boost. Continue until the climber reaches the rock or belay end of the rope, at which point it becomes far easier to yard than boing.

For both these techniques a skilled belayer who responds quickly, and whose movements are synchronized with the climber's, is essential. Before a climber starts to yard or boing he should give the belayer time to prepare and then ask if the belayer is ready.

Both yarding and boinging are easier if the belayer uses belay gloves with a rubberized pattern on the fingers and palm. This kind of rope work can be hard on the belayer's hands, and while leather gloves are good at protecting the hands, they don't provide much purchase on the rope—they create less friction between the rope and the surface of the glove than gloves with rubberized fingers and palms do. An auto-locking belay device makes these methods easier too, by preventing any rope from slipping through and slowing progress.

Advancing the Rope en Route

What if you can't make the moves to the next bolt? You're stuck and either the move is too hard for you or, despite repeated attempts, you can't figure it out. Repeated falls at the same place can be physically and emotionally exhausting and don't help you learn the route. It's better to advance the rope to the next bolt so you can work the challenging section on top rope.

Clip up. In some areas the bolts are close enough together to allow you to reach from one to the next. Go straight in and pull up some slack. Grab the draw in front of you with one hand, pull up, and clip the rope through the next draw.

Bring up your stick clip. At many crags you can't reach from one bolt to the next, so you need to bring up your stick clip to advance the rope. You'll need to tie into two bolts because you'll be off belay when you lower a loop of slack down to the ground for your belayer to clip your stick clip to. (See page 82.)

Use your neighbor. In some sport climbing situations, the routes can be close together. If the distance between

the anchors is not too great, you may be able to use a neighboring route to set up a top rope on your project.

Here's how you do it: Climb to the anchors of the adjacent route, place two draws, and clip in your rope. Carefully traverse to the anchors on your target route, place two draws, and clip in your rope.

You have effectively created top ropes on both routes using the same rope. If a rock projection between the anchors causes the rope to drag, you may need to go straight in after traversing to your target route and then create a top rope on that route alone. Either way, lower off the targeted route, set a draw on every bolt, and clip your rope in. This will give you directionals as you climb on top rope. Recover your draws on the neighboring route by climbing the target route, reversing the

Use a neighboring route to set a top rope on your project or target route.

traverse you made previously, and cleaning the neighboring route in the usual way.

Make sure before you attempt this method that the climbing between the anchors is easy and the rock quality sound; you want to avoid the severe pendulum that would result if you fell while climbing from one set of anchors to the other.

Leave a biner. You may decide that the route is too hard for you, or you are particularly frustrated and just want to get down, or you need to retreat quickly because of sudden bad weather or the onset of darkness. The simplest thing to do is to leave a biner, usually one that is old or outdated but still in good condition. Go straight in, place the leave-it biner on the bolt hanger under the draw, and move the rope out of the draw and into the leave-it biner. Ask your belayer to take, and remove all the draws on your way back to the ground. It's a good idea to carry a leave-it biner on working burns just so you can escape quickly and easily if you need to.

Route Cleaning

Spending time wisely is key to organizing your climbing days. You should be able to quickly and easily retrieve your draws after you're done with a route so that you can move on to the next project expeditiously. The most efficient process is to thread the anchors and then ask your belayer to lower you. Rappelling involves unnecessary risks (such as lack of a backup anchor and having only one hand free to retrieve draws), takes longer, and makes cleaning the draws on overhanging or traversing routes virtually impossible.

Get in the habit of asking your belayer to lower you back to the ground. Your first step in cleaning the route is to thread the anchors (see page 86).

You can save a step or two if the lowest rings on the anchors are large enough to allow a bight of rope to pass through them. Here again you pull up about ten feet of slack after going in straight, but this time instead of immediately tying an eight on a bight, pass the bight through the anchor rings and then tie the eight on a bight. Clip the eight on a bight to your belay loop with a locking biner. Then untie your original knot and pull the loose end through the rings. Do a quick safety check, ask your belayer to take, remove the draws from the anchors, and you're ready to lower off.

After you've threaded the anchors, use these tips to save time retrieving the draws. Lower to the highest bolt and ask your belayer to stop. Remove the rope from the draw before removing the draw from the hanger. Even a small outward pull on the rope makes unclipping the hanger first more difficult. It is much easier to push the rope inward, pop it out the open gate, and then remove the loose draw from the hanger. Then lower to the next bolt and repeat the process until you've retrieved all your draws.

Steep and traversing routes complicate the cleaning process; without tethering yourself somehow to the

To clean a draw, first remove the rope.

Then remove the draw from the bolt.

Threading anchors

After placing a draw on each anchor and clipping the rope into both, ask your belayer to take. Clip a third draw to the bottom biners of the draws clipped to the anchors. (You'll need to carry one extra draw or preplace it at the anchors in anticipation of your redpoint.) Then clip your belay loop into the lowest biner. Tell your belayer you're straight in and call for slack.

Pull up about ten feet of slack, bend it over in the middle, and tie a figure eight on a bight. Attach the eight on a bight to your belay loop using another draw or use a small locking biner. (You'll need to carry that along too.) Do not clip the eight on a bight to a gear loop, which won't hold your weight if something goes wrong and you fall onto the rope.

Retie the threaded tail back into your harness with a figure eight follow-through knot.

Next unclip and untie the figure eight on a bight. Double-check that the rope leads up from the belayer, threads through the anchor rings, and is tied securely to your harness.

Untie your original figure eight follow-through knot and pull the loose tail of rope free from your harness.

Take that loose tail and thread it though the lowest point on both anchors, typically the lowest chain links or rap rings.

Pull yourself closer to the rock and give the "take" command. Check one more time that the rope comes up from the belayer, goes through the anchor rings, and is tied into your harness. Test by weighting the rope.

Remove the draws from the anchors and give the "lower" command. When you reach the last bolt, command "stop" and retrieve the draw.

Using a tether can help keep you close to the rock on overhanging routes.

Grab a hold to keep yourself near the rock.

Before attempting to clean a draw, first move the tether below that draw.

Wrap a leg around the rope to hold yourself in.

belay line, the lower you go, the farther away you end up from the route. To recover your draws, use a tether by first clipping an extra draw to your belay loop and the belay side of the rope. This will keep you close to the gear and the route. Lower to a point where the rope is horizontal between your tether and the next draw you want to retrieve, and then, using that horizontal section of rope, pull yourself toward the route. When you reach the bolt, move your tether from above the bolt to below it. Then unclip the belay line from the draw you wish to retrieve by grabbing the draw with one hand to hold yourself in and pushing the rope out of the biner with the other.

Get close to the rock and stable. The more difficult part of retrieving a draw is unclipping it from the hanger. Your job will be easier if you use keylock biners instead of the traditional hook-and-pin variety. The hook portion of the hook-and-pin biner has a tendency to catch on the hanger especially while you're pulling on the draw as you try to get it free. In either case you need to get weight off the draw—you can't hold yourself in with the draw and hope to get it off the hanger. One way to do this is to use the rock itself. Simply grab a hold, pull yourself in with one hand, and remove the draw with the other. You may need to get your feet on the wall as well. If the holds are small and you can't stabilize yourself by using the rock alone, wrap a leg around the belay side of the rope and pull.

You can also use momentum to remove the draw. This is tricky to perform but can save time and energy. With one hand on the biner clipped to the hanger, hold the gate open and pull yourself with force toward the bolt such that momentum is generated. At the deadpoint, or apex of the momentum, pop the biner off the hanger.

Take care in removing the first draw, which leaves you open to a potentially large swing. Before popping the draw off and cutting loose, be aware of all the possible obstacles you might impact. Remember that you will be much closer to the ground at the bottom of the swing path because of the downward arc of the swing and rope stretch. Obstacles such as boulders, tree stumps, briar bushes, and rocks protruding from the ground may appear to be far below but have an odd habit of reaching up and biting you.

You can pull yourself in to the rock to remove the first draw if the swing is clear of obstacles and you're

Use momentum. Grab the draw so you can hold the gate on the bolt end biner open as you pull yourself forcefully toward the bolt.

far enough off the ground. Look carefully to be sure trees, boulders, people, and any other obstacles are not in the path of the swing. Remove your tether and unclip the first draw. Take the swing and lower to the ground.

If you are in danger of hitting obstacles or are too close to the ground, you can use one of several other methods to remove the first draw. First, if the climbing is relatively easy above the first bolt, unclip the belay

To remove the first draw on an overhanging route, clip the belay end into the second draw and lower to the first.

Climb or yard back up to the second, remove it, and swing free.

side of the rope from the second draw and clip your end of the rope in. Remove your tether and then lower to the first draw and remove it. Climb back to the second bolt, remove that draw, and swing free. This can leave you clear of any ground obstacles.

Second, use your belayer and tether for assistance. Stay tethered after retrieving the first draw. Your belayer should take a firm stance with her back to the wall in anticipation of a sharp pull away from the rock. After you've removed

the draw, let go and your belayer can lower you. This method can be difficult to use as the climber can drag the belayer along the ground. Ask your belayer if you can use this method before committing to it.

Third, lower off the route after retrieving the second draw and use your stick clip to remove the first draw.

Fourth, if the landing area is level and you're confident in your ability to easily boulder up to the first bolt and then back down, you can retrieve the draw that way.

If the landing area is clear and the climbing easy to the first bolt, you can boulder up to retrieve the first draw.

✓ Establish clear communication between belayer and climber and learn the proper response to common climber commands such as "take" and "yarding."

✓ Remember that beyond the primary job of keeping the climber safe, a belayer's goal is to make the climber's tasks as easy as possible. Feed out and take in slack to reduce risk to the climber and facilitate his ascent.

✓ Provide a dynamic belay whenever feasible to soften the forces of impact on the climber by learning to jump off the ground as the climber falls past his high protection point.

✓ Provide a static belay in situations where a falling climber could impact a ledge or other projection.

✓ As a belayer, be aware of your climber's condition and the environment around you and respond appropriately.

✓ In general the belayer's position should be near the rock and just to the side of the first protection point.

✓ Use a variety of rope-handling methods to more quickly, easily, and safely learn the route and retrieve your gear. Use the appropriate technique to avoid swinging into an object or the ground after removing the first draw.

Longtime Gunks climber Russ Clune reflects on the common attitude of climbers to the new practice of redpointing in the early and mid 1980s, and how they compared the new style to what was then the common practice of yo-yoing, or lowering off after a fall with the next climber top roping up to the high point and continuing the lead from there: "What we didn't understand was that the sport was about to embrace difficulty at the expense of what we thought of as style. . . . At that time the redpoint seemed really contrived. Sure, being held in place would make it easier to learn the moves, but that's just choreography, that's not climbing. . . ." At that time choreography was considered unacceptable. Thirty years later, choreography is still an appropriate term, only now it doesn't express disappointment, but rather a positive description of the work, challenge, and aesthetic potential of redpointing.

Learning choreography is a process. If you've ever watched dancers practicing, you know how they break their routines into sections, frequently working on very short sequences or even individual moves that are particularly challenging. They focus on the details of each section and strive to understand it physically, emotionally, and intellectually. They practice timing and the best approach to take, and they seek to understand how each part of the dance fits into the whole. In addition they try to quickly and accurately memorize these movements as they learn them.

In the roughly thirty years since redpointing first made its appearance in America, climbers have come to embrace techniques and approaches that are similar to those used by dancers. Of course, there are meaningful differences. In climbing, choreography is based on what we have learned from others and on our own interpretation of the resources provided to us by the climb. These elements are combined in a way that is best for us. The choreography is not exactly a proscription; it is a matter of discovering what feels and works best for each individual climber. Learning, refining, and developing greater efficiency takes up the majority of the redpoint process and is what learning burns are all about.

General Principles

Redpointing is dominated by learning, memorizing, and refining movement and other important details of a route such as rests and clipping stances. Redpoint tactics maximize learning efficiency, increase the speed with which you can memorize a route or boulder problem, reduce the amount of energy you need to exert in order to obtain the necessary learning and memorization, and increase the amount of information you gain from each burn. Essentially, learning burn tactics help maximize the amount of learning and memorization you can do, while at the same time minimizing (or at least controlling) the amount of physical work required to gain that learning.

Developing this kind of learning efficiency takes a great deal of practice and, at times, is counterintuitive. It can seem that the most important task during a learning burn would be performing the actual moves, but in reality the most important task of early attempts is remembering the most efficient sequences so you can repeat them.

There is a difference between learning a route and making a redpoint attempt, and it's critical to distinguish between the two. Learning burns are exactly that. You are under no pressure to do anything other than learn and memorize the various components of a route. If you try to do anything else, you are distracting yourself from the central mission. You must be clear about your intent each time you leave the ground. Will you be acquiring knowledge and skill, refining moves, linking sections, or are you attempting to send? You need to be prepared before you leave the ground for a redpoint burn, and many climbers neglect the preparation and begin making redpoint attempts before they're ready. Many climbers do not know when they are ready for the redpoint and switch over to redpoint burns because they don't know what else they need to learn or what the potential barriers to getting the redpoint might be. Being able to assess the amount and quality of your learning and compare it to a reasonable estimate of what it will take to make the send are important parts of the learning process.

The Process

You need to be in the right frame of mind to learn. It can be both intimidating and exciting to get on a hard project for the first time, which means you may feel anxious or distracted by the emotions of the moment. Stay on track; your mind needs to be open to possibilities and alternatives. Linking sections is not necessary and may even be counterproductive at this stage. Further, don't stop your exploration at the first sequence that works for a given section—good enough at this stage may not be good enough down the road when you begin to put the whole route together.

Breaking the Climb into Sections

Since the first task is to learn and memorize movement and technical details such as rests and clipping stances, you need to break the climb into small sections of a few moves. On the first learning burn, when you know little about the climb or sequences, the most logical sections are those delineated by the bolts. Think of each of these sections as individual boulder problems that you need to study and learn. Working in such small sections is necessary because there is such a vast amount of information to be gleaned from the whole climb. It's far easier to find effective sequences and memorize them when working with small sections of three to eight moves. Any more than that and you'll quickly forget important details.

For bouldering you can break each problem down into its individual moves. Many times you can try out and refine each move independent of the others and then, once you're happy with all the individual sequences, begin piecing them together. The general principles that follow can be applied equally well to roped routes and boulder problems.

The typical process begins with examining the section visually before you climb it and locating the available holds. On well-traveled routes, this may simply be a matter of looking for chalked handholds and blackened or polished footholds, but don't confine your search only to these holds. For crux sequences especially, keep an open mind concerning available holds. Real rock can have a great variety of holds, and what works best for you may not be the prescribed beta, even though it can serve as a good starting point. For

The speed with which you can learn, memorize, and then execute sequences is the basis for efficient redpointing.

example, climbers who are particularly short or tall can sometimes find significant variations in crux sequences that best use their height.

The Basic Steps

1. Climb a section up to the next bolt, clip, and take.

2. Go straight in to give your belayer a break. Rest here for a bit.

First break a route down into bolt-to-bolt sections and work each segment separately. **Quinsana Plus (13a), New River Gorge, West Virginia.**

3. As you rest, review the section you just climbed. Can you look down and identify each hand- and foothold you used? Do you remember the order in which you used them? What were the specific moves? How good was the position you clipped from? How hard did the section feel? Was the difficulty in line with what you expected from a route of its grade?

4. After you have rested and reviewed the section, lower down to the bolt below you and reclimb the section. On very easy sections of a route, if you liked what you did on your first try, you don't need to go shopping for alternative sequences unless you suspect you did something wrong or a better sequence is readily apparent.

   On sections of moderate or significant difficulty, reclimb the section with several goals in mind. If you think the way you climbed the section the first time was good, then your first goal is to see if you can repeat the sequence or discover another, better sequence. Second, try to understand what makes that sequence work and how it could be better. What makes it difficult? How well does it flow? Are there any elements you are likely to forget, such as a hard-to-see foothold? How do you think you will do on this section when pumped? Will any moves be hard to do the same way every time? Based on these kinds of questions, look for modifications to make the section easier.

5. Before moving on, assess the difficulty of the climbing against the route grade. One of the challenges of this process is that it's highly intuitive, and its effectiveness depends on your level of experience. Nonetheless even less-experienced climbers can compare the difference between how the moves feel against the expected difficulty. For example, if you are on a 5.12a and the sequence you are using for the crux is V4+, there are three likely possibilities. First, and most likely, you are using a sequence that is more difficult than necessary and an easier sequence is there for you to discover. Second, you are on a one-move-wonder and all the difficulty of the route is derived from one very short sequence. Third, the route is not accurately graded and may be 12b or harder. When your sequence seems wildly out of line with the grade of the climb, you need to experiment more with sequences. If you are making a minor mistake, you may not realize it until later when you climb the section in the context of those below and above it.

6. After you have reclimbed the section, take and go straight in again. Look down and review it, comparing your second run to the first. How well did you

remember the sequence, and were you able to accurately reproduce or improve it? If you did something different, what was it and how did it affect your balance and the difficulty of the sequence, as well as your timing, flow, feeling of stability, or other salient aspects of the sequence? It's not uncommon to hear a climber comment on his sequence by saying, "That's not redpoint beta." This means that even when working on a learning burn, the sequence feels hard enough or awkward enough or has poor enough balance that the climber knows immediately the sequence will not be effective during the redpoint when he must climb the section while fatigued. When working in the fast redpoint range (one or two redpoint burns), repeating a section twice may be sufficient to discover a good sequence, memorize it, and reproduce it at will.

7. While still hanging on the bolt, if you are satisfied with what you learned from the section below, turn your attention to the section of the climb just above you. Identify as many hand- and footholds in the next section as you can. Using either beta from a climber who knows the route or your assessment of the available holds, come up with a likely sequence. When you have a good understanding of the section, go back on your belayer, lower into the last position of the previous sequence, and begin to climb. Don't skip a move or two by getting onto the rock at a slightly higher position from where you previously stopped climbing. While you're working each bolt-to-bolt section, keep in mind that each segment will eventually need to flow into the next, and if your sequence for one section leaves your hands or feet in a position that does not allow you to advance into the next portion of the climb, you'll be stuck. Take a little time to determine how the sections flow together so you're not climbing yourself into a corner.

8. When you get to the next bolt, take, go in straight, and review the section of the climb you just completed.

Experimenting on the Route

The eight steps above give the broad overview of the learning process you'll repeat on every logical section. Each section will have a different movement sequence requiring you to use different techniques; in other words, you've got to have a good repertoire of moves in your toolbox to solve the sequence puzzle in each section. Don't be satisfied with the first sequence that works; spend some time experimenting and you may discover an easier way through.

You can experiment with movement until you find the easiest way through, yet simply throwing random moves or a prescribed set of techniques at every section until you find one that works is inefficient. So

Examine and climb each bolt-to-bolt section, testing sequences and rests.

Rest at each bolt and examine the section ahead.

what's the process climbers use on difficult or puzzling moves? How do you decide what to try?

You could say that it takes experience to solve climbing sequences and that with time and practice you'll get good at it too. Climbers do rely on experience and intuition developed over the years, but you can shorten and strengthen the learning curve by learning a few simple, tested principles.

Evaluate holds. The first thing that a skilled redpoint climber evaluates on a given section is the size and configuration of the holds, which determine what movements are even possible. Make sure you see all the holds; underclings have a nasty way of disappearing from view as you move above them, and unchalked small holds are sometimes the key to success.

As you pull onto the wall after scanning the available holds, you'll probably use the biggest and most chalked handholds as well as the largest, most polished footholds first. You'll experience the type and quality of the balance they provide. Most climbers experience balance kinesthetically by how a move or body position feels, how much physical effort it requires, how stable you are when you let go with a hand or foot, and how quickly or slowly you need to do the move. It also helps to understand the basic rules that govern balance, which can take the guesswork out of envisioning sequences. Finding the best balance for each move is essential for discovering an efficient sequence.

Improving balance is a large topic (we devoted an entire chapter to it in *The Self-Coached Climber*). Here's a primer: First, the quality of balance is determined by the relationship between your center of gravity and base of support. Stable balance occurs when the center of gravity is positioned well within the base of support. Offset balance describes any situation in which the center of gravity approaches the limit of the base of support. Dynamic balance is when the center of gravity moves beyond the limit of the base, requiring a new base to be established. All three types of balance are on a continuum; there are positions and moves of higher and lower quality offset balance just as there are higher and lower qualities of dynamic and stable balance.

You improve your balance by broadening your base of support. Altering your base may not change the type of balance, but it can improve its quality. An offset balance position can often be improved by broadening the base of support in the direction you are moving. For instance, you can sometimes improve an offset balance move to the left by placing the left foot a little farther to the left.

Changing the path or the position of your center can also improve your balance. For a back step it's common for your center to be one side of the base (the line between the hand on a hold and the back-stepped foot). Simply arching your back can bring the center closer to the base and improve balance. On sloper moves, keeping the center of gravity low and close to the rock in relation to the holds provides an advantage.

Also, experiment with momentum to improve balance. Some offset balance moves, often those with slopers, require you to move very slowly and maintain maximum core tension as the center of gravity approaches the limit of the current base. Other offset balance moves benefit from moving faster, thereby limiting the amount of time you spend with your center of gravity at the limit of the base of support. When your center must move outside the base to reach the next hold, you always need to use momentum; you can't make a dynamic balance move without momentum. But how much momentum should you generate? And how will it originate? Will you throw your hips? Kick off a foothold? Will your hips start away from the wall and then move in or will they maintain a constant distance from the rock for the move? There are many ways to create momentum, and you'll only find the right answer for any given situation by experimenting.

As a rule, easier climbs have many moves of stable balance, while harder climbs have more offset and dynamic balance situations. Thus you will often find that the primary task in learning a sequence for a redpoint project is improving the balance on difficult moves. Sometimes this means making nuanced changes, such as using a foothold in a slightly different way. Other times you'll need to apply more substantial changes, such as altering a foot sequence altogether or switching from a back step to a drop knee.

The wall angle gives a clue for finding efficient sequences, letting you know whether turning, or back stepping, will provide any advantage. On less than vertical terrain, back stepping isn't of much use, but as the wall steepens, turning provides powerful leverage by bringing the center of gravity closer to the rock.

Turning will many times yield an advantage on steep terrain.

On vertical and steeper walls there are other standard movements to try. If you are failing on a back step, see if there is a foothold available to turn the move into a drop knee. This will broaden your base of support dramatically compared to a back step. If you are performing a difficult foot match, try substituting an inside or outside flag.

Beyond hold configuration, balance, and wall angle are a whole host of specialized movements to apply to any sequence. Look for any of the following movements in every sequence, and after a while you'll develop a sense of when each might be useful. Think of this as experimentation, like a game you are playing with the climb.

Working long reaches. If you're having trouble making a reach, use the following three-step approach.

Dynamic movement is often the easiest way to reach the next hold. Spyro Gyro V6, Stone Fort, TN.

A stem can relieve significant weight from the hands and arms.

Kids who routinely have difficulty reaching the next handhold have good results with this method.

1. Move your feet to higher holds. First simply step higher. If this doesn't work try. . . .

2. Turn, back step, or flag. Inside flags tend to lengthen your reach, while outside flags tend to shorten it but can create a very stable position to reach from. If this doesn't work try. . . .

3. Dyno. If you can't reach the hold using step one or two, throw for the next hold. The terms dyno and deadpoint are many times used interchangeably, typically describing a move in which you use momentum to reach the next handhold, and if you miss that hold, you fall. Dynos and deadpoints are

many times the easiest way between two handholds. Often a long lock off is a waste of energy when compared to a deadpoint or dyno.

Stemming. A stem broadens the base of support, thus improving balance in many situations. A solid stem places your center of gravity between the base of support described by the line between your feet and the rock, instantly relieving weight from your hands. When you find yourself in an inside corner, no matter how shallow, or when you are near features that stand out from the rock, look for a stem.

Some hand jams, like those where your wrist can be slotted into a constriction, can take weight off your fingers, allowing them to rest.

High step, rock over, and lock off. Use a high foothold and then rock your weight over that foot and reach to the next hold.

Look for hand jams. Jams are useful because they allow you to apply force in several directions. Any crack or narrow pocket is a potential source. Search for underclings, which are often overlooked. Horizontal cracks, huecos, and large pockets are good candidates.

Heel hooking. If the route is steep or you're following an arête, try to involve your heels by hooking. A good heel hook can act like a third hand and either support a significant amount of weight or counter a barn door.

Intermediate holds, even poor quality ones, can sometimes put you in a slightly better position for reaching the target hold. Try making two shorter moves in a row with the same hand rather than one longer reach.

Knee bars. You can sometimes lock your entire lower leg by wedging your knee and foot between two opposing holds, called a knee bar. Knee bars can provide rests in unlikely positions, like on extremely steep routes, and by locking your lower body into the rock, they allow you to use handholds that might otherwise be unusable.

The tenuous positions involving offset balance can many times be improved by tinkering with the speed of the movement.

Twistlocks, especially with opposing feet, can suck your hips into the wall and allow your core and upper back to greatly assist in reaching the next hold.

The New River is famed for its many high steps. Magnatude 11d, New River Gorge, WV.

Underclings are often overlooked even when chalked heavily.

Make good use of your heels on steep routes.

Using your heel on an arête can help control a barn door.

An intermediate hold can provide a slightly better position from which to reach the next hold.

Knee bars are common on blocky, steep routes. Apollo Reed 13a, Summersville Lake, WV.

Opposing feet can help lock your hips in to the wall.

A heel-toe cam can lock your leg in place. Lactic Acid Bath 12d, New River Gorge, WV.

Heel-toe cams and hooks. You can make a heel hook even more powerful by locking it in place with a toe, applying pressure in the opposite direction, i.e., the side of the heel pushes down while the toe pushes up.

Hooking a toe on steep terrain so your feet don't swing loose allows you to use poor handholds.

You can occasionally find a ledge or protrusion to sit on or straddle, creating an instant, hands-down rest.

Certain movements work repeatedly on certain types of rock. The high step, rock over the foot, lock off, and reach technique is common in the New River Gorge. At Rifle, knee bars are often used to good effect. Look for the common holds and movement types everywhere you climb.

Performing Moves

While climbers tend to use the movement skills described above, there are many moves that don't have names or fall into tidy categories. In addition, many times a climber uses the correct sequence but doesn't execute it with sufficient efficiency to achieve the redpoint. Working moves is not simply a matter of finding acceptable sequences, but also includes learning how those sequences should be performed. This includes movement initiation and speed, the path of the body through space, the distribution of effort through the body, and so on. The more difficult the moves are, the more important the nuances of execution become.

Ask questions about moves. What is the best starting position for a move? The starting position plays a role in determining what happens in the rest of the move. Understanding how much momentum is required and the quality of balance both at the start and end of the move will help determine the best starting position.

What part of your body is doing the most work? It's hard to imagine a climbing move in which the total muscular force necessary is evenly distributed between the arms, legs, and trunk. Different parts of the body naturally make different contributions to different moves. The question is what is best for the move under consideration. How can the effort of the move be better distributed? You often need to experiment to determine just how much work you can shift to the lower body and trunk and off the upper body. With experimentation you may discover that the obvious sequence

Hook your toe to prevent your feet from swinging free.

requires a great deal of pulling with the arms, but that adjustments such as pushing harder from the legs make the move easier.

Low-percentage moves are those you can complete only some of the time even when you feel like you are performing them exactly the same way each time. Low-percentage moves often combine dynamic movement and great precision, such as hitting a target handhold with the fingers positioned in a very specific way, and timing the move is often difficult. In order to hit a hold just right in these situations the body needs to continue its movement toward the rock longer than is necessary to simply reach the target hold. The difference between successful and unsuccessful movement isn't visible to the unaided eye, but you can look for clues. On a poorly timed move you'll feel as if the target hold is being yanked away from your hand at the moment you touch it. On a well-timed move you will be able to grasp it properly. In reviewing video of climbers on precise dynamic moves, we learned that a fraction of a second is all that it takes to make a difference, a slim margin for error. When facing a move of this kind, you are likely to focus all your energy on grabbing the next hold since that appears to be the primary issue in a successful attempt. Rather what you should do is work to be more consistent in the inward movement of your body and then maintain body tension at the end of the move. Don't let any part of your body relax at the moment of contact with the new hold.

Many low-percentage moves are the result of extreme offset balance in which you start to fall just before reaching the target hold. In these moves the center of gravity is moving close to the limit of the base of support, requiring great physical effort to maintain balance and stay on the rock. These moves often feel extremely insecure, or you feel like your strength is failing just before you reach the next hold. Experiment with your footholds to make sure you are using those best suited to the move. In this situation, hold position can be more important than the size of the hold, and even very slight changes in the position of a foot on the same hold can be advantageous. Also experiment with the speed of the move. Sometimes offset balance moves must be done slowly; other times momentum can be used to move you through the worst balance in less time, making your performance more consistent.

Repetition. Despite the emphasis on learning everything you can about a move, there may be some aspects you will never be fully aware of or understand. This is what makes repetition so important. Even when you know a move fairly well, repetition allows the brain to learn it better and to make subtle changes you will not be consciously aware of. This is one reason that it can be so hard to know when you are ready for the redpoint. There are times when there is a discrepancy between what you know about a move or sequence intellectually and the brain's ability to consistently produce movement with the necessary level of refinement.

One sign that more repetition is necessary is your emotional response to a move or sequence; if you have doubts or feel less confident than you should, more repetitions of the sequence may help. Perform a number of high-quality, consistent repetitions in a short period of time. Depending upon the difficulty of the sequence, this might mean dedicating multiple learning burns to only one short section of the route and repeating it three to five times per burn with a few minutes of rest between efforts until you can perform a number of high-quality repetitions in a single day. For extremely difficult sequences it may take several days to achieve this.

Learning by Watching Others

It's common to see a group of climbers or boulderers working on the same route or problem together, providing each with the opportunity to watch and learn from others who are attempting the same moves. Cognitive research suggests that watching other athletes can be helpful. You may think that watching better athletes is desirable and watching average or bad athletes less so. Research suggests, however, that we can learn equally well from average and elite athletes as long as our observations are guided by a coach or more experienced climber who can lead our eye to the more salient features of the movement we are observing. You can guide your own observations if you know what matters and what does not.

It's easy to be distracted by the less important aspects of movement, such as how smooth or graceful climbers

Repeat a sequence until you can consistently complete it.

look. But you need to compare the effectiveness of movement. The first and easiest thing to compare is climbers' sequences, particularly the footholds. Compare their hand and foot sequences to your own. What differences do you observe? What are the advantages and disadvantages of the options? Also look for the use of intermediates and very slight differences in hand and foot sequences. Two climbers might use the same hold differently, and this difference might be meaningful.

Look for variations in body position. Climbers using the same hand and foot sequence will not always be performing the exact same moves. Look for variations in how close or far from the rock a climber's body is, the degree to which he turns his body, or the horizontal and vertical relationship of his body to the holds. These elements tell you a lot about the kind of balance he is using as well as how the move is initiated.

You can get a general sense of movement timing by comparing the degree to which different climbers are static or dynamic in their execution of sequences. If you see one climber perform a move statically and another climber doing the move dynamically, then you can try to figure out what the differences between these methods are and which works best for you.

Our brains are good at seeing movement and interpreting how it feels to produce that movement. This is particularly true if you have experience with the kind of movement you see. You can perceive how moves will feel and thus what you can expect at different points in the route. This can tell you what makes particular moves difficult and give you ways of addressing that difficulty.

Many routes or boulder problems have sequences that contain a specific difficulty you need to address in order to be successful. Examples include a barn door or a foothold that is particularly difficult to use. Watching others can give you insights into how best to tackle such issues and add to your understanding of why certain things happen at that point in the problem.

Other Details and Emotions

In addition to deciphering sequences you'll want to locate rests, clipping stances, protection points requiring special treatment, and possibly even chalking points. Discovering and testing rests is covered in

Find the rests and then use them to recover between sequences.

detail in chapter 8. Don't overlook their importance, and be sure to determine how long to stay at each rest—if you rest too long or not enough, your recovery may be suboptimal.

Many times a route won't feel difficult in the learning phase because you're hanging between attempts at different sections, so the endurance you need may not be immediately evident. Recognize that the rests will be important later and that you'll need to invest time in locating them for future reference.

Practice clipping stances in which you've got to hold on with one hand while the other clips. Find the best stance for clipping every draw and commit it to your sequence memory. Occasionally you'll need special protection such as a longer-than-normal sling placed under an overhang to prevent rope drag.

You should also address your emotional response to each section, particularly those emotions that are negative. Is there anything that creates fear or discomfort? Are you intimidated by anything about the route? It's common to be concerned about a run out, difficult clip, bad hold, or hard crux, so part of the learning process is to recognize the elements of the route that cause fear or discomfort and then find good ways of dealing with them.

Visualization (see chapter 10) can help improve your emotional responses a great deal, allowing you to mentally climb the problem section of the route over and over again while staying calm and focused. Physically repeating the route can also be very helpful. Climbing a section over and over again will often help you refine your movement as well as improve your emotional comfort.

In cases where you fear a run out or potentially scary fall, the section can be rendered less intimidating by taking controlled falls to ascertain the real, rather than perceived, consequences. This is important. If it's a fall you fear, repeating the section without taking the fall may not help since the unknown consequences are likely causing the anxiety. Develop a safe and not too scary way to experience the potential falls in that section. For some climbers this will mean taking the fall from the most intimidating part of the sequence. For others it will mean taking a series of smaller falls first. See chapter 11 for a detailed prescription for dealing with fear.

How will you know when you're ready to move to the next section of the climb? That depends upon the relative difficulty of the climb. On fast redpoints you need to successfully repeat a sequence several times without hesitation or mistakes, especially at the crux, to fully learn it. On more difficult redpoint projects, you may have to repeat each section many times even after you feel you know it.

Depending on your skill in learning a route and its difficulty relative to your climbing abilities, you may or may not be able to create a workable plan in one learning burn. Your maximum time on a learning attempt shouldn't exceed forty minutes to an hour or you'll become fatigued and less able to learn. Efforts beyond an hour may even be counterproductive because you may become frustrated by your inability to execute precise movements.

Don't Get Pumped

You'll learn and memorize movement better when you are fresh and relaxed as opposed to fatigued or tense. As you become fatigued your motor coordination is impaired. Attempting to learn moves when you're tired often leads to ambiguity—it can be more difficult to determine the best movement since different methods can feel equally hard due to diminished coordination.

Unlike redpoint attempts, your learning routine should contain lots of hanging rest en route. Try a move or sequence and then take, rest, and recover before getting back on the climb. It's important to rest frequently and prior to the onset of a pump; you never want to feel pumped on a learning burn. Taking frequent rests before the onset of even a mild pump will allow your

Take lots of hanging rests on learning burns. Use the rest to review the previous section and look ahead to the next segment.

rests to be shorter and will help you feel less fatigued at the end of the burn as well as allow time to review. If you feel a pump developing, stop and rest immediately. Remember that your objective at this point is learning about the route; getting pumped is counterproductive. While resting, consider the segment you just climbed. If you're still working on an efficient sequence for this section, go over the holds in your mind while considering possible alternatives. If you've developed a workable sequence, then go over the moves in your head one more time, committing the look and feel of the holds and the proper sequence to memory. Once you've committed the movement to memory, advance to the next section and repeat the process.

Reviewing on the Route and on the Ground

Reviewing moves and sections is an essential aspect of going bolt to bolt. When you get back to the ground after a learning burn, it is just as important to review the route as it was when you were on the wall. After the first burn, the details of the route are usually not well engrained and need reinforcement. It's easy to forget details when you turn your attention to other tasks. Granted, you need to get ready to belay and support your partner, but before you move on, take a minute to review the climb or sections of the climb that you are likely to forget. Then while you are belaying your partner, use his rest periods to visualize and review sequences on your own project.

We cover visualization in chapter 10, but at this stage all you really need to do is remember the important parts of the route. Which hand or foot goes to which hold in what order? This is the basis of any sequence: the simple ordering of holds by hand and foot, without the nuance and refinement that will come later with subsequent learning burns and visualization. For a fast redpoint of a route within your limits, this may be all you need, but for bigger, more difficult projects, refining movement and visualizing it on the ground become more important.

Learning Burns and Linking Burns

There are two kinds of learning burns: straight learning burns when the goal is to learn and memorize short sequences of moves, and linking burns in which you are both testing your knowledge of individual sections

Review your sequences, stances, clips, and rests on the ground immediately after a learning burn.

and seeing how they work with the sections above and below them. Once you know the details of the sequences, rests, clipping stances, and chalking points for each bolt-to-bolt segment, you're ready to begin linking the segments together.

On subsequent learning burns, try to put longer segments of two or more sections together. The best way to do this on climbs that aren't too steep is to make your way to the anchors and set up a top rope. A highly effective approach is to lower to the last bolt and execute your sequence to the anchors. Then lower to the next-to-last bolt and climb to the anchors. Repeat by starting at consecutively lower bolts, always attempting to climb to the top of the route. Notice that the sections that are climbed most are near the top. The top-rope method forces you to climb the upper sections repeatedly and in this way learn them better than lower sections. On redpoint runs you'll likely be pumped when you near the anchors, impairing your judgment and coordination, but having repeated these sections a number of times, you'll know them best and therefore have a better chance of performing as planned. Note that even though you are on top rope you will want to either unclip each directional or pause for a moment in your clipping position to simulate a lead clip. Practicing on top rope without incorporating clips won't allow you to learn the appropriate rhythm and pacing for the section.

On severely overhanging routes, don't use the top-rope linking method. Lowering to the next lower bolt means pulling yourself back into the rock and clipping

Use a top rope on climbs that are less steep to practice sequences and begin linking sections together.

draws into your end of the rope, a difficult and taxing proposition. Instead work the climb from the ground up by attempting to link sections together. The classic steep climb approach is to apply your planned sequence to the first section, and if you make it through to the first bolt, continue on to the second, third, and so on until you need to take and rest. Begin again from your rest and try to link together the next sections. Again, take and hang when you become fatigued. Continue in this manner until you're at the anchors. This initial linking run sets a benchmark on which you'll try to improve.

These classic linking methods work well in many cases; however, leave room for variation and adaptation as you'll have indications about which sections will be easiest to link and which will need extra effort. The more experienced you are at redpointing, the more likely it is that you will note sections that are of higher linking priority than others. Linking sections from the ground or top may not be as important as linking sections in the middle of the route, so you may need more practice, time, and effort for these and less for sections high up or low down. Further, you'll often want to combine some linking and some learning into a single burn. If you need to learn sequences higher up on the route, you can try to link the lower sections, if they are easier, on your way up to the section you still need to learn.

Your first linking run will likely result in at least one and possibly several hangs, depending on how well you memorized the route and on its difficulty. On successive burns, many climbers try to reduce the number of hangs to one. Then they attempt to push that hang higher on the route even if only by a move or two. Once you've reduced the hangs to one very short hang, you're close to switching over to redpoint burns.

An alternative to the one-hang strategy suggests that the hang is less meaningful in terms of progress than it is in revealing a lack of knowledge or learning. When you fall, look for what you missed or what you did wrong, and then correct the error. If you fall two times on a linking burn, your goal for the next burn may not be to do to it with one fall but to correctly apply the new learning. This latter method may be best employed on routes that push your limits, where you'll need every move to be as efficient as possible.

Many climbers attempt to reduce the number of hangs to one and then push it higher on the route as a redpoint tactic.

As you link sections, you may discover that one sequence doesn't flow into the next and that your hands or feet are in the wrong positions to advance. You'll need to rework the section, possibly invalidating your planned sequence. Sometimes the easiest sequence for a particular segment can't be used because it leaves you unable to progress into the next section. In this case you'll need to come up with a different, and probably more difficult, sequence that leaves you in a position to move into the next section.

In addition to practicing your planned sequences in each section of the climb, linking burns can provide additional helpful information. First, you may learn that a redpoint crux exists apart from the crux. The crux is the most difficult individual sequence on the

route while a redpoint crux would follow the crux higher up where the moves aren't as difficult as those at the crux but the pump can take you out. Not all routes have separate cruxes, but if there is any question in your mind be sure to practice the higher redpoint crux section thoroughly so that on redpoint burns you won't hesitate in this crucial section.

Are You Ready to Send?

When are you ready to make redpoint attempts? This topic is covered in detail in chapter 7, but in general you're ready to send when you can consistently perform all the sequences, use the rests, and have reduced the number of hangs in your linking burns to one—although a good bit of variation to these rules of thumb exists.

Three Ranges of Redpoint Difficulty

There are three broad redpoint ranges depending on the route's difficulty, your experience at redpointing, and your recent climbing history.

Redpoints that are one or two letter grades above your consistent on-sight level can be completed in two to five attempts. In terms of skill and fitness this is a range of difficulty where you are working well within your established base. Emotional pressure is not very great at this level, and success is almost guaranteed. What makes this level challenging is learning, memorizing, and applying a large amount of new information quickly. It takes focus and a reliable memorization technique to quickly complete these routes. The difference between a three- and five-try redpoint is most likely how fast and well you can memorize.

Fast redpointing can be differentiated from more difficult levels by the nature of the first learning burn. You need to determine what is necessary for the redpoint and learn it all on the first learning burn. Some sections of the climb will be easy enough that you need not memorize them in detail. For example, just climbing through the 5.9 section of a 5.11c one time should give you all the information you need. Your efforts will be best spent focusing on the crux, the redpoint crux, anything that is not obvious, or aspects of the climb that are a personal weakness. Don't link large sections in the first burn in a two- to five-try redpoint, but rather assess what will prevent the redpoint from happening quickly and address those issues in detail; experience and skill will allow you to get though the remainder of the route. The next run will either be a redpoint burn or more learning and memorizing for a redpoint attempt on the third or fourth try. You can link a number of sections when you visualize the route. At this level, it's possible to complete several quick redpoints in a day—a rewarding exercise that helps refine learning and memorizing tactics and builds confidence by providing a consistent diet of success.

The next redpoint level consists of those climbs three or four letter grades harder than your consistent on-sight level and that generally take somewhere between seven and twelve attempts to complete. This is a very popular range for redpoint climbers, and it's common to see a four letter grade difference between a climber's on-sight level and best redpoint. The challenge at this level is to persevere through the sometimes much longer learning and memorization stage involved with sequences at a higher level of difficulty. The higher level of difficulty means that fitness starts to play a larger role too, and you may need to refine your moves to make them more efficient than you would on an easier route. You may need to make four, six, or even more learning runs before you begin serious redpoint attempts. Some burns may require learning and memorizing short sequences. Later you'll need to repeat and refine difficult moves even after you know the sequences well to stress-proof your performance. In later runs your focus may change to linking longer and longer sections together.

This is the type of route that best fits into the redpoint process described earlier in the chapter; it's all about finding and learning the efficiencies a route has to offer and then applying your current skill set to them. You'll need to find most of the weaknesses of the route, which requires significantly more effort than sending a route within your limits. A good sign that you're ready to redpoint is one hang, but keep your options open to see if you can discover better, more efficient movement even after you've reached the one-hang goal. A single hang that lasts for a minute or two at the same bolt on consecutive redpoint attempts may be a sign that you are inefficient on lower parts of the route or need greater fitness.

The last redpoint level is made up of climbs that are five or more letter grades harder than your on-sight level and that can take many tries, perhaps fifteen, twenty, or even more. These megaprojects require you to work far enough beyond your established base of skill and fitness that success is less likely, and you may invest many days of work and still come up empty-handed. You may need a dozen or more learning runs and many redpoint attempts over many months for routes so far beyond your current abilities. It can be very hard to know when you are ready to start making redpoint burns, and the transition from learning to having a chance at the send may be quite gradual; you may not have the same level of awareness that you would at the other redpoint levels.

If this sounds daunting, you're not alone in your assessment. It would be easy to argue that you should avoid routes beyond your current limits, especially if you lack redpoint experience or have an obsessive personality! Focusing on a route at this level necessarily means passing up the opportunity to send a number of other routes in the same amount of time. However, very hard routes can, in the end, be instructive and rewarding.

Really difficult routes first require learning not just most but all the efficiencies a route has to offer, and then executing flawlessly. Typically every move, rest, and stance must be the most effective and efficient possible, and this effort in learning the underlying nuance is most instructive in advancing redpoint skills.

At this extreme level it's difficult to say when you're ready to send; you need to feel comfortable with the planned sequences and have confidence in your ability to carry them out. The one-hang rule shows progress, but it may not be a good indicator of readiness since learning may not be complete—remember that you need to be able to execute the most efficient sequences with confidence.

Finally, these climbs produce a great amount of learning at a subconscious, imperceptible level. You may feel movement becoming more stable and consistent with practice but not be able to identify why this is happening. The brain makes meaningful adjustments to variables, such as the timing of movements, that you cannot perceive directly. This occurs at all levels of movement learning, but it has a greater impact on success or failure at this difficult level, which means that you'll need to make a greater commitment to repeating sections. At easier grades you may only need to repeat each difficult section three to five times, but at this more challenging level you may need to repeat each hard section seven, ten, or fifteen times.

Except for the easiest redpoints, the number of attempts necessary to complete a route at each redpointing level varies greatly. This wide range occurs for two reasons. First, climbers vary greatly in their ability to learn, memorize, and apply the necessary tactics. For example, a climber new to redpointing may have difficulty completing a route one letter grade above his consistent on-sight level in two tries because he simply does not know efficient methods for memorizing movement and the technical aspects of a climb. Thus his learning will be inconsistent and have gaps, and he will repeatedly make mistakes that he doesn't eliminate until later. It will therefore take more tries to redpoint relatively easy routes.

Second, even experienced redpoint climbers can have difficulty memorizing and executing sequences. The speed with which you redpoint a route depends on the style and difficulty of the route in relation to your base level of skill and fitness and your ability to learn, memorize, and then execute movement under duress. The farther outside your base level of skills a route lies, the more difficult it will be to learn and redpoint. A climber who specializes in extremely steep routes should expect a vertical route one letter grade above his on-sight level to take more than two tries as he is tasked with learning and memorizing the movement as well as adjusting to a completely different style of climbing. It's a safe assumption that in this situation efficiency will be harder to come by.

For each range of redpoint difficulty, completing a route is a somewhat different task requiring different expectations, tactics, and emotional investment. Determining when you're ready to send is rooted in experience and not based on a proscription, and at the highest levels, you might be ready to redpoint and not know it. You may need to experiment to determine the next step. It's OK to try linking sections before you know all the individual sequences of a route. You can also make an early redpoint attempt to assess where you stand. These things can be helpful; however committing to redpoint burns too early in the process can unnecessarily extend the learning process.

First Attempt: On-Sight or Learning Burn?

The goals of the first attempt vary greatly depending on the level at which you are working. If you're attempting to redpoint a route in two tries, the first attempt is the only learning burn. You should end the first burn having repeated each section a few times, memorized the crux, found the redpoint crux, and noted any idiosyncrasies that might cause problems on the redpoint attempt. At the level with twenty or more tries, you may not be able to do all the moves on the first burn and may only come away with the draws in place and a general overview of what the route is like. While that would be considered a failed burn for a fast redpoint, it's a successful learning run for a longer redpoint.

Should you use the first burn as an on-sight attempt? Even the authors of this book disagree! The case for an on-sight attempt is based on the idea that you only get one shot and that the opportunity shouldn't be squandered. If an on-sight attempt is successful, you save time and can move to a new route on your pyramid that same day. Further, from time to time you might be surprised and actually get the on-sight for what would have otherwise been considered a redpoint project.

The case against an on-sight attempt is that it blurs the line between two distinct types of performances

Should you use your first burn as an on-sight attempt or a learning burn?

and slows down the learning process. Climbers rarely learn much about a route in an on-sight attempt, so the energy used in the first attempt is wasted. In reality, the second burn becomes the first learning run.

For climbers moving from purely recreational to more serious climbing, though, self-assessments may not reveal a clear distinction between on-sight and redpoint levels. A historical pyramid may, for instance, report a 5.10d redpoint and a 5.11a on-sight and include only a small number of routes, so the climber can't draw any conclusions. This climber has a lot to learn about his current ability, and making on-sight attempts in the 5.10d to 5.11b range can help more clearly define his current performance level.

Working at Different Redpoint Levels

There are different attitudes and approaches toward redpointing. Those who focus on fast redpoints have different values than those who focus on megaprojects. Fast redpoints refine your ability to quickly memorize and execute climbs. You can expect to redpoint two or three routes or half a dozen boulder problems in a single day. This provides a steady diet of success and can make each day of climbing fun and deeply satisfying.

The potential drawback from a heavy emphasis on quick redpoints is that you may have the potential to perform at a higher level but never learn how to do so. Further if you do attempt a significantly more difficult route, it will be hard to change your expectations and correctly assess how well you are doing. You may become discouraged by expecting the learning process to go faster than is reasonable and conclude that a route is too difficult.

At the other end of the spectrum are those climbers who put all their energy into long-term projects taking fifteen, twenty, or even thirty or more attempts. These climbers have the benefits of patience and self-confidence, and when their efforts pay off, they do so in a big way. The problem is that making megaprojects your focus will be far less productive in terms of the number of routes completed in a given period of time, and skills in other areas can sink to unacceptable levels. For example, we have seen climbers who redpoint 5.14a but can't on-sight 5.12b. This suggests that their

focus has been so narrow for so long that they've lost fitness and skills that could significantly help their performance on big projects.

Some people deride climbers who "flog" climbs into submission because they appear to climb better than their abilities would suggest by repeatedly attempting the same project. While there may be some truth in that, consider sports like figure skating or gymnastics in which athletes practice a given move or routine for months or longer before a successful performance. No one would say an Olympic gold medalist was performing above her abilities by flogging her routine into submission. The difference between the gymnast and the climber is that the gymnast receives a great deal of support from a coaching staff—encouragement, movement analysis, and practice consisting of a variety of activities that promote fitness and movement skills during the learning process—while the megaproject climber is usually on his own with a very narrow focus and little support from outside sources.

It is likely best for an individual's development to spend time working at different redpoint levels to provide a variety of learning experiences. Work up to megaprojects, if you choose to do them at all, by first developing and refining your redpoint tactics on a variety of routes one to four letter grades harder than your on-sight level. If you are well prepared, a big project can be a rewarding and positive learning experience; if you aren't, it can be miserable and discouraging.

Belayer and Rope Management

Helping you learn the route is partly the responsibility of your belayer, whose active participation is indispensable to the process. See chapter 5 for techniques you and your belayer should employ to make your job in the learning process easier.

Difficult Moves

What if you simply can't figure out how to do a particular move, or confront a move so difficult that on linking or redpoint burns you repeatedly climb into it and fall off only to have to make another attempt? Consider converting a bolt-to-bolt section into a top rope. Either pull up a stick clip and advance the rope to the next bolt (see chapter 5 for the full description of this technique) or climb through and lower back down to the difficult section. Now begin by putting yourself in a position where you can easily reach the final handholds of the difficult portion. Where will your feet need to be? Find footholds that allow you to reach the final handholds, and then ask your belayer to lower you a few inches. With your feet on the holds noted above, attempt to make the final move. If you're successful, lower a few more inches and again attempt to climb to the section's final handholds. Work each very short section, lowering a few inches each time until you can do each repeatedly and have climbed through to the highest bolt clipped. Continue until you can climb the whole section from lower to higher bolt.

If you're still not able to perform the move after exhausting all the possible holds and sequences, either something is eluding you that you can't discover on your own or you lack the movement skills or fitness to perform the move in question. It's common to first blame a lack of physical strength, but over the years we've learned that the answer is often to refine your movement. Many times, once you learn to execute the move better, you can perform the sequence flawlessly and with consistency.

Determining whether the root cause is a lack of skill or strength is difficult; first approach the problem as a movement or experience issue. If you're working within your performance pyramid, especially at the lower levels, chances are strength or fitness is not the issue. In any case you'll need to break out of your usual habits.

You can watch a friend or two on the move and ask them to describe what they are doing and why. Or try to be more playful with the move, attempting it different ways such as very slowly or dynamically while focusing on the process rather than the outcome. Occasionally trying something different can provide insights into the move even if it's not successful in itself.

You can also perform a more detailed analysis of the move starting with a description of the type and quality of balance. How might the quality of balance be improved even slightly? Also consider the difficulty of the move in relation to your current on-sight or project bouldering level. For a megaproject or a redpoint four letter grades harder than your on-sight level, a stiff crux may fall into a range of bouldering difficulty with

Progress in very small increments on a top rope to overcome difficult moves.

which you have little experience. More bouldering at that level may be warranted.

Other Learning Burn Issues

Movement skills. Movement improvement spans a wide variety of skills with a whole host of possible exercises. Those exercises most applicable to you depend on your specific weaknesses; if you don't turn well, for example, you should practice the line and flag exercise (described in detail in *The Self-Coached Climber*). Working difficult boulder problems is a great way to refine your movement skills for a specific sequence. Try to choose problems with a similar angle using holds like those on the route section that's giving you difficulty.

Fear. One of the objectives in making learning runs is to discover scary sections, giving you a chance to do something about them. For example, you may decide to preplace a long draw on the bolt above a run-out section or on a poorly placed bolt that requires a difficult clip using a standard draw.

A good learning process removes the uncertainty about all the elements that make up a climb: its holds, stances, protection, movement, falls, and so on. Reducing uncertainty helps assuage your fears by making you more comfortable with the climb.

Weather. In some parts of the country, weather can play a crucial role in your ability to execute movement. In the East, for example, summer humidity may significantly reduce the friction between your fingers and the holds, making climbs near your limit virtually impossible. During hot and damp seasons, you may need to work on the lower levels on your pyramid, saving the more difficult climbs for better conditions.

Partners. Your choice of partners can affect your ability to learn and send. You'll need someone with similar goals who can be patient while you spend thirty minutes or more hanging all over a route trying to learn its ins and outs. An impatient or negative partner can obligate you to shortchange your learning burns; find someone who is supportive, shares your climbing philosophy, and with whom you can amiably spend long hours.

Differences for Bouldering

As with learning burns on routes, the central goal of gaining high-quality learning with the least amount of effort is important for bouldering, and many of the methods for learning routes are also applicable to boulder problems. Having a goal for each attempt, taking an appropriate rest between efforts, reviewing sections immediately after you have climbed them, and using guided imagery and other tactics described above are all important tools for projecting boulder problems. Yet there are important differences.

Learning Burns

The biggest difference between learning burns on a route and boulder problem is that a problem usually ends when the climber encounters more difficult moves. Rather than hanging on the rope to study the moves, a boulderer will often enter into his second learning burn with little or no knowledge of the harder sections of the problem. Further, you can expect the moves on a boulder problem to be significantly more difficult than on a route; moves that approach the limit of your ability can be very hard to learn and repeat because it can be nearly impossible to tell why you are succeeding or failing. You can be overwhelmed by the sheer effort and therefore unable to adequately sense the balance, timing, and other variables essential to the move. This makes learning moves on challenging boulder problems more difficult and time-consuming.

The primary working tactic boulderers can use to address these problems is power spotting. In a power spot, some of your weight is supported by a spotter standing on the ground. This is a simple learning method especially for moves near your limit, but it can also be tricky to administer; providing a good power spot requires practice and understanding.

First, the amount of weight to support depends on the climber and the relative difficulty of the moves. The goal is to take off just enough weight to allow the climber to do the moves and thus learn something about them. Provide too much support and the climber won't learn much because he won't feel the balance, timing, and effort needed. Provide too little and the climber won't get through the move. The goal is to make the moves easier for the climber but not to drastically change their nature. It can take some experimentation to determine exactly how much weight to take off for a particular section of a problem.

Second, it's important to not alter the climber's body position or path through space. Supporting the climber is not simply a matter of trying to lift him up toward the next hold, but rather of adjusting to how the climber is moving or needs to move for a given sequence. Sometimes a power spot will be a matter of lightly pushing the climber into the rock or to one side. The spotter needs to observe the move, move with the climber, and apply appropriate pressure. If performed

A power spot can help you learn difficult bouldering moves.

well, a power spot will allow the climber to learn the moves more quickly than he could on his own. It's also helpful to use a power spot on repeated attempts so that as the climber learns the moves the spotter applies less pressure on consecutive attempts until the climber is able to do the moves entirely on his own.

If the crux is too high for a power spot but some of the lower moves are difficult, then you can use the power spot low down with the idea that the climber will arrive at the crux less fatigued and have a better chance of learning something about, or completing, the crux.

Resting

While an individual learning burn on a boulder problem rarely leads to a pump, keep two things in mind regarding fatigue and rest. First, on short efforts you might come off the problem feeling perfectly ready to

go again. Your muscles, however, have depleted their short-term energy supply, so even if you feel fine, a few minutes rest are necessary before you'll be fully recovered. Second, if you rest too little between efforts, you can become pumped, turning a bouldering session into a low-intensity anaerobic endurance workout. Rest between one and five minutes, depending on the problem length, intensity of effort, and your relative fitness. The fatigue you feel may not change much over the course of a few minutes, so use a watch to make sure you get enough rest. Most energy reserves are regenerated in three minutes following the short bursts of effort you use in bouldering.

Range of Difficulty for Bouldering Projects

While it's common to redpoint sport routes four letter grades above your on-sight level, it's more difficult to describe the relationship between on-sight and project levels for bouldering. For example, even though you can on-sight V6, you may not be able to complete V7 in two or three tries even if your tactics are good. There is no common and naturally occurring spread between on-sight and project levels for boulderers; many boulderers have two or possibly three number grades between on-sight and project level while others have a spread of only one or two grades. This makes setting goals for different levels of boulder projects more difficult. Also, bouldering culture tends to focus on projects and eschew on-sights. A large number of boulderers in climbing gyms put their efforts into working at or near their limits, so not only do they not know their on-sight level, but they also don't have a good idea of how many tries it takes to complete projects of a given grade.

Learning to efficiently prepare for redpoint attempts takes patience and time, and you progress through hard experience. You cannot learn the techniques and tactics in this chapter quickly; you need to spend considerable time observing and experimenting and then reviewing and assessing how you performed. This book can help send you down the learning curve more quickly, but you still need to invest the time and effort to apply it to your climbing.

QUICK TICKS

✓ Break the climb into sections of three to eight moves, most commonly by going bolt to bolt. Experiment to find the most efficient sequence and locate rests, clipping stances, and chalking points.

✓ Experiment with balance, movement initiation, momentum, turning, and all the other movement skills available to you to discover the most efficient sequences.

✓ At each bolt, review and commit the section to memory and evaluate your emotional response before attempting to learn the next section.

✓ After lowering off the climb, practice visualizing your sequences.

✓ Once you're satisfied with your bolt-to-bolt sequences, begin to link them together. Continue to visualize yourself executing the linked sequences with perfect efficiency.

✓ When you are ready, attempt to send the route. Remember that on a fast redpoint you may need only a single learning burn before trying to send.

How you transition from learning and linking burns to redpoint attempts varies depending on the difficulty and nature of the route, your emotional state, and the quality of the preparatory work. In the best case, you know the route and have each move committed to memory. You have set rests, clipping stances, and chalking points and rehearsed critical sections. You're mentally ready and itching to send. If you are prepared, you can send by efficiently repeating what you've learned. You may even find the redpoint feels easy! On the other hand, a successful redpoint can be elusive and frustrating—you can lose motivation and even abandon the project. Success and failure don't just happen, they're constructed, so you need to know what variables contribute to successful redpoints.

All climbers are different: the visualization and emotional tactics that work for you may not work as well for another. General principles address the transition from learning a route to the successful redpoint, but the details and variations are what help you create an individual redpoint performance plan.

Transitioning

Begin by preparing yourself mentally for the attempt. Redpoint burns require a different mindset than learning burns: execute versus learn. Up to this point your goal has been to learn and practice sections of your project route. During redpoint burns you need less conscious effort to execute each movement because you have practiced it so many times; now you can pay attention to other aspects of the climb, such as your breathing, pacing, or fixing mistakes if they occur. Before your redpoint burn, you tried alternate sequences, searched for and changed rests, explored clipping stances, and set chalking points, but as you approach your first redpoint burn your focus shifts from learning to performance, using the emotional and physical resources that work for you.

Emotional Preparation

Transitioning from learning and linking to redpointing is emotional and intellectual. Emotions play a huge role in climbing performance; the basic fear for your safety and feeling at risk, the excitement of being on a great route, the investment of time and effort into a project, the uncertainty concerning the outcome, the stress of working near your physical limit—it's easy to see that redpointing can be a profound emotional challenge, and in fact, it's possible to be physically prepared but not emotionally ready for a redpoint attempt.

It's important to be open to new ideas and different possibilities during the learning process, to be analytical, and to devote time to memorizing what you learn. After transitioning to redpoint burns it remains important to take an analytical approach to unsuccessful attempts. Analyze unsuccessful attempts to understand what, if anything, you can change on subsequent burns. Analysis not only keeps the process moving forward, but it also prevents you from getting caught up in your emotional response to failure. At times you need to trust your intellect rather than your emotions because your intellect can correctly assess risk, tell you why a burn went wrong, assess your pacing and execution, and so on. Negative emotions, no matter how compelling, cannot give you that kind of performance assessment.

During the redpoint process you might feel discouraged, fearful, or foolish and not want to get on the climb again, but you shouldn't let emotional responses like this guide your climbing. There are good reasons to walk away from a project, but the decision should be intellectual and based on an analysis of your performance and likelihood of success.

Compare how you felt about the project at the beginning of the learning process to how you feel at the transition to redpoint burns. It's easy to feel intimidated by a project in the beginning, but now that you've worked the route you should be more familiar and comfortable with the climb. Problems arise when you do not become less intimidated over the course of learning burns. Bad falls or holds breaking can cause prolonged or increased uneasiness even as you become better prepared for the redpoint. Spend a few minutes looking at the route and letting yourself honestly respond to the idea of climbing each section. Ignoring or even being unaware of negative emotions concerning the route can cripple a redpoint.

If the crux continues to intimidate you after you have worked it, repeat it while fresh a number of times and then link it with larger sections below and above or repeat it with less than a full rest so you can feel what it is like to climb that section tired. You may need to repeat it a number of times, depending on how negatively you view the crux. Prove to yourself that you can climb the section well, even when tired, and let that be your emotional focus.

Fear of a run out or a fall. Potential falls and run outs are a fact of life when it comes to redpointing, and dealing with these emotional issues is just as important as learning sequences. There are two ways of dealing with potential falls and run outs: First, acknowledge that the section is frightening to you; then give yourself something very specific to focus on in that section such as concentrating on the precise placement of your feet or the way in which a particular hold feels. The most direct benefit of this change in thinking is to reduce anxiety. Often times we focus on our fear when we get to a scary section rather than on the essential aspects of execution.

The second tactic is to take some practice falls in the sections that concern you to lessen your anxiety over the possibility of a fall (see chapter 11 for exercises designed to reduce your fear of falling). Start small and take a series of falls. Work with your belayer to create the kind of fall that you feel is most suited to that part of the climb and then work up to taking longer falls if necessary. After you take some practice falls, the consequences are no longer an unknown. In addition, you've learned you can trust your belayer to give you the best fall possible.

Expectations. Some people thrive under the pressure of expectations; others are crushed by their weight. Someone who loves trying to send a route on the second try on a fast redpoint may be crippled by long-term projects. Take note of your responses to expectations in different contexts, and whether those expectations are motivating or impede your progress.

Visualization. During learning burns you use visualization primarily to memorize and refine sections of a climb. For redpoint burns visualization is a way of refining and planning the full ascent. When you are practicing redpoint visualization, watch for periods when you lose concentration, become tense or fearful, hesitate, or don't perform the sequence as planned. These issues can impede your success, so it's important to note and correct them, often simply by altering your visualization; however if the problems persist, you may need to work the route on top rope or take some mild, controlled falls. Merely visualizing a climb one, two, or three times likely won't benefit you unless it's for an easy redpoint. Projects taking multiple days may require many visualizations; you should eventually be able to visualize the climb all the way through from stepping off the ground to clipping the chains using the proper sequences, performing the moves in the most efficient manner, staying focused, calm, and aggressive with no lapses in concentration. If you can do that, consider yourself prepared for the redpoint.

If your first few redpoint attempts are not successful, compare your actual performance to your visualization. If you find differences, address how and why they are meaningful and whether you need to change the visualization or the actual sequence. You should be able to figure out which by climbing the section a few times and then comparing it to your visualization. Reconcile the differences and perform the visualization again.

Physical and Mental Preparation

If your learning runs and redpoint attempts are spread over a series of days, you'll have the opportunity to prepare away from the route based on what you learned in chapter 6. For example, you can sometimes manipulate an indoor climb to mimic a large section of a redpoint project or at least the crux. Practicing the sequences while away from the cliff can give you confidence and increase your fitness in situations similar to your project. If your gym won't allow you to alter a route or boulder problem to suit your specific needs, then practice on routes that have similar characteristics to your project, like the wall angle, the type of holds, and the overall physical nature of the climb. Using both interval and repetition training methods described in chapter 9 on routes with similar characteristics to your project is a pragmatic way to increase your readiness for the redpoint. (See *The Self-Coached Climber* for more on these methods.)

Use warmup routes to prepare yourself physically and mentally for more difficult climbing.

You can also take a more general approach to preparation. A redpoint project that takes you outside your comfort zone—onto steep ground if your expertise is with vertical climbing or using slopers if you have a strong preference for crimpers—may require you to work on weaknesses. Indoor facilities typically have a range of wall angles and holds for you to practice on and improve, especially in those areas for which you are deficient.

You can also prepare mentally while away from the crag. Have a few minutes to spare? Find a relaxing position, close your eyes, and concentrate on your breathing until you are in a relaxed state. Now see yourself ascending your project, executing the movement flawlessly, recovering well at the rest stances, making every clip perfectly, and feeling confident in your movement and imminent success. Your mental imagery should include the details that are meaningful for your performance and end with you successfully clipping the anchors while feeling happy and relaxed. These mental practice sessions might only last a few minutes at a time, but they provide a powerful sense of achievement that carries through to your actual attempts.

You should also learn a relaxation cue that works for you. You want to be able to relax when you reach a rest stance to enhance both mental and physical recovery. If you can relax quickly, you can conserve energy and recover more rapidly. One cue used by the author is simple face relaxation—when you relax the muscles in your face, your other muscles follow suit. This cue allows you to quickly relax once you reach a rest by simply relaxing the muscles in your face. Find a cue for yourself and then practice using it both away from and at the crag.

Warmup

Upon reaching the crag, you need to warm up properly. Your body must be prepped for the difficult redpoint effort to come. Gradually increase the intensity of effort over several climbs so that your body gears up for hard exercise. Warming up dilates blood vessels so blood can flow more easily to and from your muscles. You need to warm up tendons and other connective tissue and acclimate to the overall feel of intense activity. Failing to warm up gradually can lead to a flash pump.

Upping the intensity too soon or too fast can mean that your body is not prepared for the work and is forced into an anaerobic state before it's ready to deal with the byproducts. Climbers sometimes don't recover from an initial severe pump like this, thus ruining their chances of performing well that day.

Warming up also allows your mind to adapt to the day's activities. Just as your body needs help adjusting to the demands of difficult climbing, so too does the mind.

Concentration. Prepare yourself to concentrate on the important details of your climbing. Outside thoughts don't distract you, and you are in control of where your focus lies. It's easy to get overexcited for a redpoint, so you may need to calm yourself down during the warmup. The key point is that you want to be in control of your thoughts and emotions. If outside thoughts are intruding or you can't hold your focus, the warmup allows you to tune in to the task at hand. Choose one simple thing to focus on for a specific amount of time. For example, you might focus on breathing for the first four bolts. Or concentrate on pacing for an entire route. It's up to you; just set your concentration by focusing during the warmup.

State of mind. Your state of mind should be determined by your performance plan, as described later in this chapter, but in general it's beneficial to be calm yet aggressive. Since you have rehearsed the moves, a somewhat elevated arousal level is optimal. You want to be calm and focused yet ready to work as hard as necessary.

Positive talk. Provide yourself positive self-talk in preparation for redpoint burns. The kinds of messages should be based on your redpoint performance plan, which takes into account what has previously helped you to be successful. In addition to your plan, take into consideration your needs for the day. If you are feeling overly excited, your positive self-talk should place more emphasis on being calm and focused than if you're feeling tired and unsure of yourself.

Begin warming up well below your project's grade and work your way up through more difficult routes. A proper warmup might consist of three, four, or even five pitches before you make the first redpoint run. For example, if your project is 12a, you might begin by doing a couple of laps on an 8 or possibly a 9. You'd then move on to an easy 10 and 11 before making your first burn on the 12. Rest anywhere from twenty to thirty minutes between warmup routes that require moderate to strenuous effort and never allow yourself to get a deep pump. A wise climber once said, "There's no glory in a warmup." Better to hang and rest mid-route on a warmup than acquire a flash pump that you might never recover from. A mild pump is beneficial on the more difficult warmups, however, to prepare both your body and mind for the difficult work ahead. Rest another thirty to forty minutes before making your first redpoint attempt.

Route Prep

You can do a number of things to prepare your project for redpoint burns, each of which can save you considerable effort when it is time to send. The first is rigging the draws. Preplacing draws saves the effort of making a rigging run, or a run to equip the route prior to making a serious redpoint attempt. If you're lucky enough to be able to reach the top of your route by foot, you can rappel down and accomplish all the steps in this section at once, and if your walk in to the crag includes descending to the base, you can simply rap down your project before even warming up. If you can't reach the top by foot or the route is severely overhung, you'll need to rig

While preplacing draws, take the time to brush crucial holds.

the route by climbing it. Of course some routes, including many steep routes, are fixed with permanent draws eliminating the need to pre-equip.

While preplacing draws, you can also ready the route in a couple of other important ways. Chalk can build up on well-traveled routes, especially if they are overhung and out of the weather. Brush off crucial rest and crux holds to remove chalk that is imbedded in the rock. Cleaning off the rock improves friction between skin and rock so that you need less force on the hold. Always use a natural-bristle or nylon brush—steel or brass brushes can damage the rock by removing its texture.

You may wish to place or emphasize certain tick marks that allow you to quickly find and use tricky holds. Many chalk bags have a small zippered pocket to carry a piece of chalkboard chalk that is easier to use and more precise than smearing a chunk of gymnastic chalk. Blind holds that require accuracy are particularly good candidates for ticks. Mark a specific part of the hold that corresponds to a particular finger, for example where you want your index finger to impact the hold. Tick blind footholds under small roofs or bulges and crucial footholds that are easily confused with others. Try not to overdo it; place only as many ticks as you need, and make them as small as possible. There's nothing worse than a route covered with huge lines drawn to every semi-important hold. And remember to remove your ticks with a brush once your send is complete.

As you're rapping down, stop at crucial sections and go over the sequence and movement in your head one more time. Touch the holds and fix them spatially so that on your redpoint attempt they will be that much more familiar to you.

Redpoint Gear

Take as little gear as possible when making a redpoint burn. The route is already equipped with draws, so a harness, shoes, and chalk bag with small hold brush are all you really need; leave everything else on the ground. That includes an extra draw, a belay device, daisy chains, and any other gear. You probably bought a thinner rope, a smaller harness, and lightweight draws to save weight, so don't lose those benefits by carrying unnecessary equipment.

Tick marks can be used to mark a foothold or handhold, and the direction and style of the mark often tells us about the hold and how to use it. Tick marks generally serve three purposes: ticks make it easy to find the hold (top); they distinguish the specific hold a particular climber wanted to use from the other available choices (middle); and they help locate a hold or a specific part of a hold that can't be easily seen because it's obscured by a feature such as a bulge (bottom).

Mental Prep

A few minutes before putting on your shoes and tying in, take a moment and visualize once more the performance you are about to execute. Visualization prepares you mentally for the task ahead by setting up the framework and fleshing out the details of your imminent performance so that your body can complete what your mind has visualized.

In the minutes before leaving the ground for a redpoint attempt, sit somewhere quiet, close your eyes, and visualize your performance from start to finish. Imagine making every move perfectly, recovering at the rests, clipping flawlessly, and feeling strong and relaxed as you glide through the sequences. See yourself hitting every hold perfectly and feel its texture as you flow across the rock. Make all the clips and per-

Take a few minutes prior to a redpoint burn to visualize a successful performance.

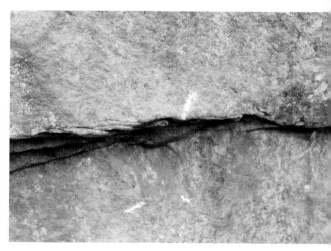

A climber properly outfitted for a redpoint attempt.

form each move following the plan you developed previously. In other words, imagine a perfect send where everything falls into place and you flow over the rock with power and grace. Once you've worked your way through the route, bring yourself gradually back to the moment at hand.

The Attempt

Redpoint burns are about executing a plan, letting your body perform the learned routine while focusing your mind on what is most important at any given moment. Usually this means controlling your pacing, correcting mistakes, and staying aggressive in the harder sections or as you become fatigued. You should not be wondering which hold to use or what sequence to take or questioning whether you'll complete the route. There is no room for such debates on redpoint attempts, and you

need to find pragmatic and positive thoughts to replace any doubts.

Rests are important not just to provide recovery but because they give you time to review and plan for the next section. Take a moment to mentally rehearse the next section of the climb. What lies below or several sections ahead doesn't concern you at this point. Concentrate on the next section alone, complete it, and then focus your attention on the subsequent sections, each in turn. While at a rest stance, try to relax as much as possible. Relaxation cues, such as relaxing your face, can help you to ease the tension on critical muscles, give your mind a break, and generally allow a quicker and more thorough recovery.

It's very important to use the rests to full advantage on a difficult redpoint. Don't be in a hurry; take the rests and recover as much as possible at each stance. A hands-down rest such as a ledge or seat can provide an almost total recovery, so use it even if it takes several minutes. The quality of a stance depends on a number of factors more fully described in chapter 8, but how much time to spend at each rest boils down to a simple rule of thumb: Stay just long enough to recover as much strength and endurance as possible. There is an optimal time to rest that varies with each stance—wait too long and you'll begin to fatigue, too little and you won't have recovered enough. Moving on before optimal recovery or staying too long means you start the next segment in a less than ideal physical state. The amount of time spent at any given rest may vary somewhat from attempt to attempt, but you should have a good idea of how long to remain at each

A successful redpoint is one of the most satisfying experiences in climbing.

While resting, look over the next section and review the details critical for success.

rest from the information you gathered in your learning runs.

If you've prepared adequately and executed your plan well, you may find yourself standing at the anchors accepting congratulations on a successful redpoint. There are few things in climbing as rewarding as sending a difficult project, and a successful send deserves recognition and reward. Treat yourself afterward to commemorate the accomplishment.

If you're unsuccessful, rest thirty to forty minutes before making another attempt. Ideally you want to clear as much lactic acid from your muscles as possible while restoring reserve energy supplies, without cooling off so much that your blood vessels constrict to where they were before you warmed up. In colder weather the rest period may be reduced because your body cools faster. Making three to five strong attempts in a single day is possible if you're in good condition.

Learn from Failed Attempts

Before immediately jumping back on the route after a failed attempt, take a few minutes to evaluate your effort. Begin by determining why the failure occurred. Did you fail at the crux? Given that you did your homework and already worked out a good sequence for the crux, you may just need another try or two. Be

After a failed redpoint attempt, critically review your mistakes before making another burn.

sure to take full advantage of any rests so that you are as fresh as possible upon reaching the crux, and mentally rehearse the crux sequence just prior to your next burn so that the memory of the moves is also fresh.

Did any of your planned sequences fail under the stress of attempting the entire route? Sometimes a sequence is not viable and needs to be altered, and if you have a failed sequence, it's important to rework that section before making another attempt. Be sure your new sequence is an improvement in some way over the old.

Did you fail somewhere above the crux because you pumped out? You might believe failing at the crux or above it happens because you lack physical conditioning. It may feel as though you just pumped out before making it to the anchors, and all you need is to do is train harder. Possibly, but becoming more efficient at your sequences may help you succeed faster. Or you might have skimped on practicing the easier sections, believing that on redpoint you could cruise through them. Be sure you're well rehearsed on any section that could cause you problems and that you're following your plan and taking advantage of every available rest.

Did you flub a sequence and come off? Botching a sequence is a clear sign that you haven't practiced it enough. You'll benefit more from practicing any troublesome segments than jumping right back on with no clear and practiced plan. Get the sequences down cold and then make another attempt to send the route.

Learn from Successful Attempts

Ticking off another route on your progressive pyramid is one of climbing's great pleasures and calls for celebration, but it's also an opportunity to reflect, learn, and then apply useful lessons to subsequent routes. Begin your post-send analysis by reflecting on the initial work you completed, that is, discovering sequences, rests, and clipping stances. Determine if all these steps went as planned during your burns or if they had to be altered somewhere along the way. Based on your observations, should you take more time or less on the discovery portion of the learning stage next time?

Next examine how much practice was useful. For optimal efficiency, you should rehearse moves only as much as is necessary to send the route. It is certainly possible to practice a route or sequence so much that you gain little, thereby wasting time. Upon reflection, do you think you could have gotten away with less practice? Did your last rehearsals help you remember or perform the sequences any better? Were there sections that went poorly on redpoint that would have benefited from more practice?

Did you discover any weaknesses that training might help correct? For example, if the sloper crux was difficult, you may need to work more with slopers. Or perhaps you could only make two solid burns in a day and need to improve your stamina. Address movement skill and physical conditioning issues through training.

How would you rate your mental preparation and performance on this route? Was the route fun or all work, and why? Your mental preparation and condition during burns greatly affect your ability to climb, so take a close look at how you felt before each attempt and afterward.

The Redpoint Performance Plan

Another way to learn from your success is to create a redpoint performance plan. A plan can make your performances more consistent by assessing what has worked and listing what to do on future redpoint attempts. While not yet widely used among climbers, performance plans are used by Olympic and professional athletes; they're a great tool for recreational athletes as well since these athletes typically have less time to practice and train. Every effort needs to count, and having a daily plan for success helps make that happen. While we can give general advice on how to proceed through redpoint attempts, only you know why some days are discouraging or merely average while others are extraordinary.

Creating the Performance Plan

Examine your best and worst redpoint experiences of the recent past. The first two groups of questions given on the worksheets that follow help you assess these experiences while the third consists of a comparison between best and worst. The last group of questions will help form your new performance plan.

Assessment of Past Redpoint Performance

Recall a high-quality redpoint experience of the past year or so—the more recent the better, as you'll need to recall the details of the climb. Answer the following questions.

Now recall your worst redpoint experience for which you have a detailed memory. This may be a route that you tried repeatedly to redpoint but were never able to send. It may be a route that took longer than expected. As with the best performance, the more recent, the better, since remembering the details is critical. It's often easy to select one great burn (the successful one), but the worst redpoint experiences evolve over time. They don't usually immediately stand out as being a worst redpoint experience; rather, they become so after numerous failed attempts. Try to recall specific burns, such as your last on the route, and also think about how the experience developed over a number of tries or a number of days.

Comparing Best and Worst Performances

Now that you have created portraits of your best and worst performances, examine the similarities and differences between them.

By documenting the differences between best and worst performances, the characteristics of success begin to become clear. It's typical to find some similarities and some radical differences between best and worst.

The Redpoint Performance Plan

After examining some of the characteristics of your best and worst performances, use the final worksheet to create a plan to foster more consistent success.

Your answers to this last set of questions make up your performance plan, and by combining the specifics in your plan with the general guidelines laid out earlier in the chapter, you will have a powerful set of tools for creating success. A word of caution: Creating a performance plan is not always easy, and there are several common challenges you'll face.

Some climbers, particularly those with only a few years of experience, may have trouble identifying a

Successful redpoints also deserve a critical post-send analysis. What did you do right? What could you have done better?

best climbing experience. Sometimes the difference between an average and best day is small. Your best day may not have been a standout, but simply a day when you were more successful than usual, when you had more fun, or when success came more easily. If you are having trouble deciding on your best day, think about the nuances that distinguish your climbing days. As you gain experience and progress, you are likely to have more high-quality days, thus giving you more successful and enjoyable days to choose from.

Sometimes climbers don't take the time to fully reflect on the details of their performances or record information to refer to in the future. Take the time to recollect as many details as you can. A performance for which you can recollect details, even if it is not your very best performance, is the best candidate for creating your plan.

The performance evaluation identifies the features that contributed to your best performances, but not everything you identify is equally important. For example, the volume and intensity of the warmup may have felt inadequate, yet it was part of your best performance. Perhaps the warmup was excellent despite not feeling right at the time. The point is to think critically about the details and discern the important differences between a great day and one that is poor or merely mediocre.

Finally, as you use your performance plan, you'll find ways to modify and improve it, but do so only when you have a good reason. The first step is to apply it to your climbing and let it work for you.

Best Redpoint Performance

Name of route: _____

Grade of route: _____

Location: _____

Date: _____

1. Describe what made this your best performance. What are the features of the performance that stand out to you? Give as much detail as you can.

2. Describe your warmup. How many routes of what grades and how long did it last? If you can, list the climbs and grades that were in your warmup. What were you thinking about and how was your emotional energy focused during the warmup?

3. After your warmup, as you prepared for your best redpoint burn, what were you doing and thinking? Did you use guided imagery or visualization? What sort of things were you saying to yourself? Were you focused on the outcome or something else? Did you pre-equip the route or preclip any draws?

4. Rate your level of emotional excitement prior to the climb with 1 being completely relaxed and 10 very tense.

    1   2   3   4   5   6   7   8   9   10

5. Rate your level of fear prior to the climb with 1 being a complete lack of fear and 10 being petrified.

    1   2   3   4   5   6   7   8   9   10

6. What were your goals or expectations prior to the successful redpoint attempt?

7. What were you thinking as you started the route?

8. What was your emotional state as you climbed the route? What kinds of messages were you telling yourself and how did you respond to them? How did you respond to the climbing itself?

9. If anything unexpected happened during the climb, how did you respond to it? Did you need to correct any mistakes? Did you need to react to sudden changes in the route or environment, such as a hold breaking?

10. Who was your partner that day and what were your interactions with him or her like? How did you respond to your partner emotionally?

11. How well did you know the sequence and other details of the climb? How confident were you in this knowledge? Give some detail.

12. How did you deal with aspects of the route that you didn't like or that intimidated you? Were you able to overcome this intimidation? If so, how? During the learning and redpoint process, how long did it take you to admit that you were fearful or intimidated?

Worst Redpoint Performance

Name of route: _____

Grade of route: _____

Location: _____

Date: _____

1. Describe what made this your worst performance. Be specific and give as much detail as you can.

2. Describe your warmup. How many routes of what grades and how long did it last? If you can, list the climbs and grades that were in your warmup. What were you thinking about, and how was your emotional energy focused during the warmup?

3. As you prepared for your worst redpoint burn, what were you doing and thinking? Did you use guided imagery or visualization? What sort of things were you saying to yourself? Were you focused on the outcome or something else? Did you pre-equip the route or preclip any draws?

4. Rate your level of emotional excitement prior to the climb with 1 being completely relaxed and 10 very tense.

   1   2   3   4   5   6   7   8   9   10

5. Rate your level of fear prior to the climb with 1 being a complete lack of fear and 10 being petrified.

   1   2   3   4   5   6   7   8   9   10

6. What were your goals or expectations prior to the worst redpoint attempt or attempts?

7. What were you thinking as you started the route?

8. What was your emotional state as you climbed the route? What kinds of messages were you telling yourself and how did you respond to them? How did you respond to the climbing itself?

9. If anything unexpected happened during the climb, how did you respond to it? Did you need to correct any mistakes, or were there any sudden changes in the route or environment, such as a hold breaking?

10. Who was your partner that day and what were your interactions with him or her like? How did you respond emotionally?

11. How well did you know the sequence and other details of the climb? How confident were you in this knowledge? Give detail.

12. How did you deal with aspects of the route that you didn't like or that intimidated you? Were you able to overcome this intimidation? If so, how? During the learning and redpoint process, how long did it take you to admit that you were fearful or intimidated?

Comparing Best and Worst Performances

Now that you have created portraits of your best and worst performances, examine the similarities and differences between them.

1. Was there a difference in your warmup routine between your best and worst performances? What did you do differently and how did you feel during those warmups?

2. Was there a difference between the way you used guided imagery or self-talk as you prepared for each climb? Think about the quality and quantity of both for each performance.

3. What were your relative levels of emotional excitement prior to the climb? Fill in the rating scores you recorded above.

   Best:

   Worst:

4. What were you levels of fear prior to your best and worst performance? Fill in the rating scores you recorded above.

   Best:

   Worst:

5. Was there a difference between your goals and expectations prior to your best and worst redpoint performances? Again, pay attention to details as well as the nature of those goals and expectations.

6. Note any differences in your self-talk at the beginning of your best and worst climb. Between the ground and the first bolt, what were you saying to yourself?

7. Compare your emotional states on your best and worst performances. Describe the differences between your emotional states as you progressed through each climb, and note any important details, such as disparities in your emotions and changes in your emotional state.

8. If anything unexpected happened, describe the differences between your responses to these events.

9. Describe any differences between your partners on your best and worst performances. How were the interactions different?

10. Was there a difference between how well you knew the sequence or how confident you were on your best and worst redpoint attempts? Give the details.

11. Were there differences between how you dealt with adversity on the best and worst performances? Provide the details.

The Redpoint Performance Plan

After examining the characteristics of your best and worst performances, use these ten points to create a plan to foster more consistent success.

1. On a day when I expect to make redpoint attempts, I want my warmup to consist of the following:

2. After my warmup, as preparation for redpoint attempts, I want to think and say the following things to myself:

3. On a scale of 1 to 10 my level of emotional excitement will be:

   1   2   3   4   5   6   7   8   9   10

4. On a scale from 1 to 10 my level of fear will be:

   1   2   3   4   5   6   7   8   9   10

5. My goals and expectations for redpoint attempts are:

6. During redpoint burns I will say the following things to myself.

7. During a redpoint attempt I prefer to be feeling:

8. During a redpoint attempt, if anything unexpected happens, I will respond in the following manner:

9. On days when I'll make redpoint burns, I need a partner who:

10. When it comes to the sequences and details of a route I want to redpoint, I will know and do the following on redpoint burns:

✓ As you make the transition from learning to redpoint attempts, change your mind-set from acquiring information to executing what you've learned.

✓ In evaluating whether you're ready to send, examine your visualizations—are there gaps indicating more learning may be necessary? For a fast redpoint, however, gaps in the visualization of the climb's easier sections might not hinder performance.

✓ Warm up well by climbing several routes of increasing grade, ending at about one number grade below your targeted redpoint.

✓ Prepare the route for redpoint by preplacing draws, brushing critical holds, and placing tick marks.

✓ Before leaving the ground on a redpoint attempt, visualize a perfect performance.

✓ During the attempt use all the rests to their full advantage.

✓ Take time afterward to evaluate a successful or failed attempt.

✓ Using your best and worst redpoint experiences and what you learn through evaluating successful and failed attempts, construct a redpoint performance plan to help you recognize the elements that contribute to a successful redpoint.

This chapter addresses four categories of skills and tactics that will improve your on-sight and flash performance. The first is learning and anticipating as much as you can about the route and its possible movement before leaving the ground. Work you do on the ground toward learning and understanding the route is work that you don't need to do while on the route.

The second category is the ability to improvise, such as when you're faced with sections of the climb that you couldn't see from the ground or when you discover that the sequence you planned won't work. It's impossible to know everything about a route before climbing it, and at some point you'll need to either assess sequences while pausing at a rest stance or improvise moves in real time.

The third category is managing fatigue, which entails recognizing rests and using them to your greatest advantage. It's common to arrive at a rest pumped to near failure and needing significant physical recuperation, mental calming, and refocus. Managing fatigue also includes the ability to create the best rest possible in a given situation and use that rest to maximize recovery.

Fourth is the ability to solve problems when faced with unusual or unanticipated situations, such as a back clip, loose rock, or other problems that arise without warning. Recognizing problems and knowing how they are best solved makes them easier to address when they occur.

Before You Leave the Ground

The goal of reading a climb is to get the most detailed understanding possible of the route's characteristics, its protection, its movement, and different possibilities for how it might be climbed prior to your attempt. Learning a route from the ground also includes memorizing a flexible plan that you can apply to the climb. In short, you are trying to remove as much uncertainty as possible before you begin climbing.

While reading a route is a somewhat fluid process that isn't the same for every climber, it is aided by working within a structure and having goals for what you wish to learn in the process. True, it is impossible to see, understand, and correctly anticipate many details of a climb from the ground, but you can learn a great deal from visual inspection that will increase your likelihood of achieving the on-sight.

Reading a route usually begins with general observations and then moves to greater specificity and detail. Begin the process by examining the route's general line all the way to the top. Follow the line of bolts, chalk marks, natural features, or obvious places for protection and simply take in what the climb presents, making sure you can spot the anchors on a sport route, the top belay on a trad pitch, or the top out on a boulder problem. This may sound self-evident, but in practice climbers often skip this step. It can be hard to see an entire pitch from the ground, which means you need to move around and take the time to understand where the climb goes and get a sense of what you can and can't see from the ground.

During this phase, resist getting too specific; you just want to discover the route's general line. The difficulty of this task will vary. At an unfamiliar or lightly traveled trad area, finding the beginning of routes can be a real challenge, and it can be extremely difficult to distinguish between routes that are close together—oftentimes guidebooks don't provide enough information to make such distinctions clear, so you may have to study several routes to figure out which climb is your intended target.

As you are getting a general sense of the line, consider safety issues. On a boulder problem you might look at potential landings from different parts of the problem. On a sport route, count the bolts and assess the spacing. If the route goes through a roof, zigzags, or consists of lateral moves such as starting on one crack system and then jumping to another, bring some longer draws. Mention this to your belayer so he can remind you to place those long draws when the time comes. Check the nature and placement of the anchors. On a trad route, assess the gear you will need. Are there any objective hazards on the route, such as obvious loose rock? In some areas climbers are in the habit of placing a large chalk X on features that are loose or might break off, so keep an eye out for such markings before getting on the route.

On traditional climbs the planning process for protecting a route takes experience. The only way to really assess from the ground which cam might work best in a flaring horizontal thirty feet up is experience. Even then, the climber may not have the perfect answer while on the ground, but experience leads to more accurate expectations. This is an important point for less-experienced trad climbers. If you are not already in the habit of doing so, always take a few pieces that are bigger and smaller than what it appears you will need.

Naturally while you are making the general assessment, you will become aware of other details. You'll see the climb's natural sections, holds, and some sequences, but at this point it's piecemeal. This infor-

mation is examined in detail in the next step of reading a route.

Reading Sequences and Reading Moves

Getting the general information described above prepares you for the most important tasks: Reading sequences and moves. These tasks are both interpretive and creative; it takes time to do them well, and experienced climbers have a significant advantage. What's so interesting and enjoyable about reading sequences is that when you first look at a climb it's little more than a pattern of features, or of white spots on the rock, an abstraction with little meaning. By reading the sequences, patterns become concrete and understandable, ultimately evolving into the movement you will do on the climb.

We consider reading sequences and moves closely related but different tasks. When you read a sequence, you are gaining an understanding of what the hand and

This route traverses to the right. Look for the dangerous spot where the climber is above and to the side of his last protection.

This trad route doesn't follow an obvious crack. Look closely for points of protection before leaving the ground.

footholds are, how they will be used, and the order in which they will be used. Reading moves takes the analysis further, to subjects such as what kind of move will be used in each sequence, the quality of balance likely to be found, movement initiation, pacing, and so on. We make this distinction because in application reading a sequence does not always lead to reading the moves. There are a couple of reasons for this. First, reading sequences and reading moves require different skills, with reading moves being the more advanced,

requiring a great deal more knowledge to do well. It's far easier to visually identify holds and suggest a basic hand sequence than it is to determine the exact type of move or body position that will work best—for example, deciding that a flag will work better than a back step. It's also difficult to describe the type of balance that may occur in a move, how hard the move will be, or how it would be best initiated. These things require knowledge and experience that picking a sequence does not. Climbers who do not have much experience

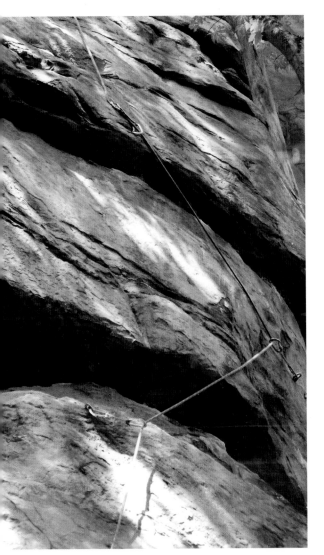

A long draw on a zigzag portion of a route can reduce rope drag.

Make a general assessment of this route. What basic information can you see? Where does the route go and what is its nature?

reading routes can find it challenging to identify the holds and create a basic sequence, much less see the nuance in potential moves.

Finally, in some situations you may not need to read the moves as well as the sequence. A climber reading a route well below her limit may not need to know anything other than the basic sequence in order to do the climb well, because she is working at a level where her skills are well developed and she can intuit the moves as she goes without sacrificing movement quality. Nevertheless, it is impossible to interpret the critical details of moves without first understanding what the available sequence options are.

Reading Chalk

In many situations, reading a sequence is a matter of interpreting the patterns of chalk left by other climbers. If you know what to look for, chalk can provide a great deal of information. The following photos and descriptions show some common patterns.

The shape of the hold and the location of chalk are the most basic features to look for when reading a sequence; they reveal the hold's size, orientation, and type—whether it's a sidepull, undercling, Gaston, pinch, jug, crimper, and so on.

Note how the chalk reveals an undercling.

Thumbprints leave little doubt about which hand climbers have used on a hold. This thumbprint reveals where the right hand is typically placed.

Again, thumbprints outside the usable part of the hold show where and how to place the right hand.

In order to see and interpret chalk, you need to view the climb from as many angles as possible. Look at the climb from the far left and far right and get far enough away that you can see the top. Try to get up high to see the climb. If there is a tall boulder nearby, get on top of it. If there is a steep hillside that would allow a better view, walk up the hill. If there are trees that are easily climbed near the route, climb them. The more perspectives you gain on the route, the more likely you are to get new information. Look for holds that aren't obvious as you follow the line of the route, and look farther to the right and left than you think you need to. Even though looking at the chalk is important, it is possible to miss important details because you are too focused on the chalk. Guard against tunnel vision by making sure you look for holds and features that are not chalked.

The presence of chalk does not make reading a route a simple matter. Any climb can have ambiguous sections. To address such ambiguity, start with what is known. Look at sequences immediately before and after the section giving you trouble. Having a good idea about the sequence leading into an ambiguous section should give you clues for the first move or two at least. Considering how you need to exit the unclear section may provide similar insights for the last move or two. Also, look at the details of the tricky

Sometimes chalk is an impediment. Some climbs have so many chalked holds that it's difficult to tell which are best. Sometimes a large number of chalked holds signals many good choices. This can indicate that you have a number of options and may not need to identify an exact sequence.

section. Can you find any holds that are most likely used in a specific way? If you can't come up with a sequence from the ground, at least develop a good understanding of where holds and features are so you are well prepared for the improvisation to come.

Activity 5: Reading Sequences

The following photos show sequences two to four moves long. Determine the order in which each hand should move to each hold. Answers can be found in the appendix at the end of the book.

Interpret the hand sequence for this boulder problem that traverses from right to left. The next handhold off the picture is far to the left.

What is the hand sequence for this route that trends from the bottom right to the upper left?

A longer section to sequence. You're looking at the last three bolt-to-bolt sections of the climb from 70 feet away.

Activity 6: Comparing Sequences

Perform this activity in a gym with a partner. The goal is to improve your skill at visualizing sequences and movements. Start by selecting a short boulder problem in the gym that is two or more V grades below your current on-sight or flash limit.

1. Working independently, you and your partner should each take several minutes to come up with what you each think is the most likely hand sequence. Note any places where there is ambiguity or where there are multiple sequences that look equally attractive. At this stage do not discuss the sequence or your ideas with your partner.

2. After you have each developed a hand sequence, start at the beginning of the problem and independently come up with a foot sequence. For each hand move, decide exactly where you want your feet positioned. You also need to determine the exact order in which you will move your hands and feet. This may take some time because you have to consider every hand and foot move on the problem. Be patient—the longer you examine the problem, the more possibilities you are likely to see. Explore each of these possibilities.

3. After each of you has a sequence, go over the route together, comparing notes. Discuss the differences, and describe why you chose each move. After comparing sequences, take turns attempting to flash the route. Watch each other closely and see if the actual sequences deviated from the plan. Compare what you thought would work to what you actually did. It's important to understand how and why these differences occurred. What did you miss when you were reading the route? Were there places where you simply misread the sequence? Did you think a reach would be possible, but it turned out to be too long? Did you choose footholds that were poorly positioned for the move? Find and define the ways in which your reading of the problem did not match what actually happened in an attempt. This important part of the activity may allow you to understand why you read the move the way you did and what you missed. As you do this exercise on multiple problems, you may see patterns emerge in the differences between what you read and how you climb.

VARIATION

It can be helpful to first videotape each other giving move-by-move descriptions of your sequences to provide an accurate record of your plan. Then videotape each other climbing the problem. Watch the video as soon as you come down and make comparisons.

In addition to reading hand and foot sequences, reading a route also involves the important tasks of identifying cruxes and assessing the relative difficulty of each section of the climb, as well as finding likely clipping and rest positions. Assessing what gives the climb its grade and how the difficulty is distributed over the route provides much-needed information that will influence your pace and rests on the route. These tasks are aided by breaking the climb into sections.

From your first look at a route, you will be aware of natural divisions in the climb. These are sometimes based on the presence of prominent features such as roofs, cracks, ledges, or slabs. Other times, features are more subtle: you might notice a jug in what is otherwise a long section of small holds, a slight change in the angle of the climb, or a place where the climb starts to traverse. These will allow you to break the climb into small, distinct sections. For the sake of understanding the route and memorizing a detailed plan, it is easier to examine, plan for, and memorize a number of smaller sections than it is to treat the climb as a single large block of information.

One of the challenges of reading a route from the ground is that you can see the lower sections so much better than you can the higher sections. Some serious on-sight climbers address this challenge by using binoculars to inspect the upper regions of a route. Even without binoculars, just getting a general sense of the features, angle, and rock quality of the higher portions may be helpful, providing a general sense of what to expect. Another way of addressing this challenge is to realize that what you can learn about the lower sections of a climb will show what you are likely to face on higher sections.

When you are breaking a climb into sections and evaluating sequences and moves, you are also gaining an understanding of the difficulty of each section and the nature of the climb. Is it sustained? Is it a one-move wonder? Does it have multiple cruxes and multiple rests? Does its difficulty slowly decrease or increase over the length of the route? As you examine the sections of a route, the nature of what gives the route its grade should become apparent. Accordingly, if you see an obvious crux down low, that might suggest that the climbing gets easier higher up where it is harder to see the route from the ground. If the climb looks sustained, or you can't identify cruxes down low this may suggest that the climbing remains hard or even that a crux is higher on the route. This kind of information helps you address the specific challenges the route presents. If you determine that the route has a high crux, how sustained does the climbing on the lower pats of the route look? How many likely rests do you see? Answering these questions will help you know if your plan should consist of resting as you go or getting up to the high crux as quickly as possible. If there is a clear crux down low on the route, consider what the route is like after the crux. Is it over, or do you need to plan to conserve energy and recover for sustained climbing above? The patterns you can see from the ground should aid in developing a plan for how you want to approach the climb in terms of pace and rest.

As with most issues in on-sight climbing, identifying cruxes and rests gets easier with experience, and there is no substitute for logging a lot of hours reading routes and attempting on-sights in order to sharpen your visual analysis skills. For climbers with little on-sight experience, there are some visual cues you can look for. Cruxes are often denoted by specific changes in the nature of the climb. You may see that the holds get smaller, that they get farther apart, or that they are fewer in number. The crux may be steeper than the other sections of the route.

Transitions between sections of a route can create cruxes as well. If you are attempting a route that is vertical or steep and then transitions to a slab, study the slab transition closely as this situation can often create technically challenging moves at the point when your upper body is on the slab and your handholds are smaller, while your legs and feet are still on the steeper part of the climb.

Another transition between sections that often creates a deceptive crux is found on climbs with roofs. You might assume that the roof itself will be the crux as that is the most dramatic-looking element of the climb; often though, the crux is not in the more dramatic upside-down part of the climb, but rather at the lip of the roof where you need to transition from the roof to the face climbing above. The Gunks is home to climbs like this, where good holds in a roof transition to a face with holds that are smaller and difficult to see. In these situations it may be extremely difficult to see your feet under the roof and to see the holds above you on the face. Tactically, the most important thing to do is not rush. Before you start climbing, imagine yourself at the lip hanging down so you can see footholds under the roof. Also imagine yourself calmly scanning and observing the nuances of the face above you. As longtime Gunkie Mike Freeman used to say, "Rotate your eyeballs!"

On climbs that have arêtes, a crux often occurs if it is necessary to move around the corner. Even if the actual moves are not that hard, moving around an arête can be difficult because it can be impossible to see what is on the other side of the corner before you get there, so you may need to commit to a sequence without knowing if it will work or not. Try to first find a sequence or position that allows you to see around the corner before you actually try the moves.

If nothing else, acknowledging the likelihood of these different situations should help you control your level of arousal. By recognizing and accepting such possibilities in advance, you allow yourself to plan and visualize yourself remaining calm, focused, and pragmatic in a situation that could elicit a negative emotional response if you experienced it as a surprise.

Study such transitions closely before getting on the route. There are different types of cruxes: cruxes like those just described, where just being able to see and identify holds is an exceptional challenge; traditional cruxes that are simply the most physically demanding moves on the route; redpoint cruxes, which occur higher on a route where there is a more demanding crux lower down. The redpoint crux may be significantly easier than the actual crux, but a redpoint crux is more likely to cause you to fail on redpoint burns because you're fatigued when you reach it.

When looking for easier sections or rests, the visual cues are the opposite of those for a crux; in general you look for larger holds that may be caked with chalk, more holds closer together, a less angled section of the climb, a ledge to stand on, an inside corner that allows a stem, or sections of rock that are more highly featured.

Spend as much time as necessary to gather and process route information. A climber serious about on-sighting a particularly challenging climb or boulder problem may inspect it many times over days, weeks, or even months, saving the on-sight attempt for a time when his fitness level, the weather conditions, and his knowledge of the route are all conducive to the attempt. Reading a route in a few moments while your belayer waits does not allow you enough time to discover and process all the information you need for an effective on-sight attempt.

On-sighting and Flashing at New Areas

Visiting new areas is a wonderful opportunity to improve your on-sight skills on new routes, different rock types, and unfamiliar features. Before going for the glory on any challenging routes, learn as much about the area as possible. Different areas vary greatly in terms of hold types and shapes, common crux locations, the steepness of the climbs, how to read the features, where to anticipate rests, and other factors that you need to practice before you attempt difficult flashes or on-sights. Start with a few easier routes to give you an idea of the kinds of holds available, common crux locations, and how to read sequences and gauge rests from the ground. Learn the visual cues that can guide your strategy. At your home crag the idiosyncrasies of crux types, rests, and fitness requirements are likely second nature to you, but a new area can introduce a number of variables that you'll need to study in order to on-sight well.

Consider the rock type, texture, quality, unique features, coloration, and how things look in different light. This last one is important since on some rock types the wrong light can make finding holds far more difficult even at close range. Different types of rock hide holds in different ways. On bulging, pocketed limestone, for example, footholds disappear into the curvature of the rock as you pass them. Some crack-climbing areas have helpful features such as crimpers inside the cracks that may be easier to feel around for than to see. In other areas, the crack may be all you get. At a number of sandstone climbing areas in the American West, you have to look for certain patterns in the dark patina on the surface of the rock. In the Southeast, sandstone areas like the New River Gorge have pockets that face downward, making them better as sidepulls or underclings. Every climbing area is different, and if you know an area's idiosyncrasies, you are more likely to be successful in your on-sight attempts. Take the time to do a number of easier routes so you can adapt to the unique characteristics of the new area.

Reading Moves

Reading the moves of a climb is a more advanced skill than simply reading the sequences. A sequence specifies the hand- and footholds to use, the order you will use them in, and some details about the moves, but in many cases you'll be able to do more than just read the sequence. Determining the character of the moves is the most refined level of reading a route, providing you with specific details about each move's feel, its difficulty, its quality of balance, and so on. For example, a hand sequence may consist of a hold that is an obvious right-hand side pull, followed by a high left-hand sloper. Once you know that, you can consider the best way to perform the move. Will you have your side into the wall, will you face the wall, or will you turn? Will you perform a back step, an inside flag, or something else? How fast or slow will you move? What do you think the move is going to feel like? How much effort do you think the move will require? What kind of balance will the move have? How do you want to initiate the move? When you reach the left-hand hold, do you need to maintain body tension or can you relax? How will you get to the next footholds? Your observations of the size and quality of the holds, the distance between them, the steepness of the climb, along with your strengths and preferences will provide helpful information for answering such questions, and the answers will allow you to move beyond a grasp of the basic sequence to understanding movement nuances and the challenges they pose.

Your ability to read moves depends upon your experience level, knowledge, and how you climb in other settings. If you don't consciously control your movement initiation in your day-to-day climbing, there's no advantage in considering movement initiation in preparing for an on-sight. If you don't know when

Take a look at the photo. Can you read any of the sequences? The Hole, Kaymoor, WV.

inside or outside flags are used, then you won't be able to see them when reading a route. Indeed many climbers don't read moves at all, and other climbers read moves without fully realizing it. If you've ever looked at a move and noted that it will require a lot of body tension, or if you've observed that a move looks balancy, then you are intuitively using your past experience to interpret individual moves.

The ability to read moves is a learned skill that improves with practice. The purpose of reading a route from the ground is to remove as much uncertainty as possible. Ultimately, when you attempt a climb you are working with finite resources in terms of fitness, and when near your on-sight limit, the amount of time you have before you get too pumped to keep climbing is short. The learning and planning that you do while on the ground is learning and planning you won't need to

do while on the climb. See *The Self-Coached Climber* for descriptions and exercises to help you learn and recognize common movement patterns.

Improvising

Improvising is a complex skill that is difficult to teach. Experience plays a large role—you are probably not generating completely new moves but rather applying known moves to a new situation. Beyond this, though, in on-sight situations your planning and tactical decisions help structure the context in which you will improvise.

More often than not, a climb will have sections that can't be seen from the ground. In many cases you won't even be able to see these sections very well from just below them. There are two approaches to addressing this situation. If there is a rest not too far below the

Locate natural breaks to divide the climb into sections. The left route is Jesus is My License Plate 10d and the right is For What 10b, Summersville Lake, WV.

Several bolt-to-bolt sections from Quinsana Plus in the New River Gorge. Can you come up with possible sequences for the holds shown?

Several indoor boulder problems. Examine the size, shape, and orientation of the holds, plus the angle of the wall, and come up with a likely sequence for each. Sequence the problem marked with orange tape. The starting handhold is marked with an upside-down V. See the appendix for answers.

Sequence the problem marked with black tape. The two starting handholds are marked with upside-down Vs.

Sequence the problem marked with purple tape. The starting handhold is marked with an upside-down V.

unseen section, one approach is to do some reconnaissance climbing. Knowing that you have a rest you can retreat to, the goal is to climb a few moves into the section, assess its sequences and difficulty, and then after looking around a bit, climb back down to the rest for a recovery. You may need to climb up, look around, and then climb back down several times before you can push through the section. If the down-climbing is not too taxing and the rest is reasonably good, getting as much information as you can like this before attempting the scouted section is a reasonable approach. This tactic can also help you control your emotional state. By seeing down-climbing as a tool, by gaining experience on the opening moves of the section and removing uncertainty, and by gaining knowledge and making a plan, you decrease the anxiety associated with the unknown and increase the likelihood of success.

Sometimes climbing up and down a section will be too difficult or awkward, or there is no rest close by. In these situations you only have one option, to fully commit to climbing through the section on the first try, improvising as you go. First, before you make this commitment you need to have evaluated the closest rest and determined that it is not good enough to allow recovery. Depending on the nature of the rest, this decision may not be an easy one. You also need to assess down-climbing back to the rest and estimate its relative difficulty. Based on these observations, choose your approach to the section that you can't see. Be aware and analytical as you climb. Further, when you decide that down-climbing is not the best approach, you will need to control your anxiety and arousal. Consider how hard the climb has been up to this point—has it earned its grade yet? The answer to this question often gives you a good idea of what to expect and how to respond to the climbing to come. Emotionally, you may benefit from taking a moment to commit so that your dedication and focus are keen and unrelenting and that you are giving your best effort no matter what happens or how pumped you get. You will not stop or give up. Without such a commitment, fear or unexpected developments are more likely to alter your focus and erode your confidence. Commit to focusing on the basics that are likely to get you through, such as avoiding tunnel vision by actively scanning for holds.

Commit to making good foot placements, keeping your breathing steady, and responding to the balance that each new move provides.

Pacing

Even experienced climbers can have a hard time controlling the pace of their climbing. Keep in mind that completing a sequence slowly usually requires more energy than finishing it quickly. This is not to say you should speed-climb; rather, you should eliminate pauses in movement. Climbers frequently move at a fairly slow pace, pausing for long periods before moving again. These pauses occur often and without regard for natural rest positions and, therefore, waste energy.

The first part of learning to control the pace of your climbing, then, is to become aware of the pauses in your movement. Identify where you are pausing and why. Sometimes you pause when you're trying to identify handholds and footholds, which is unavoidable. Additionally, extreme offset balance moves must often be performed slowly. Other times, you may just be hesitant, may not want to commit, or may be worried about the fall. These are common reasons to pause, but they are counterproductive and with practice can be reduced or eliminated.

Activity 7: Video

Have a friend record you on a number of different routes, both on-sights and routes you have done previously. The camera should roll for the entire climb, even if you stop and rest at one spot for an extended time. Afterward, look at the general pacing of your climbing. How often and where do you stop to chalk? How often do you stop to look for holds and how quickly do you find them? Are you finding the best holds in each section? Do you put your foot on the first hold you see or the best hold you see? Think about your attitudes toward climbing and how they affect your pace. Some climbers intentionally move slowly because they think that good climbing consists of slow, deliberate movement. It may be aesthetically pleasing, but as a rule, unnecessarily slow movement wastes energy. If your review of the video reveals pauses, try to remember why you paused. Repeat the climb again and try to eliminate pauses.

Record this second ascent and compare it to the first. Were you successful in eliminating the pauses? Was there a difference in the speed of your ascents?

Activity 8: Controlling Your Pace

Perform this activity on a moderately difficult route you know well and that gives you a mild pump. Break the climb into hard and easy sections. An easy section is any part of the climb where you can recover while climbing; hard sections are those in which you develop a pump. The ideal route will have multiple hard and easy sections, but a route with only one hard section is fine too. Examine the route from the ground, decide on the exact holds where each section begins and ends, and then climb each difficult section without pausing. The goal is to climb continuously while maintaining high-quality basic movement—for example, placing each foot accurately and precisely with no adjustment.

When you reach a hold that marks the beginning of an easier section, immediately slow down and pause between moves so you can rest. Upon reaching the next difficult section, once again climb without pauses. After practicing on moderate routes, move to slightly harder routes. The goal is to become more aware of your pacing, learn correct pacing on different sections, and control your pacing. Don't try to speed-climb; rather, move at a pace where you can maintain high-quality movement. If you discover that you can't eliminate pauses in your movement or climb at a slightly faster pace without your movement suffering, you may need to revisit basic hand and foot placement activities such as glue hands and silent feet (see *The Self-Coached Climber*).

Resting

Recognizing and effectively using rests are critical skills for an on-sight climber. Even a small recovery en route can mean the difference between success and failure. Rests come in different forms—sometimes they are brief and only allow for a momentary break from the climb, but in the best cases they allow your forearms to recover and your heart rate and breathing to return to more normal levels. Rests also provide emotional recovery; as you climb, get more pumped, and have to move faster, you can lose focus, become distracted, and miss important details. A good rest can help you pull back

from this excited state, calm down, refocus on pragmatic aspects of the climb, and get into an emotional state appropriate for the climbing ahead. While you rest you can also inspect and evaluate upcoming moves.

Many times effective resting takes creativity and attention to detail. Accomplished climbers can find rests where other climbers thought it impossible. Finding and using creative rests is a great advantage in on-sights and flashes. Like any other skill, it takes experience and practice.

Before getting into the details, it's important to understand the physiology of resting. During low-intensity muscle contractions, your aerobic energy production system can sustain activity for extended periods of time. The blood flow to the muscles is not interrupted, or if it is, the interruptions are short and intermittent. The intensity of work is low enough that the muscles rely mostly on the highly efficient aerobic system.

In contrast, during more intensive muscle contractions, the aerobic system can't produce enough energy to keep up with demand. When this happens, you have crossed your anaerobic threshold and an increasing percentage of energy is produced anaerobically. Anaerobic production of energy is inefficient; large amounts of waste product accumulate in the muscles, further restricting aerobic processes and producing a pump. To rest, you must find a stance or sequence where the movement intensity is brought back down below the anaerobic threshold. The aerobic system can then produce the required energy and the waste product can be cleared.

In the simplest case, resting is a matter of finding a stance where most of your weight is on your feet and you can alternate your hands on a hold while keeping your arms straight. Or you can find a position in which you don't need good handholds, such as a good stem. Ideally, find a position in which your center of gravity (COG) is between the rock and an imaginary line drawn between your feet. In this way your body leans into the corner so you can drop both hands off of the holds. On a vertical route it's often best to keep your COG as close to the rock as you can, but on overhanging climbs the position of your COG depends on a number of factors such as the size and quality of footholds or the availability of heel hooks. Focus on keeping your arms straight and doing what you can to get weight on your feet. Finally, it's often better to begin a rest by switching your hands on and off the rest holds rapidly, and as you recover and feel less pumped, you can switch out more slowly.

In most cases you hold on with one hand while the other arm hangs comfortably and rests. Some climbers also alternate between holding the resting arm over their head and letting it hang down. In order for a rest stance to be effective, the recovery gained in the resting arm must be greater than that lost by the other in holding on. In other words, you reduce the average intensity between the resting and active arm until it's below your anaerobic threshold, which allows your body to remove waste products from and deliver oxygen to the forearm muscles. If you don't switch quickly enough, you'll find the working arm stays pumped or gets more pumped.

The pace at which you switch hands depends both on the quality of the rest and your level of fatigue. If you are very pumped, you can often recover better by rapidly switching hands back and forth so the forearms go through a larger number of work-rest cycles in a shorter period of time. As recovery progresses, you can switch hands more slowly.

A less experienced climber can find resting counterintuitive and believe that if he stops climbing to rest he'll simply pump out sooner and fail lower on the climb, or he can feel like a rest stance isn't producing any recovery, so he'll continue climbing too soon. As you become pumped it's more difficult to remain calm and stick to a plan. You may need to spend several minutes at a stance while a pump diminishes in order to get a good recovery. This takes patience, and it's a common mistake to leave a rest too soon. It is also common for beginners to attempt to rest with both hands on holds, but in order to rest, one hand holds on while the other hangs relaxed at your side. It takes experience to gauge the optimal time to remain at a particular rest; if you leave a rest as soon as the pump feels like it is lessening, you'll very quickly return to a fatigued state.

The most basic elements are keeping your arms straight, finding the best position for your center of gravity—often by keeping your hips close to the rock—and taking weight off your fingers.

Good general advice for resting: Keep your arms straight and hips close to the wall.

There are three types of rests for on-sights: those you can see from the ground, those you can't see from the ground but find en route, and those you create out of necessity. Rests you can see from the ground tend to be large, heavily chalked holds, large ledges, inside corners, and any other obvious features that allow you to take weight off your forearms. As you climb you will likely discover other rests you didn't recognize from the ground. Sometimes you can create an effective rest from small holds when the angle of the wall relents or footholds are particularly large or well located. Shallow inside corners or features protruding from the rock can yield a solid stance that you also may not recognize from the ground. And you can sometimes create a rest out of what seems like nothing by shifting your center of gravity, hanging with straight arms, dropping one foot off to keep your hips close to the wall, or any number of creative balance and body position combinations. Here are a few common types of rests to look for.

Stems. Stems are often excellent rests because they increase the base of support by making it wider and usually moving it farther out from the rock. Stems are especially restful if you can get your center of gravity between the rock and an imaginary line drawn between your feet. This position allows you to lean into the rock and drop both hands simultaneously, achieving a hands-down rest. Not all stems are as obvious as an inside corner. Sometimes a face will have a contour that is slightly concave, allowing for the same relation between center of gravity and base of support as a corner.

Pushing. Look for holds or wall features that will allow you to palm or push off rather than pull. You might try pushing down on a jug at waist level, pushing off a shallow corner, or even pushing up into a small roof. Pushing off a feature allows you to open your hand and rest the flexors of the wrist and fingers.

Jamming. Another way to take weight off your fingers is to jam a body part into a crack or other feature. Certain kinds of hand jams, especially those where you can lock your wrist in place without using your fingers, are an excellent way to rest the forearms. Although trad climbs that follow cracks come to mind here, many sport climbs have excellent finger and hand jams. In addition, look for places to jam with a foot, elbow, arm, shoulder, or leg. Creative climbers often find ways to shove a body part in a crack or pocket in order to get a good rest.

Knee bars. In the 1990s knee bars were a controversial technique. At Rifle Mountain Park in Colorado hard routes were downgraded because climbers began using knee bars to rest in places that the first ascentionists hadn't noticed. With the added knee bars, the routes became significantly easier, and since the first ascentionists didn't want their best lines downgraded, they argued over the legitimacy of the new technique. These days climbers use knee bars when they're available. Knee bars, however, can be very painful if some form of padding isn't used; at Rifle climbers often wear pads on both knees. Many climbers use neoprene knee braces and other materials to craft pads that make knee bars more comfortable.

Stemming is a powerful tool in your resting arsenal.

Pushing off features takes weight off the fingers, allowing your forearm muscles to relax and recover.

Thumbs and heels. Sometimes simply using your hands and feet a little differently can help you recover. For instance, on less steep sections of rock it's often possible to hook a thumb on a feature and relax your fingers.

Look for good-sized footholds too where you can place your heel instead of your toes. This gives your toes a break and can make it easier to pull your hips into the rock. Climbs with vertical sections may have a large foothold or feature that stands out from the wall with some options for footholds below. Place your heel

Above and below: You can often find hand jams at a constriction in a horizontal or vertical break.

Above and facing page, top: Knee bars can be used in a variety of situations, such as the severely overhung Lactic Acid Bath (12d, right) Kaymoor, WV, and the slightly overhanging Toxic Hueco (11d, above) Meadow River, WV.

and as much of your foot as possible on the higher foothold. Place your lower foot on a hold you can toe into. This position provides a good base of support that in some cases will allow you to create enough force with your legs to rest both hands. Look for this protruding upper foothold on indoor climbing walls and highly featured routes.

Lying down. Although it is not common, you can occasionally lie down or wiggle into horizontal cracks

or ledges. By wiggling your body into large horizontal features, you can often get that coveted no-hands rest. Sometimes large horizontal cracks have ledges, and with a little creativity you may find a variety of ways to use such features. Horizontal rests can, however, take considerable work to get in and out of.

Bat hangs. Steep routes sometimes have horizontal features that allow a rest position known as a bat hang, that is, hooking your toes on features or jamming your feet or lower legs between the features and then letting go with your hands and hanging upside down. A well-known bat hang is on Spray-a-thon in Rifle, Colorado, and another is atop the popular Apollo Reed at Summersville Lake in West Virginia. They both have sections where you can jam both feet in a horizontal crack and hang upside down in relative comfort.

Hooking a thumb lets you relax your fingers.

Sitting on a high heel is another good method for taking weight off your arms.

Activity 9: The Contortionist

This activity will help you become better at finding rests in a variety of situations. It has two variations. In the first, choose a route of moderate difficulty and then find as many rests as possible on a single route. Try stems, shifting your center of gravity, dropping a foot off, and using your heels, knees, and thumbs. Make the known rests better by using the same tactics.

Do the second variation in a gym. Have a friend select two to four hand holds of varying sizes four to six feet off the ground. Use any footholds you like. Experiment with different body positions and ways of using the selected holds to create a rest, get the pressure off

Large horizontal features can provide seats and other platforms. Psycho Wrangler 12a, New River Gorge, WV.

A bat hang on the Trophy (12c), Red Rocks, NV.

your arms, or find even a slight recovery. You may need to try things far out of your comfort zone, such as turning your back to the wall, hooking your heel, or even sitting on a hold. Try this activity a number of times, starting with configurations that are easy and then working your way up to more challenging situations.

Finding rests is a real challenge, especially on rock you're not familiar with. Rock type often dictates the sort of rests you're likely to find, for example Southern sandstone is characterized by horizontal stratifications that yield large rails and deep horizontal cracks, which lend themselves to heel hooks and leg jams. Limestone often has blocks or large pockets with knee bars. Some rock types like basalt have many inside corners that you can stem. To develop an understanding of the rests for a given rock type and area, climb a number of easier routes before attempting a difficult on-sight. Keep an open, inquisitive mind and try a variety of rest tactics that you might then use on harder routes.

Problem Solving

You can't expect things to go perfectly when attempting an on-sight or flash. You might mess up some sequences, miss rests, break holds, or inadvertently back-clip. You may discover that you do not have enough draws to get to the top of a route. Unexpected problems are fairly common, but if you acknowledge that they can happen, know in advance what to do when they occur, and have an attentive belayer who can help you identify the problems, you'll be able to keep climbing in situations where others would fail.

Fixing Sequencing Errors

It's common to climb into a sequence and realize that your hands need to be reversed, that your right hand should be where your left is or vice versa. There are four methods for dealing with this situation. First, if possible, climb down to a rest so that you can recover and figure out whether you skipped a hold, made an unnecessary match, or started the sequence with your hands reversed. Reevaluate so you can identify the mistake and commit to a different sequence that will get you to the same spot with your hands on the correct holds. Second, if you can't or don't want to climb

down to a rest, consider changing your sequence by matching on one of your current holds or down-climbing to a hold where you can match and then reverse your hand order. Third, sometimes it's often possible to fix a sequence error by crossing to the next hold. This is most likely to work on moves with stable balance and shorter reaches. Finally, look for other possibly unchalked holds that may be used to fix your mistake. Remember that it's easy to get tunnel vision and lose the ability to critically analyze the situation when you're under stress. This is exactly what your tactics should help you avoid.

Holds Breaking

A hold suddenly snapping off in your hand or breaking under a foot is perhaps the worst thing that can happen during an on-sight. A fall is often unavoidable, but sometimes holds crumble or peel off slowly. When you feel this happening, don't assume your flash attempt is over; you may have a moment to finish your move or to retreat from the hold. If you retreat, you might still be able to use a breaking hold if you know how to apply force to it. Sometimes a hold that won't withstand a hard outward force can survive brief downward or sideways forces. Or you may choose to remove the breaking hold and see what's left—sometimes, if you are lucky, what remains is as good as or even better than the broken hold. Also look for other sequences. Can you reach past the broken hold? Might a match be possible on a nearby hold? Stay focused on solving the problem.

Back Clips and Z Clips

Back and Z clips are common in gyms and at sport crags. The best way to deal with them is to prevent them from happening in the first place. For example, as soon as a belayer sees his climber pulling up rope from below the previous quickdraw, he should warn the climber and prevent him from making a mistake. If a Z clip does happen, it is easy to fix. Unclip the lower of the two draws from the rope and reclip it to the belayer's end of the rope. Don't fix a Z clip by unclipping the rope from the top draw. This is unnecessary, more difficult, and exposes the leader to a longer potential fall.

You can fix a back clip most easily by leaving the rope clipped into the draw and unclipping the draw

1

A Z clip occurs when you reach below your last draw to pull rope for the next clip.

2

To correct a Z clip, first simply unclip the lower draw from the rope.

3

Next, clip the lower draw back into the belay side of the rope.

4

The completed correction with draws properly clipped.

Below: A back-clipped draw.

Right: The easiest way to correct a back clip is to simply remove the draw from the bolt, rotate it 180 degrees, and clip it back in.

Bottom right: The corrected clip.

from the bolt. Then rotate the draw so it is no longer twisted and reclip it to the bolt.

Skipping Clips

On rare occasions skipping a clip can be advantageous. When a bolt is poorly placed on a climb that is otherwise well-protected, stopping for the clip may take more energy than it is worth. Your chosen sequence might be effective in terms of its movement but make clipping more difficult. You may not have a long enough draw, and using a short draw would make the rope drag significantly worse. Or you might be so fatigued that stopping and clipping may be enough to push you to failure, and you must choose between clipping and then falling or skipping the clip and potentially reaching more moderate moves just above.

Caution: skipping clips can be unsafe. Contemporary sport climbs tend to be very well bolted, so skipping a bolt may only result in the prospect of a slightly longer, but still perfectly safe, fall. The trick is to be able to identify these situations quickly and make an informed decision about the potential risk. Your belayer should also be able to provide advice and be ready to catch the potentially longer fall.

To less-experienced climbers, a number of situations mentioned here may sound highly unlikely, but they are more common than you think, and if you climb enough, you will encounter them. Committing to success has to include an understanding of things that can go wrong and knowing procedures for fixing them. This will help you react calmly and decisively and get the send.

Practicing On-Sights

This section covers a number of skills and tactics for sending a route on the first try. Perhaps more than in other aspects of climbing, experience is central to performance. Developing this experience means being methodical, setting aside time, and creating high-quality learning experiences for yourself.

Remember to practice on-sighting at as many different climbing areas as you can, as often as you can, so you become familiar with different types of rock and routes with different characteristics.

Work below your current consistent on-sight level. (Consider the grade where you have a success rate of 70 percent or higher your consistent on-sight level.) You should have a good deal of movement experience at this lower level, and you should have an easier time recognizing patterns of holds and the moves they suggest. Don't focus on getting the on-sight itself, but instead work on your on-sight skills and tactics. Work through the process below step by step.

1. Examine the route from the ground from a variety of perspectives. Start by getting an idea of the general line and see where the route goes and what its protection is like.

2. Break the route into sections and identity all the available holds you can see.

3. As you identify the holds, begin to think about sequences, look for rests, and get a sense of the general difficulty of each section.

4. Begin to visualize how you will climb the route. Since you are operating well within your abilites, the sequences you visualize should be should be fairly accurate. Take your visualization as far as you can until you can really see yourself on the route.

When you feel you have all the knowledge that can be gleaned about the route from the ground, have visualized the sections of the climb, have a solid plan including variations where the route is ambiguous, and you're calm but ready to work hard, you're ready to go for the on-sight.

This kind of practice may seem arduous, but keep in mind that although we break down the process step by step, in practice the distinctions between these steps are not so clean. They often occur, quite naturally, simultaneously. Consider going through these steps on short routes or boulder problems before trying it on longer routes. Finally, remember that all the work you do on the ground really pays off on the rock.

On-sights are a test of your experience, fitness, knowledge, and most of all, creativity. Learn and have fun on-sighting.

✓ The purpose of reading a route is to eliminate as much uncertainty as possible before starting the climb.

✓ Reading a route often depends on interpreting the chalk left by other climbers.

✓ Reading a route means reading sequences, as well as reading moves, rests, clipping points, and other variables such as pacing.

✓ Planning for an on-sight means memorizing details and having very specific ideas about how to climb the route, while at the same time being flexible and ready to respond to new information as it is revealed during the climb.

✓ Skills such as resting and down-climbing are of great value and need to be practiced in many contexts to best benefit your on-sights.

✓ Knowing about and planning for mistakes such as back clips and Z clips will make them easier to address.

In addition to finding effective and efficient sequences, rests, and clipping stances for your redpoint projects or making a careful visual assessment of a route's characteristics for an on-sight, your physical capabilities will need to be up to the level the route or boulder problem requires. If you lack the aerobic or anaerobic endurance, strength, or stamina to meet the demands of the routes or boulder problems you'd like to attempt, your progress will be severely limited as surely as if you choose inefficient sequences.

Redpoints, on-sights, and boulder problems have somewhat different fitness demands, and therefore your training may vary depending on the nature of the climbing and your current condition.

Roped Redpoints

As you begin to understand a route's nature, you'll become aware of its physical requirements. Is it short and bouldery or long and continuous without good rests? Is there a distinct and difficult crux section? These elements help define the physical abilities you'll need to possess to work and send the route.

Fitness Elements

Local aerobic and anaerobic endurance. Aerobic endurance is defined as your muscles' ability to use oxygen to produce energy. Local refers to our primary area of interest, the forearms. All athletes have a limit to the exercise intensity they can sustain with aerobically produced energy. The higher the grade at which you can climb relying mostly on aerobic energy, the greater your ability to continue performing when the climbing is difficult or prolonged and the less you'll need to rely on the inefficient and pump-producing anaerobic energy system. Anaerobic energy production begins to take over as the level of intensity rises above your anaerobic threshold (the highest intensity of effort you can sustain aerobically). Raise the threshold and you can climb more difficult terrain aerobically, thereby holding off a pump longer.

It's important to distinguish between the endurance requirements of different route types. For example Horse Latitudes (14a) in the Virgin River Gorge is 110 feet long with no solid rests and requires a high level of aerobic fitness. In other words, most of the moves are not hard for the grade, but there are a great number of them. If your local aerobic endurance level isn't 5.12, the climb will pump you out. On the other hand, the Beast in Rifle, at 45 feet of bouldery movement, entails a severe taxing of the anaerobic system. Both are called endurance routes, but for different reasons.

You'll typically have reasonably good endurance when working near the level at which you have well-developed skill and fitness (say, the bottom two levels of your performance pyramid), unless you're venturing into unknown terrain such as attempting a 120-foot endurance march when your primary experience is with one-move wonders and short anaerobic endurance routes.

If you're on familiar ground and still find that you pump out while attempting to link sections together, you should first examine your movement, pacing, and rests to see if there are efficiencies you're missing. As a last resort, you may need to train your aerobic and anaerobic systems to develop an improved capacity, but before beginning a training program be sure you've thoroughly examined your sequences and searched for all possible rests.

Stamina. Stamina allows you to make multiple runs in a single day; it's a measure of how much work you can sustain in a day. To be efficient at redpointing, you need the ability to make repeated, full-strength redpoint or learning burns. A reasonable target for redpoints one to four letter grades above your on-sight level is four to six solid learning burns or three to four redpoint attempts in a given day. If your current fitness level falls short of this goal, stamina training may be warranted.

Strength. We define maximum strength by your bouldering level. Since bouldering typically does not require the endurance of roped routes, its essence is the difficult move, and therefore your ability to pull short, difficult sequences can be used as a proxy for strength. At the mid- and megaproject redpoint range, strength can affect your ability to move through the more difficult sections and can sometimes be the limiting physical factor preventing you from sending the route.

Improving Fitness

Local aerobic endurance. Continuous climbing is the best way to improve your local aerobic endurance (forearm, mostly). Low-intensity exercise over an extended period promotes the expansion of capillaries in the muscles, increasing the intensity or difficulty under which that muscle can function aerobically. And since the aerobic energy system is anywhere from fifteen to sixty times as efficient as the anaerobic system, you can go a long way toward improving your overall endurance by improving your aerobic capacity.

Anaerobic endurance. Anaerobic endurance is the capacity to perform without oxygen when your muscles are forced through increased intensity to use the anaerobic energy production system. Improving anaerobic endurance means being able to climb longer while pumped, and you can accomplish this by using interval training methods such as bouldering circuits or roped laps.

Stamina. Stamina is the ability to climb at a sustained intensity during repeated attempts over the course of the day or session. The best way to train for stamina is sending repeated difficult climbs at your on-sight level, known as continuous intensity repetitions (CIR) or variable intensity repetitions (VIR) in a narrow range.

Strength. Many climbers prefer bouldering for increasing maximum strength. Bouldering advances movement skill along with muscle strength and intermuscular coordination, promoting the effective and efficient use of newly acquired strength gains. Strength gained through isolation exercises, such as pull-ups, can't be applied as effectively as strength obtained in conjunction with the intermuscular coordination that you use in climbing. In fact, it's likely that intermuscular coordination is much more significant than the strength of any individual muscle or group of muscles. When you see someone who looks very strong when he climbs, don't assume that what you are seeing is raw power. It is, rather, the ability to apply strength in a precise way that is most effective.

There are a variety of good training regimens that can improve your strength, endurance, and stamina. A short list of the best methods is provided below, but for detailed descriptions see *The Self-Coached Climber*.

Fitness Considerations for On-Sights

The great diversity of routes and boulder problems makes it difficult to generalize about the fitness demands of on-sights. The athletic demands of a fifteen-foot boulder problem are very different from those of a multi-pitch trad route. Yet one general idea applies broadly to on-sights and flashes: Due to the amount of cognitive work, the duration of a flash or on-sight will always be significantly longer than a redpoint of the same route. This difference is meaningful and tells us something about the nature of our sport.

On-sights, flashes, and redpoints are not timed performances (except in some competition settings), yet the duration of an ascent is a critical factor in climbing and has a direct bearing on success or failure, on whether a route feels hard or easy, and on whether a climb leaves you totally drained or ready for more.

The athletic difficulty of a climb or boulder problem depends on its length and the intensity of its movement. The grade is essentially the sum of the movement intensity of its parts, but there are a number of different ways climbs earn their grades. For example, a 5.12b could be a one-move wonder V3+ boulder problem or it could consist of forty feet of 5.11 climbing with several rests. In either case the movement intensity and the length of the route are fixed, and the physical effort required to send is a function of its intensity and duration.

One way of thinking about an ascent is to consider whether it is more or less physically demanding to climb sixty feet of 5.11- in three or in four and a half minutes. You might think the three-minute ascent would require you to sprint up the route, and that your movement would be lower quality and less efficient and that the ascent would take more effort, but this is typically not the case. If at your normal pace the route would take four and a half minutes to complete, then reducing your ascent time by a minute or so would not require sprinting. Rather, it would merely require eliminating pauses in your movement. Perhaps because climbing is not a timed event, climbers tend to take their time and move artificially slowly, pausing and hesitating even when they are not stopping to evaluate a sequence. Thus they often waste a tremendous amount of time. Simply eliminating pauses or slightly increasing your pace will dramatically reduce the time spent on the route without impacting the quality of your movement. Note though that we are not advocating shortening the amount of time spent at rests. Rests can lengthen the duration without affecting the likelihood of success because a rest's movement intensity is below the climber's anaerobic threshold.

On any ascent, controlling your pace is important. On difficult redpoints, part of the learning process should be to increase your climbing speed over the course of learning burns while maintaining high-quality movement. For on-sights and flashes, you can control the pace of some sections, but your pace will be slower in those that are more complex or physically demanding. Thus climbers who want to excel at on-sights benefit from well-developed local aerobic endurance with an associated high anaerobic threshold. A climber without adequate local aerobic endurance will have to rely more heavily on his anaerobic energy production system, which means he'll need more recovery periods of longer duration. Further, after recovering from a severe pump, he may get pumped faster on subsequent sections of the route, especially if the movement intensity is sustained.

Generally if you have a higher anaerobic threshold, you can stay on the route longer without getting pumped and, when you reach a rest stance, you can recover more quickly. This is more important for longer or more continuous routes than for short, powerful problems or one-move wonders.

For less-sustained climbs, think about how much energy the climbing leading up to the crux will take. Will you arrive at the crux feeling fresh or will the climbing preceding the crux tax you? If the crux is low on the route, can you recover enough after the crux in order to finish? A great example of this kind of route is Killer, a 5.12c at Sinks Canyon in Wyoming. The route is over sixty feet long, and the crux is a boulder problem at the start of the climb. Killer ends, however, with a short, steep section at the very top. For a climber with adequate local aerobic endurance, the route provides a number of opportunities for rest, recovery, and scanning the rock ahead; however, what would be a rest position for a climber with good local aerobic conditioning may be too strenuous to allow a less conditioned climber to recover. Those lacking adequate aerobic endurance are likely to get pumped and have fewer opportunities to rest before the final steep section, effectively creating a second crux simply due to inadequate fitness.

In gym climbing, bouldering, competitions, and short, continuous sport routes, on-sights and flashes are often a race to the top: the object is to climb as far as possible before being overwhelmed by the pump. Rests on these types of climbs are rare and the movement intensity is high; you need highly developed local anaerobic endurance and the ability to stay calm and focused when pumped.

Perhaps the longest-duration performances in climbing are trad on-sights in which you not only need to decipher the moves, but manage your protection as well. Trad climbers tend to do significantly more up-and-down climbing in order to establish protection, learn moves, and retreat to rest. Therefore, the trad on-sight climber benefits even more from highly developed local aerobic endurance than other climbers.

On-sight competitions

Typical on-sight route competitions tend to favor climbers with well-developed local aerobic and anaerobic endurance, although the role of local aerobic endurance may be more difficult to grasp. Consider two climbers trying to on-sight a 5.13 in the first round of an international competition. The route is sixty feet long and consists primarily of continuous 5.12 climbing with a few tricky sequences but no distinct crux. The first climber has a local aerobic endurance level of 5.12b while the second climber's is 5.11c. The second climber is at a distinct disadvantage because most of the climbing is above his anaerobic threshold. He will start to develop a pump sooner than the first climber and be very pumped for any tricky sequences in the second half of the route. For the first climber with an endurance level of 12b, a good deal of the climbing on the route will be near or even lower than his anaerobic threshold. All else being equal, the first climber will develop a pump at a slower rate and have more time to examine each sequence than the second climber, who needs to move faster as he is relying more heavily on anaerobic energy production and has less time before pumping out.

Today, there are a number of different competition formats designed to give competitors plenty of opportunities to climb, such as those with several rounds consisting of multiple routes or boulder problems per round. Another is the open-ended format, in which competitors attempt as many climbs as they can within a set time period. These formats are used for both bouldering and route based competitions and require a high volume of climbing, often with a time limit for each climb or a timed rest between climbs. In order to do well in these formats, you need to be able to make many high-intensity efforts in a single day, while minimizing the pump and maximizing the recovery you get during rest periods. In addition, in many competitions the later climbs are harder, and finals are at the end of the day. Climbers have to perform at a higher level after they are already fatigued. These formats are demanding; they reproduce the structure found in interval and repetition training methods. Competitors need to have a high base level of stamina and local anaerobic endurance if they expect to do well. See *The Self-Coached Climber* for more about the specific interval and repetition training methods needed to develop such fitness.

Clearly, stamina (the ability to climb at a sustained level over numerous attempts in a day) and local anaerobic endurance (the ability to continue climbing at a high intensity after experiencing a pump) are important for such competitions. But does local aerobic endurance play a role? For any competition that involves routes, the higher your local aerobic endurance level, the better, as it directly affects how much climbing you can do prior to a pump setting in. In bouldering competitions it's unlikely that your local aerobic endurance level plays much of a role in your success on a problem as the movement intensity is always going to be very high in relation to your current ability level. Local aerobic endurance may be helpful in a bouldering competition during the recovery period between problems, however. The climber with greater local aerobic endurance should be able to recover faster and more completely than climbers who lack such endurance.

Fitness Considerations for Bouldering

Redpointing Boulder Problems

Strength. The essential physical requirement involved in bouldering is strength, and increasing it is paramount to making progress. See strength training methods in *The Self-Coached Climber*.

Endurance. Problems that take over thirty seconds to complete will have a local anaerobic endurance component. But even a longer boulder problem tends to be short enough that you won't often develop a huge pump, you will just tend to feel less able to perform high-intensity moves. Local aerobic endurance is probably not a factor in your ability to complete even a long problem. If local aerobic endurance is at work in bouldering at all, it would come into play in aiding recovery between problems.

Stamina. As with learning burns on routes, the number of high-quality attempts you can make in a day is an essential component of your success in bouldering. Since the intensity of movement is so high and the duration of each attempt so short, you need a specific kind of stamina for learning boulder problems. The best way to develop it is through continuous and variable intensity repetition (CIR and VIR) workouts. Determine the highest grade at which you can do ten to thirteen boulder problems in a given session. Do several workouts at this level, and then begin to work the grades up. See *The Self-Coached Climber* for more information on repetition training methods.

On-Sighting Boulder Problems

Sending a hard boulder problem on the first try is one of the most exciting challenges in climbing due to the intensity of effort and the need to give everything you've got in a short period of time. It's also dramatically different from on-sighting a route. You can see a much greater proportion of the climb, allowing you to study difficult problems up close before your attempt. Study the problem in full detail.

The movement intensity on a hard bouldering on-sight is much higher than what you face on a roped route. And it takes practice to be comfortable on-sighting moves at such high levels of relative difficulty.

Starting around V5 there is a much higher percentage of offset and dynamic balance moves, and above V7 stable balance becomes increasingly rare. With more offset and dynamic balance comes a greater need for body tension and accuracy in movement. In that context even small mistakes are very difficult to recover from. And even though bouldering is considered a power game, in an on-sight your pace of movement will slow down considerably. The duration of on-sight attempts can more than double just like on a route. Thus, depending on the length of the problem, an on-sight might take a couple of minutes, increasing your reliance on anaerobic energy production.

Sending a boulder problem on the first try is a race against the clock. You might not be on the rock long enough to get a pump, but your ability to do hard moves diminishes rapidly. In the first twenty to thirty seconds of an attempt you can probably do moves near your current maximum, but if you are working near your limit, the difficulty of moves you can complete decreases rapidly the longer you climb. So if your maximum movement intensity for a single move in the first thirty seconds is V6, you may find that the hardest individual moves you can do in the second thirty seconds are only V3 or V4, and even less after that.

This varies from climber to climber depending on your fitness level, but the point is that you can't work at or near your maximum movement intensity for very long. Therefore you have to gather as much detailed information as possible and plan well before leaving the ground to minimize the amount of thinking you have to do on the problem. It also helps to train high-intensity anaerobic endurance through intervals such as 4x4s, and it might also be worth trying other formats such as 6x2 or others, which decrease the number of problems per set but raise their intensity level while also increasing the total number of sets.

Flashing and on-sighting boulder problems are a good way to practice general on-sight and flash skills. Since you can see so much of a boulder problem before starting, you can practice reading sequences and planning movement in detail. Further, because the movement intensity is so high, it can help develop confidence for other situations with lower movement intensity. Finally, even recreational climbers should be able to get several high-quality on-sight attempts in during a given session, whereas they may only have the fitness for a single, high-quality, roped on-sight attempt. On-sighting and flashing boulder problems are both good practice for climbers who want to refine their on-sight skills and tactics for routes.

QUICK TICKS

✓ Fitness requirements vary according to the type of climbing and the nature of the route. Redpoints, on-sights, and bouldering are physically demanding in different ways.

✓ Address your weaknesses in all four areas of physical conditioning—local aerobic endurance, anaerobic endurance, strength, and stamina—depending on the type of climbing involved.

✓ On-sights and flashes vary a great deal from bouldering to competitions to multi-pitch, but the one principle common to all of them is that they take longer than performances in which the moves have been rehearsed. Knowing this can help us understand the fitness requirements.

✓ In general a faster pace is better as long as you are not rushing or sprinting. Practice reducing the pauses and hesitations in your movement.

✓ Each different on-sight setting (competition, boulder problem, route) requires somewhat different fitness characteristics.

A researcher once broke equally talented basketball players into three groups to test methods for improving free-throw performance. The first group practiced making free throws for twenty minutes each day. The second group, through guided visualization, simply imagined themselves making perfect free throws for twenty minutes a day. The third group did nothing. At the end of thirty days the researcher tested each group's performance at making actual free throws. The third group's performance remained the same or declined slightly, the first group's performance had improved 24 percent, and the second group had improved 23 percent! Vivid imagery had been almost as successful as actual practice.

Free throws are easy to practice, so perhaps it doesn't make much difference to basketball players whether their improvement comes from actually shooting or from visualization. But for climbers attempting to learn the moves on a difficult on-sight before leaving the ground or preparing for a redpoint, visualization is an essential tactic. For a difficult redpoint, repeated physical practice takes a significant amount of time and effort, and if that time and effort can be reduced by simply visualizing the climb, the climber can save energy and reduce the number of redpoint attempts necessary for the send.

Visualization is part of mental training and includes a variety of techniques from positive self-talk to guided imagery to forms of hypnosis. Mental training in its various forms can be a vital part of climbing success, and this is particularly true of visualization. Popularly described as mental practice, or as creating a mental movie, visualization is an excellent method of rehearsal that assists athletes in attending to crucial details and refining the many aspects of their performance. The visualization process creates and then uses a highly detailed, precise, and clear mental image of you successfully climbing the route from beginning to end. The better you are at visualization, the more detail you can include in your mental movie, and the more effective it becomes. Visualization can be applied to any climbing situation—on-sight, flash, or redpoint—and for each there is a different method for achieving the best results.

During redpoint learning burns, use visualization to help memorize the many details of the climb, refine the different aspects of how you will climb, and create a positive mental picture of a successful outcome. Chief among the details are the exact hand and foot sequences that you will use as well as how and where you will clip protection, how you will initiate and time moves, the necessary pacing, and the emotional states that are best for different parts of the climb.

Visualizing a route will also reveal gaps in your knowledge of the climb. Many times, even when you

Visualization means replaying a highly detailed mental movie of an imagined performance.

believe you know the route well, in fact a number of important ambiguities remain. Such ambiguities are easy to find during visualization—you'll find yourself aware that you don't know what to do next. You'll then need to either see if you can remember what you did by attempting to visualize the section a few times or get back on the climb and find real answers to the questions.

Early attempts at visualizing a redpoint are often defined by hesitation or lapses in concentration that disrupt the mental movie. It takes a good deal of practice to be able to visualize a climb, in detail, all the way through without mistakes, gaps in your knowledge, or any lapses in concentration. Visualizing your performance is rarely a one-time activity; some climbers visualize a route many times before being ready to send. If you're using visualization as part of the redpoint process, the mental movie will develop over the course of your learning burns.

Components

Visualization is like making a mental movie. The process of assembling such a mental movie is like editing an actual movie. In filmmaking, editors get the footage from the production team and then begin a multistep process that will end with a completed film. First they put together a rough cut that strings together the scenes of the film without much refinement. Then they produce a fine cut in which each scene is attended to and refined in great detail. This leads to the creation of a final cut, which is achieved when the overall structure of the film has the pacing and development that best tells the story. Creating a mental movie of your climb can follow a similar process.

The Rough Cut

The rough cut begins with your first learning burns. As the editor of your mental movie, you begin to piece together each scene, or section, of the climb. The goal of visualization at this point is to simply memorize the sequences for sections of the climb and to distinguish between segments in which you have the sequence memorized and those you do not. At this point you won't visualize the entire route; it is enough to play back the sections you are most comfortable with. As

you learn more through working burns, the visualization grows until you have a sequence memorized for the entire route.

Inexperienced climbers often don't learn sequences in much detail, and more experienced climbers tend to leave gaps in their knowledge, but it's important to memorize a precise sequence. If you don't know your sequence, it's impossible to refine the execution of each move and unlikely that you'll be able to visualize the climb all the way through. Under these fuzzy circumstances a redpoint is more difficult.

The Fine Cut

In this stage, the film editor works on polishing scenes, refining them by bringing out the nuances in the performance, trimming each shot, and eliminating shots that don't work. The editor also thinks about how each scene contributes to the whole. You'll add critical details to each move by taking what you learn from additional burns and adding information about the exact nature of each move and section. You can also take note of what you're most likely to do wrong on important moves and visualize yourself performing those moves perfectly.

Some details may seem like minutiae but can be very important. It might be critical, for example, to visualize exactly when and how you will look down for a foothold that's hard to see. It may be important to visualize placing your hand just right on a tiny hold or initiating a move by arching your back. Any given route will contain a number of such details, and at this stage you'll incorporate them into your movie with great visual and kinesthetic clarity. You should really see and feel yourself doing the moves exactly as desired. You should also be able to visualize the climb all the way through. If, however, you find there are places where you are hesitant or lose concentration, work on refining these in the next stage.

The Final Cut

The third step is similar to working on the final cut of a film: it focuses on the whole of the climb, looking for any last-minute changes needed in individual scenes and working with the complete movie while gaining a greater awareness of the total structure. The goal is to visualize the complete climb, including all the meaningful details for each section while eliminating gaps, hesitation, or breaks in concentration. This can be harder than it seems; it can take significant practice to visualize the route all the way through without stopping.

Once you can visualize a route all the way through in great detail with no mistakes or hesitations, it's important to run through the movie in your mind a number of times. Repeatedly playing your finished mental movie will help you gain confidence in your knowledge and your readiness. It's important to be able to play back your completed mental movie with ease, visual clarity, and understanding of the details, thereby developing the confidence and precision necessary for a great redpoint.

How to Visualize

Now that you understand the concept of visualization and the overall process, let's have a look at some of the practical aspects. Visualization is a skill learned through practice, and the following activities will help you develop the ability to create effective mental movies.

Activity 10: Introduction to Visualization

The goal of this exercise is to provide those not accustomed to visualization with a basic introduction.

1. Visualization works best when you are in a relaxed and comfortable state. Lie down in a quiet place without distractions. Close your eyes and concentrate on your breathing, in slowly through the nose and out through the mouth—try to empty your lungs by sighing. Think of nothing but your breathing for several minutes, and then begin to feel your legs become heavy, so heavy they sink into the surface you're lying on. Feel the same in your arms, head, and then torso. After a few minutes you should feel very relaxed, heavy, and comfortable.

2. In this relaxed state, observe a single stationary object such as a photograph or person. Study it for as long as you like. Then, when you're ready, close your eyes and create a mental image of the object, go over it as a whole, and then zoom in and examine some of the fine details. Take a minute or two,

keeping your attention focused on the image. Zoom in and out as you like.

3. Next imagine looking at the object in motion. If you are examining a photograph of a river, for example, imagine that the water begins flowing and the image comes to life. Take notice of what details stand out to you. Is your visualization silent or do you hear the sound of the water? Do you see sparkling reflections of light on the water? These sorts of details make visualization more vivid and help create a fuller picture of the scene. Spend several minutes working with this moving image, keep it in motion, and add details as they occur to you. End the visualization when you can't hold the desired elements in mind, become distracted, or feel mentally strained. This activity should be pleasant, not work.

Guidelines

What to Include

The details that you include in your visualization should be the elements that directly affect your movement, ability to remember the sequence, and state of mind, including environmental aspects that impact your performance. These are the core elements, starting with the sequence, the look and feel of the holds, how you initiate movements, the pace of your climbing, patterns of tension and relaxation in your body, clips, rests, and other elements that are essential to a smooth, successful ascent. Less essential elements may be part of your visualization but should not be emphasized. The sound of the carabiner when you clip, or the color of your rope, help make visualization feel real, but these elements have no direct bearing on your performance, so spending time filling out your visualization with such details is not necessary.

Point of View

Point of view is the vantage point, either external or internal, used to observe yourself in the guided imagery. An external point of view is like watching a video of yourself on the climb. You can see your entire body and the nature of the moves very well, but you are observing from a distance, so the imagery is not the same as it is when you're actually climbing. Using the internal

External visualization is seeing yourself from a third-party vantage point.

Internal visualization is seeing your imagined perform-ance through a first-person point of view.

point of view places you in the first person, seeing everything as if you are actually on the climb. You see the image change as you look down for footholds and then up for handholds or perform other tasks, such as clipping or scanning higher up for holds.

One point of view is not necessarily better than the other; they both provide helpful information. Depending on your preference, you may only use one or you may switch back and forth between them. You may want to use the internal perspective for visualizing foot placement on small holds and external perspective for the movement. Any variation that feels natural and helpful to you is fine.

When and Where to Use Visualization

There are no rules for when and where to use guided imagery. It's great to do it at the crag because this is where you're examining and learning the details of the climbs you want to complete, but there are two poten-tial issues when using guided imagery there. Depend-ing on how fast you and your partner are moving, you might find it challenging to take the time to complete quality visualization. And if others are nearby, you may be interrupted. It's important to take the time to visualize properly and not be distracted or interrupted. Take just a few minutes, move away from other peo-ple, and get a good view of your climb. Looking at the climb while you visualize not only helps you remember your sequences, it also makes switching points of view easier. You can see yourself from a distance on the moves and then zoom in to get a look at each hold from the proper perspective.

Goals for Your Imagery

Determine specific goals for your visualization. Do you want to control anxiety on an intimidating section of the climb? Or will you be testing your memory of individual sections? Be sure you know what the goal is so that your visualization helps you meet it.

Visualize the Climb Correctly

As we described, visualization is a process that begins with learning the sequence and then adding more detail. By the time you reach the final cut of your movie you should be visualizing everything about the climb correctly. Research suggests that athletes who incorrectly visualize their performance will suffer a decline in performance. Your brain learns what you visualize, so make sure that your imagined movement is as good as it can possibly be.

Activity 11: Visualizing a Boulder Problem

If you've never tried to visualize a climb, work on a small scale so you can check your efforts. This activity has two parts; complete both on the same day.

Part 1: Choose a boulder problem that is moderately difficult for you. Climb it several times while paying attention to specific details, including how you leave the ground and how each hand- and foothold appears. Note how you execute the movement, where in your body you feel the greatest effort, and what you like about each move. Now stand away from the problem so you have a clear view, and go through the sequence in your mind several times, making note of details so that there is no confusion about the order in which you use the holds or the details you selected to include in your movie.

Part 2: Later the same day, set aside some time to again visualize the boulder problem you examined so closely earlier. Do this at home in a quiet room with no distractions. Start your visualization on the ground and begin the climb by either stepping toward the rock or sitting down for a sit start. Then imagine beginning the climb, replaying the moves exactly as you performed

them earlier with all the details noted. Do not stop the visualization until you have completed the problem. Repeat the visualization several times.

QUESTIONS

How well did you remember the work you did earlier in the day?

Were you able to complete the visualization with no gaps, errors, or lapses in your concentration?

How complete was your visualization—can you think of anything you left out?

Activity 12: Visualizing to Control Stress

In this variation, visualize yourself under stress. Imagine yourself becoming pumped and afraid. Then imagine responding by controlling your breathing and continuing to climb with greater commitment. Allow yourself the option to climb down. Always see yourself moving calmly and with emotional control no matter what part of the climb you are on.

High-quality visualization and insights into improving your performance do not usually happen on the first try, so after your first effort briefly take stock of how it went and visualize the problem again. Repeat the visualization as many times as you need to in order to achieve three perfect visualizations.

Part 3: In the next day or two go back to the boulder problem and climb it again. Compare your ascent to your visualization. How similar are they and why? Did you forget any of the details? Were there moves that you did a particularly good job visualizing?

Visualization is a process, not something you complete once. We've emphasized creating imagery, but later in the process you can use visualization to create new ideas for problematic sections; it can help generate new ways of thinking about difficult sections and new sequences. You may have had many unsuccessful visualization attempts marked by lapses in concentration or errors. Keep at it until you have a complete movie— some climbers redpoint soon after succeeding in a perfect visualization.

Visualization's greatest utility might be at the crag, especially for hard climbs you want to redpoint quickly. In this case visualization is a tool for reinforcing learning and revealing what is not yet known, as well as for rehearsing and perfecting movement without expending the energy needed for the actual moves.

All of the practice and effort put into visualization may seem arduous, and in the beginning it does take a great deal of work, but with practice visualization can become an easy, useful tool that you can rely on in many different environments.

Route Maps

A route map is a form of imagery unique to climbing. It is a diagram or map of the entire route you draw out on paper. Route maps tend to begin as drawings of the hand- and footholds. They grow in detail and go through a number of versions as you refine your knowledge of the route and include notes and symbols marking which moves are the most difficult and why

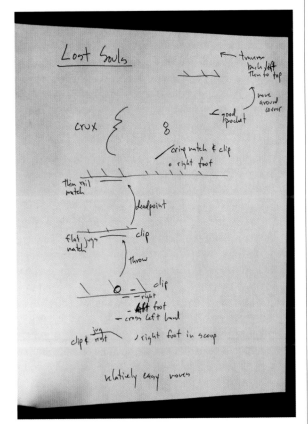

A route map of Lost Souls (12a), Kaymoor, New River Gorge.

and aspects of the climb that need special emphasis or points where mistakes are likely to occur. Like visualization, route maps provide an excellent way for you to discover any gaps in your knowledge of the route. Creating a route map can be an enjoyable exercise, and developing the details can help you memorize elements that will lead to the redpoint.

Looking at the Route as Visualization

The most common form of guided imagery in climbing is to look at the route from the ground and review the sequence hold by hold, which comes naturally to many climbers. The strength of this method is that you are looking at the actual holds and moves that make up the route, so the imagery fosters intimate knowledge of the route, and any gaps or ambiguities in the sequence should be easy to detect. The potential weakness is in your attention to detail. It can be easy to just review the handholds and not the footholds or examine a few sections of the route but not the entire thing. It's easy to emphasize the sequence but miss the moves, clips, and rests. Take the time to do the following.

- Visualize both the hand and foot sequence.

- Imagine the moves and how they will feel.

- Note mistakes you are likely to make and remind yourself what the proper execution is.

- Go slow and attend to the details.

- Start at the bottom and review the entire route in one push.

- Review cruxes and sections you are less familiar with more than once.

- If you lose concentration or are distracted, start over from the beginning or from a rest position below the point at which you were distracted.

Flash and On-Sight

Flash and on-sight visualizations have different goals. For on-sights your knowledge of the route will be incomplete. In some sections you'll have detailed information about the moves—so you can come up with a sequence, estimate the difficulty, and derive its feel—but for other sections you may know next to nothing. You need to adjust your visualization techniques for each situation. If you are confident that you know the sequence for a move or section, then visualizing it in detail is a good idea. In sections where more than one possible sequence is possible, use visualization to imagine yourself trying one sequence, discovering it's not right and then calmly reversing a few moves and trying your other ideas until you get it right. In other words, use visualization to create and reinforce options. Since controlling your emotions is so important for on-sighting, focus on visualizing yourself as calm, confident, and efficient.

For those sections where a sequence is not clear, try to visualize how you would respond to different situations. For example, a climb may transition from an obvious sequence to an ambiguous section. This might make you anxious, so your visualization should include your emotional response. Imagine yourself on that part of the climb, see your height off the ground, what the rock looks like, what the section above looks like, and so forth. Imagine you're controlling your anxiety level; see yourself calmly examining the holds above you while your breathing remains calm and steady. Allow yourself time to assess the sequence before committing to it and moving higher with confidence. Visualize calmly reaching for the first holds of the new section while remaining focused and confident as you advance.

A similar tactic is to assess the route for anything that might increase your anxiety level, such as run outs, sections of the climb that have an angle or style with which you are uncomfortable, or a potentially awkward fall. Again, focus your visualization on the emotional aspects of your climbing. Imagine yourself climbing these frightening sections with confidence. Imagine yourself calmly looking for holds while run out or moving in a confident, fluid manner during a severe pump. In any intimidating circumstance, acknowledge that you are afraid while at the same time imagining that you will have a positive response despite your fear.

Imagine your body is relaxed, your breathing normal, your mind calm and focused. Rather than ignoring the things that frighten you or letting anxiety grow, address them directly. This might not make you fearless, but it will give you a way of practicing a positive response to such situations.

Visualizing flashes is slightly different, depending on whether you've observed other climbers on the route. In the best case you will have seen more than one climber redpoint the route, so you can use their sequences as the basis for your visualization. This can be a tremendous advantage in your visualization, but be aware that you won't necessarily know how that sequence will feel to you. The climbers' familiarity with the route may have masked just how awkward or difficult some moves are going to feel.

The first goal when visualizing flashes is to learn and memorize the sequence other climbers use, and the second is to give yourself options based on that sequence. Options might include down-climbing back into a rest if a section doesn't go well or using different footholds. Another possibility is to visualize yourself climbing more slowly and being more tired than the climbers you observed. It's impossible to list all the possibilities; your solution depends on you and the nature of the route. Look for the details that will affect your performance and deal with them through visualization.

Visualization can be an effective tool for on-sight, flash, and redpoint climbing. Use it to help you remember sequences, discover gaps in your learning, and control anxiety. For redpoints, start small by simply visualizing critical sequences and gradually work your way up to seeing the entire climb, including balance, pacing, movement initiation, and other important details. Your goal is the perfect vision of your upcoming redpoint attempt.

On-sight visualizations require significantly more flexibility. A redpoint allows you to acquire perfect information, but an on-sight will always entail uncertainty. Gather visual information and envision sequences as best you can, but keep an open mind as you begin to climb, and adapt as necessary.

QUICK TICKS

✓ Treat the creation of a visualization as if you were producing a movie: create a rough cut, then a fine cut, and lastly a final cut.

✓ Include as much pertinent detail as you can, and use either internal or external points of view.

✓ Use visualization to help you remember critical sequences and movements and refine them.

✓ Gaps in a visualization can signal that additional discovery and learning may be necessary.

✓ An on-sight visualization will have gaps. You'll have to plan and improvise as you climb to compensate for the lack of preclimb information.

✓ A visualization for a flash attempt can help you remember sequences but cannot help you with movement nuance such as balance.

✓ Try creating route maps to help remember details and solidify your understanding.

CHAPTER 11

Emotional and Cognitive Aspects

edpoints, on-sights, and flashes place different cognitive, emotional, physical, and tactical demands on climbers, but the most fundamental and striking differences are cognitive and emotional.

Emotional Aspects

The emotional pressures of on-sight climbing can be immense: The fear of the unknown, the pressure of only getting one shot to on-sight, and the specter of self-doubt raise the stakes, adding tension and anxiety to the task. These kinds of pressures are routine in on-sight climbing, and they can be crippling. One of your central tasks is to control these fears and focus precious emotional energy on the pragmatics of the climb. (See chapter 8.)

Cognitive Aspects

On-sight climbing is tactically and cognitively different from other styles of climbing. It is also unique in the sports world in the way it requires you to develop and execute precise movement based on limited information and in the way the process of gathering information and then executing movement occurs.

In general there are two common situations in sports. The first is sports in which an athlete rehearses the exact movements of the performance. This includes sports such as figure skating, gymnastics, diving, and redpointing. In these activities athletes practice specific movements for days, months, or even years before including them in a high-level performance or competition. This amount of practice is necessary because the athlete's movements are of high cognitive and motor difficulty. Lengthy rehearsal periods allow athletes to refine these difficult movements to the point where they are precise and nearly automatic. By the end of the rehearsal process, these athletes do not need to focus on each specific detail of their movement as they might have earlier.

The other common situation is found in sports like soccer, tennis, or basketball. In these sports, the athletes'

movements are organized to achieve what are called higher-order goals, such as blocking an opponent, returning a shot, or scoring points. It's the outcome of the moves in relation to the overall game that matters rather than the specific character or quality of the moves. In these situations the motor difficulty is moderate to low, but the speed of movement is often extremely rapid. The moderate level of difficulty is what makes such quick responses possible. Consider that tennis or basketball players do not need to place their feet on exact spots on the court—like a climber spotting footholds—before running for the ball; they just run.

So how does on-sight climbing compare to these common sports challenges? It has characteristics of both. Like ice skating or gymnastics, the central concern of the on-sight climber is the execution of movement—there is no opponent to battle, no points to score, but it is the precise and correct execution of each movement that allows the climber to continue. As in tennis or basketball, the on-sight climber can't rehearse the exact movements needed in the performance beforehand, but he can practice general movement patterns by climbing lots of similar routes.

What makes on-sighting unique is that when reading a route from the ground, or from a rest, you can identify some stimuli and start to plan your response long before you actually encounter them as part of a move, yet the information available from visual analysis is limited. The challenge is even greater given that the motor complexity tends to be fairly high and the movement sometimes must be both precise and fast. Finally climbers are tasked with identifying new visual, tactile, and kinesthetic information en route and rapidly responding to it.

Rather than needing to rapidly produce fairly simple moves like a soccer or tennis player, or having the ability to practice very difficult moves prior to incorporating them into a performance like a gymnast, the on-sight climber needs to produce fairly complex moves, fairly rapidly, without the benefit of specific rehearsal, but he can plan ahead to a degree.

How do climbers cope with the uncertainty of on-sight climbing and make decisions in such an ever-changing environment? Let's examine how information processing—collecting, sorting, and using relevant information—relates to on-sight climbing.

Information Processing

Information processing has four stages: stimulus identification, response selection, response programming, and output.

Stimulus identification is the process by which you receive and prioritize sensory information from your environment. You might be aware of many stimuli

Right: Begin by assessing the route from the ground, but adjust your plan as you climb as more information becomes available. Here the climber contemplates sequences on the ground. *Below left:* En route, the climber assesses the upcoming section of the climb in the information gathering stage. *Below right:* After choosing a response, the climber executes the chosen set of movements.

when climbing: the color of your rope, the amount of chalk in your chalk bag, the size and shape of the next handhold, the position and quality of several footholds, the distance to the next clip, the quality of balance you have at the moment, and so on. Some of this information is meaningful for the move at hand, and some of it is not. In stimulus identification you sort that information into what is useful at the moment and what is not. Your brain can ignore the color of the rope while paying close attention to more important concerns such as the position of available footholds.

The next stage, response selection, is when you decide how to respond to the stimulus selected in the identification stage. For example you may observe a larger, more positive foothold than you are currently using and decide to use it before attempting the next hand move.

In the third stage, response programming, your brain organizes your motor system to produce the desired movement. Once you identify a better foothold, your brain now knows what stimulus will be acted on. It then decides what action will be taken and prepares the nervous system to create the necessary movement.

Finally, the output stage is the execution of the movement itself, in this case, moving your foot to the new hold. Like in many other activities, the duration of the process from identification of the stimulus to the output of the movement is very brief for moving a foot from one hold to another, but a climb is made up of many such decisions that vary in complexity.

Timing

The time it takes, or more correctly the time available for on-sight and flash climbers to process information, can be as brief as a fraction of a second—or in the case of a route you have been saving for a flash, it may be months from the time you identify a stimulus to the time you actually use it as part of a move. This means that in on-sight climbing information processing can occur in dramatically different time frames. The recognition of these different time frames has led to the tactics used in on-sight climbing.

On-sight climbing has three different information processing time frames and contexts. The first is when you perform a visual inspection of a route from the ground. In the process of reading the sequences, you postulate specific responses to visual stimuli long before you have the opportunity to put this information into action. An inexperienced on-sight climber may not be able to do much information processing from the ground; he may only be able to identify some of the holds he will be using without considering the sequence or specific movements to use.

More accomplished climbers may progress through the stimulus identification and response selection stages while reading a route. Not only do more experienced climbers identify handholds and footholds, they consider possible sequences and the specific moves for each sequence. Further, they are able to make predictions about how each move will feel, its relative difficulty, the type and quality of balance, and so on. They can glean a great deal of useful movement information from a visual inspection, potentially making the information processing easier while climbing. But reading a route from the ground does have its limitations. The only information you have access to is visual, limiting what you can know about the moves. You can only see so much from the ground, so reading a route can tell you a great deal, but it cannot provide a complete understanding of a route. This means any plan you make on the ground will need to be modified en route.

This leads us to the second information processing context on-sight climbers face. When you leave the ground you have access to additional external stimuli, such as information about footholds that you could not see previously. You also get a better understanding of the distance between holds and their size and texture. More important, though, is that you have access to internal stimuli relating to balance, body position, level of fatigue, and so on. With this additional information you can compare the expectations of the moves you developed on the ground to how they actually feel en route. Based on this new information you may modify your plan or ignore it altogether and try something new.

The third information processing context occurs during the portions of a climb that you could not see from the ground. Here information processing time is condensed, and rather than having a long gap between the stimulus selection and output stages, you react more like a tennis or basketball player who responds to new information as quickly as possible. In these situations movement takes the most cognitive effort, and you will often move slower at this point despite trying to produce movements as fast as possible, and you'll expend more energy as a result. Such situations are also likely to be the most emotionally taxing part of an ascent.

An on-sight attempt requires tremendous cognitive work in a stressful situation. While a flash attempt is also stressful, there is tremendous benefit in watching other climbers, studying photos, or receiving beta. If you watch others on a short sport route or boulder problem, you can memorize exact hand and foot sequences for the entire route. What's more, you can also learn exactly where rests and cruxes are located. In observing others you can also make good estimates of pacing, where to clip, alternative sequences, and what to do if something does not go according to plan. You can pick up on many details of how the climber's body responds to each move. Additionally, discussing the route with those who've done it can provide a number of alternative movement sequences for difficult sections. If you are skilled at gathering and synthesizing the available information, you'll know the route and its moves in great detail and with a high degree of certainty. While completing a route first try is still impressive, a flash climber gains a huge advantage with this additional information.

By looking at the different information processing situations in on-sight climbing, you can better understand how to apply tactics to your best advantage. We will go into the detail of these tactics in chapter 8.

Arousal and Anxiety

Imagine a climber on his first attempt at on-sighting a 5.11a. He feels that this is an important climb and a big challenge, and he knows succeeding would be a personal breakthrough, so he is naturally a little more nervous than usual. Early on the route he climbs at a good pace and has no trouble clipping. His nervousness does show a little in his movements; they are more hesitant than usual. As he moves higher on the route a pump begins to set in, narrowing his focus so that he can only attend to essential elements such as finding handholds and footholds. Because he is starting to worry about his pump, he rushes and misses key footholds. He starts to use the first holds he sees rather than scanning the rock for the best holds for each

Controlling your arousal level is important in on-sight climbing.

move. Moving higher on the route, his pump deepens, and he misreads a move and doesn't use the best footholds. He gets a case of sewing-machine leg.

As these things happen he becomes less confident and more fearful that he will not complete the route. Arriving at the crux, he finds a series of smaller edges that he hoped would be jugs. Not liking what he finds, he shops for holds and chalks more than he should. Through this difficult sequence his entire body is shaking, his moves are slower and hesitant, he has trouble placing his feet as they smack and scrape the rock. His breathing is fast and irregular. He is afraid of falling each time he moves a hand to a new hold.

He somehow manages to get through the crux, but he is pumped to near failure, his last clipped bolt is several feet below, and now he must clip. He is terrified of falling and that fear occupies a great deal of his focus. He pulls up the rope, but at this point his coordination has deteriorated to the point that he fumbles with the carabiner and drops the rope. This sends his level of fear even higher, and anyone watching can see that a fall is inevitable. He tries to clip again but pulls up even more rope than he did before. It's a last desperate attempt to clip before he falls with armloads of slack.

This sort of scenario plays out every day on climbs around the world, but the climber doesn't usually understand why. While the climber may believe he failed because he was not fit enough, the truth is the combined effects of increasing levels of arousal and anxiety are at the heart of such performances.

Levels of Arousal

Arousal is a state of readiness, that is, the degree to which your central nervous system is activated. In a state of low arousal you may feel sleepy. In a state of moderate arousal you feel alert and energetic, and in a state of very high arousal you may be agitated, jumpy, and even find it difficult to focus your attention. The level of arousal that is appropriate for a given activity is determined by its cognitive complexity and motor demands.

Some activities benefit from low arousal levels such as those that depend on fine motor skills or have a higher degree of cognitive complexity. A good example is playing a difficult piece of classical music on the violin, where rapid, precise movements of the fingers are essential to a beautiful performance. A high state of arousal would make such precise movements difficult if not impossible. A higher state of arousal is helpful for a lineman in football, though. His job requires blocking or tackling, which are skills with moderate to low cognitive complexity, so the high state of arousal will help him explode off the line of scrimmage quickly and hit an opposing player with maximum force.

Most sports fall somewhere between these two poles, consisting of moderate cognitive challenges and moderate motor complexity. On-sight climbing requires fine motor skills and gross motor skills and has a relatively high degree of cognitive complexity. Clipping, placing protection, and using small and difficult-to-grasp holds take fine motor skills, whereas simple moves, such as a reach between jugs, rely on gross motor coordination. On-sighting also has a relatively high level of cognitive complexity since you need to make plans for specific movements and then adapt those plans to what you find on the route. On-sights also require attentiveness to subtle proprioceptive cues that tell you about the quality of your balance and visual cues such as slight differences in rock color that indicate footholds. Because of these cognitive complexities and the fine motor skills involved, climbers benefit from low to moderate arousal when on-sighting, as high arousal levels can hinder our ability to work with such subtle cues. But as many climbers have learned, anxiety can interfere with trying to maintain the optimal arousal level.

Level of Anxiety

Anxiety is an emotional reaction to the perception of a physical threat or fear regarding an outcome. Climbing differs from many sports in that the presence of an immediate physical threat is a fundamental aspect of the climbing environment; just like the climber in the example near the beginning of this chapter, many climbers have an intense fear of falling. Falling is simply part of the sport, but the fear of taking falls can be a detriment to performance. Your experiences with falling affect your emotional state while climbing.

Climbers who have taken many well-controlled and safe falls are often far more comfortable on the rock than those who have little experience falling or those who have taken a bad fall. The latter assess every aspect of their experience on the rock by the likelihood of a fall, and they may feel comfortable on large footholds but become afraid and overly cautious when they step onto smaller or polished holds. They may have the same response when moving from comfortable to less secure handholds, when getting higher off the ground, as they begin to develop a pump, or if they think their belayer is distracted.

Many climbers also fear failure, regardless of whether they fear falling. Given that an on-sight necessarily means one attempt and one attempt only, climbers often have increased anxiety in the face of pressure to succeed. Redpoint attempts, too, can raise your anxiety level; a prolonged period of repeated attempts at the same route can make many climbers extraordinarily anxious, fearing another failure will necessitate yet further attempts. Expectations play an important role in this process; a climber who believes prematurely that he is ready for the redpoint can face frustration and self-doubt. The problem may not be that the route is too difficult; rather, it may be that his expectations are wrong.

Any number of elements can influence an individual climber's anxiety level such as a run out, developing a pump, exposed climbing, or the fear of falling. What's more, they work in a cumulative fashion, so that a climber may initially experience anxiety over one element—for example, the route being a little more difficult than he expects—to which other anxiety-inducing elements are added, such as a run out, a distracted belayer, awkward moves, social pressure, fear of failure, and so on. These variables and others all have the potential to dramatically increase a climber's anxiety level, and anxiety has a direct impact on arousal; as anxiety increases so does arousal. Learning tactics to manage anxiety will improve your ability to on-sight. If you are afraid of falling, you'll need to work on becoming emotionally desensitized to it so that the potential for a fall does not hinder your ability to move efficiently.

Overcoming your fear of falling

Progressive desensitization is a technique that has proven successful for overcoming many phobias, including a fear of flying. You can use it to overcome your fear of falling by gradually becoming used to taking lead falls.

Activity 13: Taking Falls

Climbers need to practice falling so they can reduce the fear that often inhibits performance. Belayers need to practice catching falls to learn safe and correct techniques.

This activity has four progressive stages, but everyone won't need all four stages. The first two stages are for climbers with the highest degree of anxiety. Be sure you are comfortable with the falls in one stage before moving on to the next, and don't take any falls that scare you while engaged in desensitization. You should be practicing and learning to be comfortable with falls, and if you take falls that scare you you're simply learning to be fearful.

Falling is an integral aspect of climbing, and becoming comfortable with falling while retaining a healthy respect for the possible dangers is a critical element in your ultimate performance. **Rocket to My Brain (12c), Meadow River, WV.**

1. **Take very short practice falls on a top rope**. The goal here is to take falls where you have almost no fear. For most climbers this is on top rope. Start with almost no slack in the system so that a fall essentially means sitting back into your harness without

A climber practicing lead falls by setting up for a small stage 3 fall.

A climber ready to take a more advanced stage 3 practice fall.

dropping. Fall in this manner on a number of climbs at different angles and from positions on the rock where you are not entirely comfortable. Don't give yourself time to think about the fall or letting go, just let go of the rock and let your belayer hold you. Don't tell your belayer you are falling or ask if he is ready. Work at this level until you are comfortable with these falls. For some this will take a few minutes; for others it will be a few days or longer.

2. **Take slightly longer falls on a top rope.** In stage two your belayer leaves a foot or two of slack in the rope so that you can't just sit down into your harness. Every fall will include a small drop. Over the course of a few days, try this on a number of dif-

ferent climbs and get used to the slight drop when you fall. The belayer should not leave excessive slack in the rope. The goal is to get used to a small drop and not to take long falls. Take at least fifteen to twenty falls and move to the next level only after you've become comfortable with them.

3. **Take safe, comfortable falls on lead.** When you are comfortable with short top-rope falls, begin practicing lead falls. In the beginning of this step, it's important to be comfortable with the angle and style of the climb. Take your first lead falls on climbs that have clean falls. As on top rope, the initial falls should be basic, small, and not intimidating. That might mean just sitting down into your harness with the bolt at chest level. Do that as

An example of a climber ready to take a stage 4 fall. Note the draw clipped at the climber's foot.

many times as you need, and when you've become comfortable, you can either climb higher in relation to the bolt or stay at the same relative height but ask your belayer to give a little slack so that you drop a bit when you let go.

The goal in the early stages of taking lead falls is to take easy falls and not get into situations that intimidate you. You only want to exceed your comfort zone by very small increments; going so far that you get scared negates any positive desensitization work accomplished thus far. Work on these easy falls for as long as you need, whether it's a few minutes or several days. If you tend to take longer, make sure to take fifteen to twenty falls while gaining confidence and comfort before moving to the

next level. Also note how you are responding to your belayer. Is there anything he or she does that makes you more or less comfortable?

4. **Take longer lead falls.** Note that being on lead and taking falls means that your belayer will need to do more work. When you practice lead falls, your belayer should give you a dynamic belay, especially on short falls. For example, if you take a lead fall with the bolt at your knee and do not receive a dynamic belay you will slam into the rock, which will cause additional anxiety. Use a skilled belayer you are comfortable with.

After the first three steps, you should be ready to take lead falls, that is, falls with the bolt at your foot or even lower. Even after practicing with falls in steps one through three, this may still be a little intimidating but not so much that you refuse to let go. If you have a good belayer, your falls should feel gentle and you should not slam into the rock. You may need a lot of practice over weeks or longer to become genuinely comfortable. Fit this practice into your warmup, and always keep safety in mind—don't take practice falls in situations where you could hit something or where there are other potential problems. These practice falls need to be safe in order to be effective in desensitizing you. Take falls just long enough for you to be comfortable in the situations typical of your climbing. Finally, don't expect that you will overcome a fear of falling once and for all. It's more likely that you will become far more comfortable in many climbing situations, but some occasions will still frighten you. Also, it's fairly common for climbers to take practice falls or tune-up falls now and then. Don't let too much time go by without taking any falls.

Overcoming a Fear of Failure

For experienced climbers fear of falling is typically not an issue. Having persevered through countless falls, veteran climbers have learned to accept lead falls as part of the game. There is, however, a more pernicious fear that can cripple even the most experienced among us. That is a fear of failure.

Many of us think we always have to be successful, and our culture supports this view, labeling those that try yet come up short as losers. But if you can't fail, then it's impossible to take the social risks necessary to progress. If your palms sweat at the thought of casting off on a redpoint attempt or you feel queasy thinking about potential on-sights yet a fear of falling is not an issue for you, you may be intensifying anxiety because of a fear of failing.

Fear of failure is common in our culture, and much is known about dealing with its sometimes crippling effects. The following steps can help you put this fear in its place and reduce the anxiety you feel while climbing.

1. Acknowledge the fear and define it. If you're feeling anxious before climbing, admit that you're fearful. Once you've been honest with yourself and can acknowledge the fear, you can determine its cause. Identifying the source of the fear will go a long way toward resolving it; if you have determined that your fear is based on failing, then continue to step 2.

2. Evaluate the consequences of failing—what's the worst that can happen? Put the consequences in perspective. Will your relationships with others be ruined by your failure to send? Will you be put into a perilous situation? Probably not, so cut yourself some slack. If you fall off, you've simply fallen off, and the worst that can happen for a redpoint is you'll need to try again. For on-sights there are always other routes to try. By most standards those are fairly innocuous consequences that should be readily acceptable.

3. Recognize that failures are learning experiences and not personal shortcomings. Failing at an individual task does not mean you are a failure; it is simply a consequence, and not a label you must wear. Replace negative preconceptions of failure with positive ones by telling yourself you took a risk and learned something. Remember: no risk = no reward. You saw an opportunity and tried to take advantage of it. Bravo!

4. Persist. Successful people are not successful because they never fail. Quite the opposite: they succeed because they're willing to take a chance and then persist after failing once, twice, or hundreds of times. Thomas Edison tried 10,000 lighting filaments before finding one that worked. He said of that endeavor that

he didn't fail 10,000 times but rather he discovered 10,000 filaments that didn't work. The wisdom in this is that he had faith in his process, knew how to conceptualize what he was doing, and didn't expect success to come easy. Keep trying and success will find you. Be as analytical as you like about failed attempts, but never be judgmental about them.

Effects of a Pump on Anxiety

During on-sight and flash attempts, the goal is to focus your attention and emotional energy on pragmatic tasks such as identifying holds, planning moves, and selecting the best moments to clip. You also need to make decisions based on your level of fatigue, but continually assessing or obsessing over how pumped you

Fatigue can ratchet up anxiety. Learn to stay calm and focused when you're pumped.

are is a hindrance. When thoughts about fatigue overwhelm tactical decision-making, your performance will be diminished. When thinking about the pump distracts you and you start to anticipate falling, it increases anxiety. Your level of pump should remain in the background. When your pump gets your conscious attention it should be for pragmatic reasons such as when deciding how long to stay at a rest, what your pacing should be, or whether to climb higher when you face a safety risk.

Climbers are almost always wrong about when they are too pumped to continue and often have several more moves in them even when they are convinced they will fail. For on-sight or flash climbing, fatigue should remain in the background, something you are aware of but that does not change your emotional state or expectations or distract you from the fundamentals of the task at hand. This is a tall order and very difficult to accomplish by will power alone. It takes training to become desensitized to the distracting presence of a significant pump.

Activity 14: Staying Calm While Pumped

Getting pumped is often a source of significant anxiety for climbers, so it's essential to learn to stay relaxed and focused while under anaerobic stress. With practice, you will be better able to stay calmer, make decisions, and control your movement.

Your goal in this exercise is to climb continuously for ten minutes with a mild pump while focusing on specific aspects of your climbing. You can do this on top rope or on lead. Try to maintain a very mild pump for the duration, while focusing on specific aspects of your movement. This is similar to a continuous climbing workout in that you'll climb for an extended period of time, but with the notable differences that it is of shorter duration and that you'll maintain a pump. You'll need to consider how this type of mild anaerobic training fits into your physical training regimen. Don't place it after other anaerobic training. Keep in mind that though it is a form of anaerobic training the emphasis here is on the emotional aspects of climbing while fatigued.

Choose a route. Since the goal is to maintain a mild pump for a specific length of time, it's usually best to choose an easier route with a number of rests. The route should be easy enough that if you use the rests you won't get pumped but if you skip them you will. Climb up and down the route a few times without using the rests until you get a mild pump and then use the rests as necessary in order to prevent the pump from deepening, but don't allow yourself to fully recover. While you are climbing, focus on something basic such as your breathing or your foot placement.

If you choose to focus on your breathing, your goal is to maintain a deliberate and consistent breathing pattern. Don't hold your breath or allow your breathing to become shallow and rapid. From the beginning to the end of the activity, focus your attention on maintaining a consistent breathing pattern. Give yourself a few tries at this exercise to find the level of difficulty and breathing pattern that is best for you. At first, choose a short route in a quiet location so your belayer can hear your breathing and alert you to any changes.

To focus on foot placement, use the silent feet exercise described in *The Self-Coached Climber*. Your only focus is the quality of your foot placement. Be deliberate and precise, and visually guide your toes to each hold. Try to ignore the pumped feeling in your forearms and remain focused on this one aspect of your climbing. Make each foot placement flawless.

What you are trying to achieve is a mild pump that provides a slight distraction of low enough intensity that you can consciously choose to focus your attention on something else, in this case your breathing or foot placement. If you are unable to maintain your focus during the activity, it's usually because you've developed a deeper pump than desired, and it may take a number of sessions to find the right difficulty level for you. You can incorporate this activity into your anaerobic training, doing laps on routes, traverses, or bouldering circuits, but it's much harder during high-intensity physical training. Before incorporating the focus exercises into your other training activities, first learn to do the activity well at low intensity levels and then gradually increase the intensity until you can focus on your breathing or footwork during a deep pump. Experience shows that maintaining focus while pumped helps control anxiety and is an important part of expert performance; it takes high-quality practice at the right level of difficulty to develop this skill.

✓ On-sight climbing is a unique challenge because you must develop and execute precise movement based on limited information.

✓ Information processing has three contexts in climbing. The first is when you inspect the route from the ground. The second is when you are doing the moves you saw from the ground and making necessary adjustment to your plan. The third is when you have to improvise.

✓ Information processing—in the three phases described above—is the central feature of on-sight climbing.

✓ Understanding the challenges of information processing in on-sighting helps us understand why on-sight tactics take the form they do.

✓ Arousal is the athlete's level of readiness for a performance.

✓ Anxiety is concern or worry over a potential outcome.

✓ Climbers need to manage their levels of arousal and anxiety, as too much or too little hinders performance.

✓ Through training you can learn to manage arousal and anxiety in challenging situations such as when you are pumped.

APPENDIX 1
Sequencing Solutions

2. Left hand to sidepull

1. Cross right hand to here

Left hand

Start sequence here

Right hand

4. Left hand to far left jug

3. Right hand to crimp

Direction of climb

5. Left hand up and left

4. Right hand to small slot

3. Left hand to crimp

1. Left hand to slot
2. Right hand to slot—match

Start sequence here

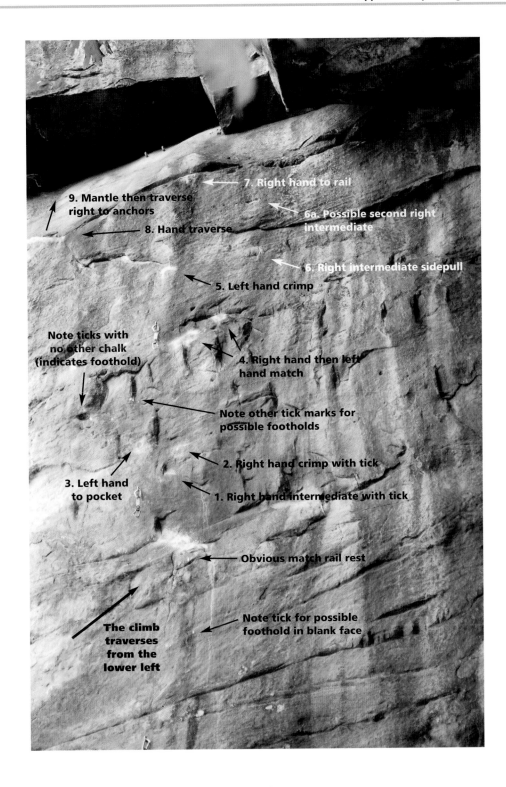

7. Right hand to rail

9. Mantle then traverse right to anchors

6a. Possible second right intermediate

8. Hand traverse

6. Right intermediate sidepull

5. Left hand crimp

Note ticks with no other chalk (indicates foothold)

4. Right hand then left hand match

Note other tick marks for possible footholds

2. Right hand crimp with tick

3. Left hand to pocket

1. Right hand intermediate with tick

Obvious match rail rest

The climb traverses from the lower left

Note tick for possible foothold in blank face

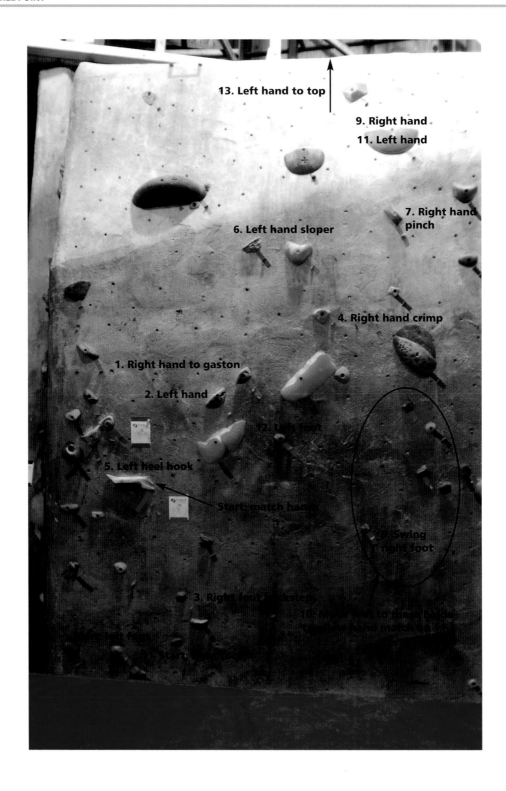

13. Left hand to top

9. Right hand

11. Left hand

7. Right hand pinch

6. Left hand sloper

4. Right hand crimp

1. Right hand to gaston

2. Left hand

12. Left foot

5. Left heel hook

Start: match hands

8. Swing right foot

3. Right foot backstep

10. Lock off to the right and match hands

Start

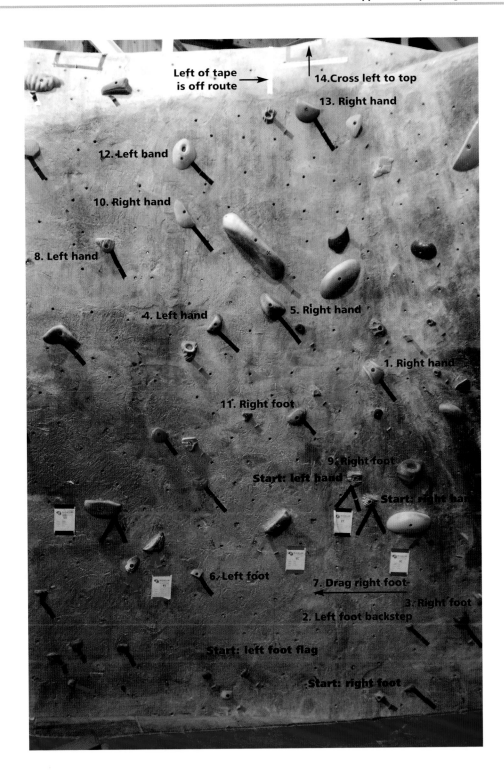

Left of tape
is off route →

14.Cross left to top

13. Right hand

12. Left band

10. Right hand

8. Left hand

4. Left hand

5. Right hand

1. Right hand

11. Right foot

9. Right foot

Start: left hand

Start: right hand

6. Left foot

7. Drag right foot

3. Right foot

2. Left foot backstep

Start: left foot flag

Start: right foot

13. Use top edge as left hand

15. Right hand

11. Right crimp

9. Left crimp

7. Right pinch

12. Left heel hook
5. Left hand

14. Right foot

4. Right hand

8. Right hand

6. Convert heel to
left normal foot

2. Left foot
Right pinch

3. Left heel hook

10. Right foot

Start: matched

Start: right foot

Start: left foot

The Physics behind a Climber's Fall

**By John Eric Goff, Associate Professor of Physics at Lynchburg College
and author of *Gold Medal Physics: The Science of Sports***

To understand the physics behind a fall in climbing, one must understand properties of the rope in use and energy concepts. If air resistance and rope friction are ignored, a climber falls at acceleration due to gravity of $g \approx 32$ ft/s² (about 22 mph/s). Of course, the climber's acceleration changes once the rope takes hold. The rope's tension, T, may be expressed using a simple model that employs the Young's modulus, Y, and is given by

$$T = \frac{YA}{L} \Delta L,$$

where A is the cross-sectional area of the rope, L is the unstretched length of rope, and ΔL is the amount the rope stretches. The Young's modulus, Y, is an intrinsic property of the rope material and may be taken as a constant. The cross-sectional area decreases slightly as the tension increases because the rope fibers get closer together. The change in A is, however, small, and A may also be taken to be constant.

Another way to express the rope tension is in a form that more closely resembles what is known as Hooke's Law,

$$T = k\Delta L,$$

where k is the stretch parameter, given by

$$k = \frac{YA}{L}.$$

Note that k is constant for a fixed length of rope but obviously changes as L changes. The simple form given

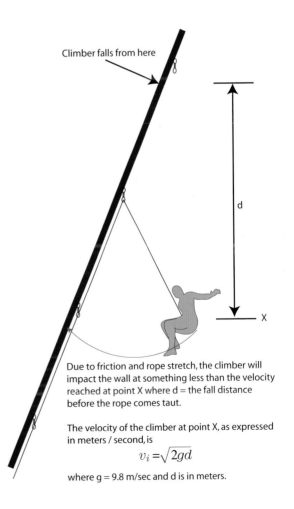

Climber falls from here

d

X

Due to friction and rope stretch, the climber will impact the wall at something less than the velocity reached at point X where d = the fall distance before the rope comes taut.

The velocity of the climber at point X, as expressed in meters / second, is

$$v_i = \sqrt{2gd}$$

where g = 9.8 m/sec and d is in meters.

by Hooke's Law expresses the fact that for a given length of rope, the amount of stretch is proportional to the tension. There is likely to be some slack in a rope just before a climber falls. The slack is one way to make L larger (or k smaller).

The qualitative analysis of a fall boils down to following the energy. As a climber ascends a cliff or wall, his gravitational potential energy increases. Simply put, the higher one climbs, the greater the potential for a large speed upon hitting the ground after a fall. Gravitational potential energy for a climber of mass m at a height h above some reference height is mgh. Energy conservation states that energy cannot be created or destroyed; only the form of energy can change. During a fall, the climber's gravitational potential energy must be converted into other forms of energy. As the climber's speed, v, increases during the fall, more and more energy is being put into kinetic energy, given by $1/2 \, mv^2$. The climber obviously wants that kinetic energy converted into some other kind of energy because he does not want to hit the ground.

There are two main types of energy into which the climber's gravitational potential energy (and subsequent kinetic energy) will go during a fall. The first is frictional energy; that energy cannot be recovered. As the climber falls, he experiences air friction (also called air resistance). As the rope slides through carabiners and along the cliff or wall, heat is generated as a result of sliding friction. Even the rope fibers experience sliding friction as the rope becomes tauter due to an increase in tension. All of these phenomena help to remove energy from the climber.

A second type of energy form that helps the climber is stored potential energy in the rope. As the rope stretches, it stores energy just like a stretched spring does. The amount of stored energy is given by $1/2 k \, (L)^2$. Note that the more a rope stretches, the more energy it stores. Increased stretching has the added benefit of slowing the climber over a longer period of time, what is sometimes called "extending the collision time." The same principle explains air bags and why we bend our knees when landing on the ground after a jump. Our speed always reaches zero; the longer it takes to get to zero the less force is needed to slow us down. A climber who has come to rest at the end of a rope after a fall has stretched the rope, which means the rope stores some of the initial gravitational potential energy. The rest got dissipated via frictional losses.

One way to increase the amount of rope stretch, and thus increase the time needed for a falling climber to come to rest, is to increase L, the overall length of the rope. Because the stretch parameter, k, is inversely proportional to L, an increase in L leads to a decrease in k. As with a weak spring, a rope with a small k value will stretch more for a given force than will a rope with a large k value.

Increasing rope length is accomplished in a couple of ways. First, the belayer could simply pay out additional slack, but without experimental data for a number of types of falls, it's impossible to say whether the increased velocity of the climber caused by a greater fall distance would be more than offset by additional rope stretch. The second method for adding slack is for the belayer to jump up as the rope begins to go taut, thus giving more rope to the climber's side of the highest quickdraw. Rope friction at that draw eventually prevents the rope from sliding back. That means that even though the total rope length is fixed, a jumping belayer can add rope length to the climber's side at the expense of the belayer's side. Of course, the jumping belayer is adding energy to the system, but some of that energy can be dissipated in the stretched rope on the belayer's side.

Another way to imagine how the belayer helps a falling climber by jumping is to think about what is called Atwood's machine. Consider two objects of different mass, one m_1 and the other m_2. Connect the objects by a string and hang the string over a pulley. To simplify the problem as much as possible, ignore the masses of the string and pulley, and ignore any friction in the system. Ignore, too, any string stretching. One can show that the acceleration of such a system has magnitude

$$a = \frac{(m_1 - m_2)}{(m_1 + m_2)} \, g,$$

where we take $m_1 \geq m_2$. If the masses are the same, the acceleration is zero (that does not mean that the *speed* of each mass is zero, only that the acceleration is zero). The qualitative idea to get out of the above equation is that having a second mass in the system reduces the acceleration. If the masses are close, the acceleration is small.

Though the problem in sport climbing is more complicated than a simple Atwood's machine, the same idea carriers over to the situation where the belayer jumps just after a climber falls. Once the slack is out of the rope, and before the friction on the rope gets large enough that the rope no longer slides through the highest draw, the presence of the belayer in the accelerating system serves to reduce the acceleration the falling climber would have felt had the belayer not jumped.

The last point is that the rope gets to a point in which it no longer slides through the highest quickdraw. We have not yet explored fully this complicated phenomenon. Our initial investigations show that friction can become so large between the sliding rope and the highest quickdraw that the rope will stop sliding. In that case, tension associated with the falling climber will cause the rope on the climber's side to continue to stretch, but there will not be any additional rope added from the belayer's side.

Resources

Goddard, Dale, and Udo Neumann (1993). *Performance Rock Climbing*. Mechanicsburg, PA: Stackpole Books.

Goff, John Eric (2010). *Gold Medal Physics*. Baltimore: The Johns Hopkins University Press.

Hague, Dan, and Douglas Hunter (2006). *The Self-Coached Climber*. Mechanicsburg, PA: Stackpole Books.

Hochholzer, Thomas, and Volker Schoeffl (Sam Lightner Jr., ed.) (2003). *One Move Too Many . . .* Ebenhauser, Germany: Lochner-Verlag.

Hoffman, Jay (2002). *Physiological Aspects of Sport Training and Performance*. Champaign, IL: Human Kinetics Publishers.

Schmidt, Richard, and Timothy Lee (2005). *Motor Control & Learning: A Behavioral Emphasis.* Champaign, IL: Human Kinetics Publishers.

Schmidt, Richard, and Craig Wrisberg (2007). *Motor Learning and Performance: A Situation Based Learning Approach.* Champaign, IL: Human Kinetics Publishers.

Ilgner, Arno (2006). *The Rock Warrior's Way La Vergne*. Tennessee: Desiderata Institute.

Macleod, Dave (2009). *9 out of 10 Climbers Make the Same Mistakes.* Rare Breed Productions.

Index

Page numbers in italics indicate illustrations.

About the Authors

Dan Hague has been an avid climber for almost 40 years. He's spent the last 18 in the indoor climbing industry, having built and managed four climbing gyms. He sits on the Climbing Wall Association's Board of Directors and two standards committees. He remains a passionate climber, winning his division of the Triple Crown Bouldering Series in 2010.

Douglas Hunter has been climbing for 28 years and coaching for 18. As a coach he has logged thousands of hours working with climbers of all levels, and he specializes in movement analysis and developing sport-specific training activities.

Dan and Douglas met in Salt Lake City in 1994 where their long collaboration in teaching climber performance improvement began. Dan's oversight of three gyms in the Washington, DC, area provided an ideal laboratory for instructional experimentation and refinement, and together Dan and Douglas molded the concepts and practices that they employ today. Thousands of climbers have been through the programs the pair developed together over a decade of experimentation, observations, and adaptation.

In 2004 Dan and Douglas began to document what they'd learned about climbing performance improvement, ultimately resulting in *The Self-Coached Climber*, published in 2006 and now widely considered the best manual on the topic. The exercises described in the book are a direct result of their 10 years of work on the subject and are the practical extension of the solid exercise theory that underlies them.

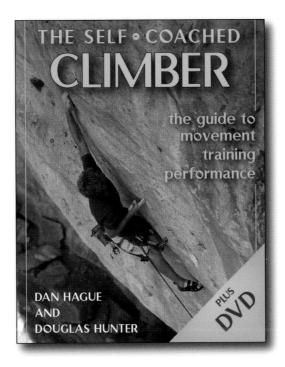

THE SELF-COACHED CLIMBER
THE GUIDE TO MOVEMENT, TRAINING, PERFORMANCE

Dan Hague and Douglas Hunter

A dynamic package of training material from the expert coaches and team behind *Redpoint, The Self-Coached Climber* offers comprehensive instruction, from the basics of gripping holds to specific guidelines for developing a customized improvement plan. Hague and Hunter base their methods on the four fundamental components of all human movement—balance, force, time, and space—and explain how to apply these principles to achieve efficient results. The DVD presents live demonstrations of training exercises and features an original documentary of a 5.14a/b redpoint attempt by Adam Stack and Chris Lindner.

The Self-Coached Climber was named a finalist in the Mountain Exposition Category at the 2007 Banff Mountain Festival.

WWW.SELFCOACHEDCLIMBER.COM